Oakland Community College
Orchard Ridge Campus Library
27055 Orchard Lake Road
Farmington, Michigan 48024

PS   Guttman
153
.J4   The Jewish writer in
G8   .

0

OAKLAND COMMUNITY COLLEGE
Orchard Ridge Campus
27055 Orchard Lake Road
Farmington, Michigan 48024

The Jewish Writer in America

THE JEWISH WRITER IN AMERICA
Assimilation and the Crisis of Identity

Allen Guttmann

NEW YORK OXFORD UNIVERSITY PRESS 1971

To Theodore Baird and George Rogers Taylor

Acknowledgments

My decision to undertake this study came shortly after some remarks of mine, on the topic of Jewish radicalism, were hotly condemned by the rabbi who had invited me to deliver them. To name him seems vindictive; to ignore him seems petty. I wish therefore to indicate my gratitude. I have learned a great deal in the last eight years. Perhaps our positions are closer now than then.

The rest of my acknowledgments are conventional enough. I find it hard to disentangle in my mind the help I have received from colleagues, from friends, and from students. I should like, therefore, to offer my indiscriminate but heartfelt thanks to Doris Bargen, Jules Chametzky, Britt Ellis, Theodore P. Greene, Hugh Hawkins, Helen Knapp, Gordon Levin, R. W. B. Lewis, Leo Marx, Bruce Morgan, Ellen Ryerson, Geraldine Thorsten, Alan Trachtenberg, John William Ward, George Edward White, and Lanny Zuckerman.

Two short sections of the book are slightly revised versions of previously published material. I wish to thank the editor of *Critique* for permission to reprint material on Saul Bellow's *Henderson the Rain King* and the editor of *The Massachusetts Review* for permission to reprint material on Stanley Elkin's first two books, © 1966 by The Massachusetts Review, Inc.

The following acknowledgments are also due:

John Hollander: Selections from "Lazienka" and "Movie-Going" in *Movie-Going and Other Poems,* copyright © 1958, 1959, 1960, 1961,

viii ACKNOWLEDGMENTS

1962 by John Hollander, are reprinted by permission of Atheneum Publishers. Selections from "Susanna's Song" and "The Great Bear" in *A Crackling of Thorns*, copyright © 1958 by Yale University Press, Inc., are reprinted by permission of Yale University Press.

Allen Ginsberg: Selections from "Howl" and "America" in *Howl and Other Poems*, copyright © 1956, 1959 by Allen Ginsberg; from *Kaddish*, copyright © 1961 by Allen Ginsberg; and from "Love Poem on Theme by Whitman" and "Sakyamuni Coming Out from the Mountain" in *Reality Sandwiches*, copyright © 1963 by Allen Ginsberg, are reprinted by permission of City Lights Books.

Irving Feldman: Selections from "The Ark," "The Wandering Jew," and "Moses on Pisgah" in *Works and Days and Other Poems* are reprinted by permission of the author. Selections from "The Pripet Marshes" and "To the Six Million" in *The Pripet Marshes and Other Poems*, copyright © 1964 by Irving Feldman, are reprinted by permission of The Viking Press, Inc. The poems quoted from *The Pripet Marshes* first appeared in *Harper's Bazaar* and *Midstream*, respectively.

Karl Shapiro: Selections from "Christmas Eve: Australia," "My Grandmother," "The Synagogue," "The Alphabet," "Jew," and "The Murder of Moses," in *Selected Poems*, are reprinted by permission of Random House, Inc.

A. G.
Amherst, Massachusetts
March 1971

Contents

The Jewish Writer in America

I

INTRODUCTION: Emancipation, Assimilation,
and the Crisis of Identity

The pantheon of the Hellenes had room for many gods and many
myths, but the deity of the Hebrews was a notoriously jealous god.
His wrathful expulsion of Adam and Eve from the Garden of Eden
was merely the first act in the long, presumably unfinished drama of
his anger. His first commandment to his chosen people warned
against apostasy: "Thou shalt have no other gods before me." But
while Moses spoke with God and heeded him, his brother led the
people astray. Exodus 32 (Revised Standard Version) tells the story:

> And Aaron said to them, "Take off the rings of gold which are
> in the ears of your wives, your sons, and your daughters, and
> bring them to me." So all the people took off the rings of
> gold which were in their ears, and brought them to Aaron.
> And he received the gold at their hand, and fashioned it with
> a graving tool, and made a molten calf; and they said, "These
> are your gods, O Israel, who brought you up out of the land
> of Egypt!"

When Moses came down from the mountain with the Tables of the
Law, he found the golden calf and grew angry. He

> threw the tables out of his hands and broke them at the foot of
> the mountain. And he took the calf which they had made, and
> burnt it with fire, and ground it to powder, and scattered it
> upon the water, and made the people of Israel drink it.

3

Then, despite his wrath, Moses returned to the mountain and asked God to forgive his people. "But the Lord said to Moses, 'Whoever has sinned against me, him will I blot out of my book.'" The Lord then sent a plague, of which the Bible tells us little.

Aaron was an apostate, blotted from the Lord's book. But was he still a Jew? The question is, of course, absurd, and I do not intend to venture an answer, but the vexed question of the Jewish apostate's religious identity has been raised countless times since Aaron worshipped his idol and will presumably be raised *ad infinitum*. Since the Emancipation of the European Jews from legal restrictions, in the late eighteenth and early nineteenth centuries, and especially since the emigration of Jews to America, the question has been asked with increased frequency and—to the degree that one can judge these matters—with increased passion.[1]

In the beginning, or what will have to serve as the beginning, Jews defined themselves as a biological group, as the seed of Abraham. Anyone born of a Jewish mother was thereby a Jew. But not all Jews were literally of the seed of Abraham. The Book of Ruth tells of Naomi, a Jewish woman who lived among the Moabites. When Naomi lost her husband and her two sons, she was accompanied on her return to Israel by her daughter-in-law, Ruth the Moabite, who said to Naomi,

> "Where you go, I will go, and where you lodge I will lodge; your people shall be my people, and your God my God; where you die I will die, and there will I be buried. May the Lord do so to me and more also if even death parts me from you." And when Naomi saw that she was determined to go with her, she said no more.

Ruth went among the Hebrews, worked amid "the alien corn," married Boaz, and became the great-grandmother of David. To this day, female converts to Judaism are spoken of as daughters of Ruth. There is rabbinical agreement that converts to Judaism are really Jews by Talmudic law (with minor qualifications for the convert himself but not for his children). The convert is considered to have been born anew, to be unrelated to the relatives of his previous life, to be literally a descendant of Abraham.

The legitimation of conversion *to* Judaism raises the problem of conversion *from* Judaism. Is the convert to another faith still a Jew? Historically, this question was asked most insistently in the time of the Inquisition, when the Roman Catholic Church sought reassurance that the tens of thousands of *conversos* of the fourteenth and fifteenth centuries really had given up the faith of their fathers. The Church was satisfied that Tomás de Torquemada and St. Teresa were sincere in their religious faith despite the fact that both were descendants of *conversos* from Judaism (as, indeed, was Pope Anacletus II). The Church finally reassured itself in the difficult matter of the scholarly humanist Luis de León, who was made to endure four years in prison when it was discovered that his ancestors had been Jews. But racial definitions linger on. The status of converts from Judaism remains uncertain, as shown in the recent, almost incomprehensible legal quarrels over a Catholic priest who claimed the right to emigrate to Israel because he had been born a Jew.[2]

The problem is complicated by the fact that Judaism and Christianity, despite their common origins, are religions of two very different types. While the history of Christianity is in large part a chronicle of the bitter competitions through which one interpretation emerged as dogma and another was stigmatized as heretical, Judaism has traditionally been concerned for ritualized *behavior* rather than for creeds, for orthopraxis rather than for orthodoxy (so that the very term "orthodoxy" represents a Hellenized perspective). Despite its name, Orthodox Judaism is a way of life rather than a series of definitions and beliefs. In the epigram of one of the twentieth century's great theologians, "A Jew is asked to take a *leap of action* rather than a *leap of thought*."[3] The secular and the sacred are one, so that the commonest acts of "economic" behavior are testimonials of faith—or betrayals of its loss. When Mary Antin recalled her childhood in her natal village, the *shtetl* of Polotzk, she remembered a Friday night when her father touched a lighted lamp:

> I was petrified in my place. I could neither move nor make a sound. . . . But he did not know that I was looking; he thought everybody was asleep. He turned down the light a very little, and waited. I did not take my eyes from him. He lowered the flame a little more, and waited again. I watched. By the slight-

est degrees he turned the light down. I understood. In case
any one were awake, it would appear as if the lamp was going
out by itself.[4]

To the Gentile, the lamp was of no religious significance, but Mary
Antin realized in horror that her father had intentionally violated
the prohibition against work on the Sabbath, that he was a secret
heretic.

For the philosophically oriented Jew, there is the tradition of theological thought that runs from Philo of Alexandria through Moses
Maimonides to Franz Rosenzweig, Martin Buber, and others who
have attempted to combine Judaism with modern thought. But for
the millions of ordinary Jews who have lived among whatever peoples gave them refuge, there has been no substitute for *Chalakah*, the
Law.* One of the foremost twentieth-century historians of the Jews
describes the Talmud (i.e. the codified Law and commentaries) in
these passionate words:

> The way of life which the Talmud so minutely illustrated and
> prescribed made the whole people of Israel one, wheresoever
> they might be found, into however many political factions they
> might be divided. It gave them the characteristic imprint which
> distinguished them from all other peoples, as well as their phe-
> nomenal power of resistance and cohesion. . . . The Talmud
> gave the persecuted Jew of the Middle Ages another world
> into which he could escape, when the vicissitudes of that in
> which he lived had become too great to bear. It gave him a
> fatherland, which he could carry about with him, when his
> own land was lost. And, if the Jew were able to maintain his
> identity in the course of the long centuries to come, under
> conditions such as no other people has ever been known to sur-
> mount, it is to the Talmud, above all, that the credit is due.[5]

Since the Emancipation, the Talmud has lost its centrality, but the
concern with behavior rather than with theory has not vanished. Re-
constructionism, the avowedly modern movement founded and led
in our day by Mordecai Kaplan, is traditional in that it sees Judaism
as a *civilization*, as faith in actions rather than in dogma. Christianity and Judaism approach each other at different levels, so that con-

* Wherever Hebrew terms are transliterated, I have used an initial "ch"
rather than "h," e.g., "Chassidic" rather than "Hassidic."

version from one to another is quite different from conversion from Anglicanism to Presbyterianism. This asymmetry between Judaism and Christianity, added to popular adherence to racial theories of definition, leads to anomalies like the "Hebrew Christians," a group that claims to be both Jewish *and* Christian.

The problem of identity becomes even more complicated when the conversion of the Jew is to a secular creed—for example, to Marxism. Many men have continued to think of themselves as Jews even while their behavior violated the Mosaic prohibitions, even while they proselytized for a millennium that is only remotely analogous to that dreamed of by Isaiah. Within Marxism, Leon Trotsky is an excellent example. Trotsky, almost the archetype of this conversion from Judaism to Marxism, was once asked to define himself as a Russian or a Jew. He replied with great firmness that he was a Social Democrat.[6] Few men have been as intellectually radical as he, and yet he is still considered by almost everyone to have been a Jew, just as Karl Marx, who was born into a family that converted to Christianity, is considered by almost everyone to have been a Jew, just as men and women almost totally assimilated into German society and almost completely ignorant of the most elementary facts of Judaism and Jewish history were considered by the Nazis to have been Jews. No wonder that some have attempted in desperation to define Jews on the basis of a *Schicksalsgemeinschaft,* a common fate, or even on the basis of *Yizkor,* the link of memory.[7]

The conversion to Marxism, or to some other form of revolutionary radicalism, is now generally recognized as conversion to a secular religion that is in fact a faith to which one can truly be converted, a creed with its appropriate rituals and forms of worship. There is, on that account, some clarity of demarcation. There may not be the incandescent, overpowering moment of conversion described in the history of Puritanism, but there is at least the sense that one has crossed the border from one realm of value to another. Within the category of secular faiths there is also what Will Herberg and others have characterized as "the American Way of Life." A form of nationalism, Herberg argues in *Protestant, Catholic, Jew* (1955), has gradually replaced the content of the traditional American faiths of Protestantism, Catholicism, and Judaism. Lack of patriotism is, for most Americans, the worst of heresies. Jews have become almost indistinguishable in their behavior from Protestants and Catholics, not because Jews have turned to Christ but because all three groups have demonstrated their allegiances to Caesar. For those who are totally alienated from American society, this transformation is a tragic one, or, at best, a shift of repression from its traditional modes to a secular form. For those who are somewhat more hopeful about American institutions, the traditional religions seem gradually to have adapted themselves to the more humane modes of behavior and the more universalistic forms of belief associated with the Enlightenment. Milton Gordon, whose theoretical model of assimilation is generally accepted by sociologists concerned with race and ethnicity, notes one of the central ironies of acculturation:*

> It is in the institutional area of religious life that one would logically expect the greatest difference between Jews and non-Jews in America to appear. It is precisely here, however, that the attractions of American core society values and the success of the acculturation process are revealed in broadest outline.[8]

One sign of this remarkable acculturation is that individual conscience has come to the fore and the sense of communal worship has weakened. Judaism has, in a sense, been Protestantized. The most eminent contemporary historian of Jewish history has written:

> To this day orthodox Jewish ethics has remained in its essence national [i.e. concerned for the people of Israel] rather than individual, and this accounts, incidentally, for the otherwise

* The key terms "assimilation" and "acculturation" require precise definition. The first refers to an entire process by which one group, usually a minority within a society, is absorbed into another group. The logical extreme of the process is the complete disappearance of the absorbed group, which may or may not contribute to the characteristics of the resultant amalgam. "Acculturation" is the adoption of the values and behavioral patterns of the "host" society. It is logically the first step. In Gordon's model, acculturation (or "cultural assimilation") is followed logically, but not always socially, by structural assimilation and marital assimilation. Structural assimilation concerns entrance by the outsiders into the political, economic, and social institutions of the "host" society, i.e., into political parties, businesses and professions, schools, cliques, and clubs of the dominant group. Marital assimilation is usually known as intermarriage. Gordon carries his analysis further, but American novelists have focused upon the acculturation of the immigrant and upon the problem of intermarriage.

incomprehensible legal theorem of the common responsibility of *all* Jews for the deeds of each. . . . What really matters in the Jewish religion is not the immortality of the individual Jew, but that of the Jewish people.[9]

That many American Jews assume the opposite demonstrates the degree of their acceptance of Protestant conceptions of religious response.

There is, moreover, the phenomenon of the secularized Jew for whom neither political radicalism nor the newest forms of Judaism are of any particular significance. One can easily construct a mythical prototype whose traits are familiar enough. The American secular Jew is ignorant of any language other than English. His parents, themselves second-generation Americans, attended religious services infrequently. He attends not at all or, at most, only during the most important holidays, and then because his parents urge him to. He keeps no dietary law nor any other law peculiar to the "chosen people." He lives and works among nominal Christians and has married an agnostic who was reared as a Christian. He identifies himself as a Jew and is thought to be a Jew by others because he relishes smoked salmon and because his speech still reveals intonations derived from medieval German, but he does not want to discuss the kind of Jew he is.

The problem of identity is further complicated by the sociological position of Jews, situated as they have been among the believers of other faiths. Moses himself was enjoined to be wary of the prior inhabitants of the land of Israel: "Take heed to yourself, lest you make a covenant with the inhabitants of the land whither you go, lest it become a snare in the midst of you" (Exodus 34). The snares of the Gentiles were difficult enough to avoid in the land of Israel, as Samson soon learned in sorrow, but *most* Jews have, in the course of nearly two thousand years, lived in exile in the midst of a pagan, a Christian, or an Islamic majority. They have survived, or perished, as a minority. As a minority, they have tended to adopt the customs of the larger society in which they lived. Their acceptance of the culture of Islamic Spain or of *Mitteleuropa* or of the New World has, little by little, transformed their sense of what it is to be a Jew, their notion of the kinds of behavior characterizing this religion that is characterized by behavior. A simple example is useful. In a symposium on the relationship of American intellectuals to the Jewish group from which they had descended, the novelist Herbert Gold remarked, "Chicken soup and Yiddish jokes may tarry awhile. But the history of the Jews from now on will be one with the history of everybody else." [10] An overstatement, of course, a witty synecdoche, but how did chicken soup come to be understood as almost synonymous with Jewishness? How did it happen that Americans often assume that the folkways of *Mitteleuropa* or of the Russian *shtetl* are really the essentials of Jewishness? To answer such questions fully is to tell the story of the American Jews, but this much is certain: a minority that adopted many of the traits of its European neighbors is now distinguished in the eyes of its American neighbors by these adopted characteristics rather than by the fundamental differences that originally accounted for the minority status.

By the last third of the present century, these adopted characteristics had very nearly followed the fundamental differences into oblivion. On the basis of a thorough study of one community (and their study of the scholarly work on other communities), Sidney Goldstein and Calvin Goldscheider have concluded that "it is likely that the distinctive popular characteristics and social behavior of American Jews will greatly diminish, and behavioral convergence of both populations [i.e. Jews and Gentiles] will occur." [11] Other sociologists have come to the same conclusion, which ought to surprise no one. [12] The sociological characteristics, the behavioral patterns, the myriad items that make up the tone and tempo of a subculture—these are the consequences of a common faith, of some form of shared commitment to basic values. Undeniably, many of the attributes associated with the life of shared faith continue when the faith itself has died. Attributes can and have continued for generations, but the question remains: at what point does the assimilated descendant of Jews cease to be a Jew?

The attempt to put one's finger on the exact point, to catch the fleet moment of transition from one identity to another, is—except in the dramatic case of conscious conversion—futile. Transition is often a matter of generations. The appropriate analogy is, perhaps, the creation of a new language from an older one. At what moment did the Latin spoken throughout the *Imperium* become French, Italian, and Spanish? Only a fool will argue that Ausonius and Proust spoke and wrote the same language; only a fool of a different variety will deny that Proust's language derived from that of Ausonius. The suggested analogy is, of course, too simple. We must imagine a situation in which the speaker of modern French insists that he still speaks Latin and that his language is the language of Virgil and Cicero. We must, moreover, imagine a situation in which some Frenchmen actually *do* continue to speak Latin and to scorn those who have adopted corrupt versions of their ancient tongue. They know that French is not Latin.

The example suggests a truth. The anxiety accompanying discussions of Jewish identity is greatest among secular Jews and least among the Orthodox. The latter have no doubts about who they are; they have not hesitated to condemn secularists as apostates and to deny that atheists are Jews. Among the Orthodox, there is little doubt about who is and who is not a Jew. Among secular Jews, definitions and conceptions of Jewish identity have proliferated, until a Jew is alleged to be anyone born of Jewish parents, anyone converted to Judaism, anyone who considers himself a Jew, anyone who is thought by others to be a Jew. "As everyone knows," explains Karl Shapiro, "a Jew who becomes an atheist remains a Jew. A Jew who becomes a Catholic remains a Jew." [13] Ernest Van den Haag, who also feels that Jews are born and not made, acknowledges that *Nationalsozialismus* operated under the same definition: "This was one part of the complicated truth which the Nazis grasped." [14] Not all Jews are this charmed by the anthropological wisdom of Josef Goebbels. Semantic uncertainties of this order cannot but produce ambivalence and anxiety. [15]

The questions of identity that I have raised are scarcely new ones, although my tone and implied conclusions may be relatively unconventional. Nathan Glazer, to offer one example, has written well of the history and varieties of Judaism in America. With the tools of sociological analysis, he and others have probed the tender matter of identity. Although I have utilized concepts and data drawn from the social sciences, my own concern is largely literary. This book is a study of the responses of Orthodox and other Jews in an unfamiliar country that combined new freedoms with more than a trace of old hostilities. It is a *literary* study of the conversions to "Americanism" (and even to Christianity), to political radicalism, and—on the part of those who had abandoned or never known Judaism—to some form of the faith of their fathers.

I emphasize the word "literary" because I see the achievements of Emma Lazarus, Abraham Cahan, Meyer Levin, Ludwig Lewisohn, Norman Mailer, Saul Bellow, and Philip Roth as one result of the process of assimilation and its concomitant crisis of identity. It is not simply that these and other writers have often written about the various conversions of American Jews, although novels and stories concerned with conversion are important; it is also that an analysis of assimilation suggests at least a partial explanation for the generally recognized excellence of certain writers. Saul Bellow's fiction is in large measure reflexive. It is about the very experiences of which it is the result. Bellow's achievement is the literary climax of a social process.

To approach literature historically and sociologically rather than, for instance, through the insights of psychoanalysis, is not to deny the value of a Freudian, Jungian, or Eriksonian interpretation. It is, however, to examine novels, stories, and poems in a somewhat different context and from a somewhat altered perspective. Denying neither the quirky uniqueness of the individual ego nor the universal relevance of a great writer's fables, I wish nonetheless to indicate some of the manifold social interactions that help define both self and work of art. With luck, these changes in context and in perspective will eliminate a small measure of the reverent claptrap that has all too often characterized discussions of the achievements of Jewish writers in America.

I shall speak briefly about the long period from 1654 to the last third of the nineteenth century. The experiences of those years are a necessary part of any valid generalizations about acculturation, assimilation, the crisis of identity, and the general background of literature written by American Jews, but the many generations that preceded the "new immigration" of the 1880s produced little in the way of literature *per se* (as opposed to memoirs, works of theology, journalism, etc.). Emma Lazarus is the one notable writer to have published in that period; she is important largely as a precursor.

My concentration upon the "new immigrants" and their progeny is justified on sociological and on literary grounds. In the first place, approximately 90 per cent of the Jewish population of the United

States at the present moment is made up of this group and its descendants. In the second place, American Jews have made their major contributions to American literature since the arrival of the "new immigrants" from Eastern Europe. The first great works were Mary Antin's *The Promised Land* (1912) and Abraham Cahan's *The Rise of David Levinsky* (1917), two books that dramatized the exodus from Czarist Russia. Since Cahan wrote in Yiddish as well as in English and since there was by the turn of the century a flourishing school of Yiddish writers in New York, I should like to state clearly at the outset that I am concerned with American literature written in English. For this reason, a number of writers, most notably Isaac Bashevis Singer, are excluded except to the degree that, like Franz Kafka, they are mentioned for purposes of comparison or for their influence on American writers in English.

A further word about omissions is probably in order. Although my purposes are largely literary, I am not concerned with all American writers who have been identified as Jews or with all the works of the writers I discuss. Many minor writers, whom I have often read with pleasure, are referred to in passing or are neglected entirely when more important writers seemed amply to illustrate the main lines of my argument. I assume that few readers will quarrel with my scanty treatment of Beatrice Bisno, but Nathanael West, Arthur Miller, and J. D. Salinger are likely to have their impatient partisans. West, Miller, and Salinger are, of course, nominally Jews, but they are in no important sense Jewish writers, nor does their work deal significantly with the process of assimilation and the resultant crisis of identity. For this reason, they have received only cursory attention.

Despite these qualifications, I am convinced that the themes I do discuss are central to the major works of most of the major Jewish writers in America. My purpose is to arrive at a more informed understanding of these writers and their work, but I should also like to think that my observations can be useful to historians, to sociologists, and to that hopefully imagined figment, the Common Reader. The relations between literature and society are rarely unidirectional. I assume that social scientists are interested in the works of art deriving from the society they are interested in.

Having attempted to describe my general approach and to lay out some of my specific principles of inclusion and exclusion, I should like also to say a last word about my methods. In order to communicate with readers whose acquaintance with Jewish literature is limited to Saul Bellow and Philip Roth, I have decided to proceed through a combination of paraphrase and analysis. Studies of a single author or of a single book can assume that the reader is (or can soon become) familiar with the text, but the range of my endeavor makes such an assumption unjustifiable. The proportion of analysis to paraphrase varies with the complexity of the works discussed. Saul Bellow calls for much more commentary than, for instance, Abraham Cahan. For the same reason—to reach an audience wider than the circle of experts—I have generally dealt with one author and with one book at a time.

Most of those who have written about Jewish life and literature in America have emphasized the continuities between the present and the past. I am certainly interested in these continuities, but I am also interested in the discontinuities and disjunctions, in ways in which the Jews in America have come to differ from their ancestors. Unlike most who have written on Jewish writers, I am concerned with the collapse as well as with the maintenance of community. From my own experiences as well as from my research, I know that studies of this sort are unlikely to please all readers, but I shall be happy if I am understood by those who may not agree.

Matters that we can categorize under rubrics like "assimilation" are, like the "matter of Troy," also the stuff of which poetry has been made, because these matters are the lives and deaths of men and women. An "objective" perspective is unattainable. Although I shall attempt to offer an interpretation to which all "reasonable" readers will assent, I should like also to indicate the position from which I make the offer. I agree with Sidney Hook's response to Jean-Paul Sartre's demand that Jews accept the identity ascribed to them by the accident of birth; in Hook's words,

> If individuals exist, they must exist as something. This is an analytic statement. But that they must continue to exist in the same social and cultural status in which they are born is a piece of antidemocratic presumption. The democrat wants to give all individuals the right to freely determine themselves as Jews or Gentiles, as citizens of one country or another, as cultural heirs of Socrates or Aquinas. . . .[16]

In another context, I hoped for a socialism with a sense of the past.* I still do. But the past I cherish and that I hope my children will cherish includes cunning Odysseus and pious Aeneas as well as Moses the lawgiver and Abraham the patriarch. My past includes the Ahab of the *Pequod* as well as the Ahab who lusted after Jezebel and seized Naboth's vineyard. If my references are eclectic and my commitments ambivalent, like those of Chicago-born Augie March, that too is what America is all about.

* To describe fully and to convince others of my interpretation of American society is, within the scope of this limited study of Jewish writers, impossible. Having, however, been queried in the past about my definitions, I should like to define my use of the terms "social democracy" and "democratic socialism." By these interchangeable terms, I mean simply the belief in the extension into economic and social life of some degree of the political equality that was, in theory if not in practice, the achievement of Liberal democracy. Social democrats *can* be Marxists, as many once were, but *need* not be.

II

The Promised Land

1   *Arrival in America, 1654–1882*

When the builders of Bay Colony settled at Salem and Boston, they likened themselves to the Israelites of the Old Testament and thought of their land as a wilderness Zion. They were, wrote one of their earliest historians, like "the ancient Beloved of Christ, whom he of old led by the hand from Egypt to Canaan, through that great and terrible Wildernesse." [1] Proverbially zealous even in their own day, the Puritans hoped that their city built upon a hill might be maintained as a sanctuary and a beacon, as a model of the religious life, and as a base from which they might venture out to bring the gospel to the heathen. They hoped, as a matter of course, for the conversion of the Jews to Christianity, but they were practical fanatics and proselytized among the Indians, whom many of them saw as the descendants of the lost tribes of Israel. They never imagined that millions of Jews were destined to follow them across the Atlantic and thus to complicate the metaphor that made America the Promised Land.

They were right, of course, in that no exodus of Jews from central Europe arrived in the days of the Winthrops and the Mathers, but a handful of Sephardic Jews did land in New Amsterdam in 1654. [2] The pilgrimage that brought them to Manhattan was a curiously roundabout one. It is worth a moment to look back at the earlier stages of their journey.

The year 1492 was doubly significant in the history of American

Jews. In addition to certain important discoveries made by a Genoese
sailor in the service of Queen Isabella of Spain, there was in that year
an edict, also Spanish. Ferdinand and Isabella decreed that the Jews,
who had flourished through centuries of Arab rule, were to be expelled from their homes. Thirty thousand families went into an exile
within an exile. Within the larger Diaspora, which dated from the
conquest of Jerusalem by Titus in A.D. 70, there was a new dispersion
of the Jews. Portugal quickly added its own decrees designed to rid
the peninsula of the "perfidious" Jews.

Spanish and Portuguese Jews—the Sephardim—sought new homes,
mostly in the lands that bordered the Mediterranean but also in Holland. (Of those who settled in Holland, the most famous was, of
course, Baruch Spinoza.)[3] In the brief period when Holland ruled
what is now the coast of Brazil, numerous Jews migrated to the New
World. When Portugal wrested the colony from the Dutch, the
Sephardic Jews moved on. Most of them went to the Dutch West
Indies, but a group of twenty-three sailed from Recife to New Amsterdam. After a skirmish with Spanish pirates, from which a French
captain saved them, they arrived at their destination and were taken
in by their reluctant hosts. They stayed on when the city passed into
English hands in 1664.

By that year there were several hundred Jews in the colonies. By
1776, the colonies had perhaps 2,500 Sephardic Jews, about half of
whom lived in Newport, which had received sixteen families from
Holland in 1658. The Jews of Newport gathered together in Congregation Mikveh Israel and quickly moved through every phase of
the process of assimilation. Acculturation was easy. They began to
adopt the ways of the Yankee merchants among whom they lived, so
that, when they decided to build themselves a synagogue in the
1750s, they chose Peter Harrison for their architect. Touro Synagogue remains today one of the finest examples of Georgian architec-
ture in America.

Economic assimilation into colonial life was relatively easy for the
Sephardim of Newport, New York, Philadelphia, and Charleston,
the main colonial centers of Jewry, but political assimilation was
slower. The barriers erected by colonial and state governments
began to come down when the Constitution of 1787 and the various
new state constitutions of the revolutionary and early national period

were instituted. The Jewish response to civic equality and religious freedom was enthusiastic. For the Newport congregation, Moses Seixas wrote to President George Washington and told of the "cordial affection and esteem" felt by the "children of the stock of Abraham" for their President. Seixas went on:

> Deprived as we hitherto have been of the invaluable rights of free citizens, we now—with a deep sense of gratitude to the Almighty Disposer of all events—behold a government erected by the majesty of the people—a government which to bigotry gives no sanction, to persecution no assistance, but generously affording to all liberty of conscience and immunities of citizenship. . . .[4]

Washington's response suggests the mutual satisfaction that acculturated Jews and rationalistic Christians found in their American arrangements:

> It is now no more that toleration is spoken of as if it were the indulgence of one class of people that another enjoyed the exercise of their inherent natural rights, for, happily, the Government of the United States, which gives to bigotry no sanction, to persecution no assistance, requires only that they who live under its protection should demean themselves as good citizens in giving it on all occasions their effectual support.[5]

Enthusiasm for American conditions led from political to religious acculturation, to a reformed Judaism compatible with the doctrines of the Enlightenment. As early as 1825, the Sephardic Jews of Charleston rejected the Orthodoxy of Congregation Beth Elohim and organized the Reformed Society of Israelites. Their statement of principles repudiated rabbinical interpretations of Talmudic law and accepted Mosaic codes only as far, in their words, "as they can be adopted to the institutions of the society in which [we] live and enjoy the blessings of liberty." [6] The group was addressed on its second anniversary by Abraham Moise, who proclaimed:

> We look not to the antiquity of rites and ceremonies as a just criterion for their observance by us, but to their propriety, their general utility, their peculiar applicability to the age and country in which we live, to the feelings, sentiments, and opinions of Americans.[7]

The Reformed Society of Israelites rejoined its parent congregation in 1833, but the Reformers soon became a majority, as evidenced by the success of their campaign for the purchase of an organ. Gustavus Poznanski, the German-educated rabbi who led Beth Elohim from 1836 to 1860, ratified the Reformers' efforts in 1840 when he said, "America is our Zion and Washington our Jerusalem." [8]

The adaptation of Judaism to American conditions meant that intermarriage and formal religious conversion were bound to increase. By the time that Henry Wadsworth Longfellow visited their graveyard in 1852, the Jews of Newport had disappeared as a group. He commemorated their fate:

> How strange it seems! These Hebrews in their graves,
>   Close by the street of this fair seaport town,
> Silent beside the never-silent waves,
>   At rest in all this moving up and down!

He commented on their disappearance:

> But ah! what once has been shall be no more!
>   The groaning earth in travail and in pain
> Brings forth its races, but does not restore,
>   And the dead nations never rise again. [9]

The poem has been derided because other Jews have resisted the attractions of assimilation. The State of Israel testifies to the tenacity of the Zionists, but Longfellow was certainly true to that moment and that place.

Complete assimilation—the total disappearance of a group into the "host culture"—was not the rule, but instances of a nearly complete assimilation were many. In Philadelphia, for example, David Franks and Samson Levy, members of the upper-class Dancing Assembly in 1748, both married Gentiles and reared their children as Christians. The majority of the descendants of the founders of Mikveh Israel are said, by sociologist Digby Baltzell, to have intermarried and dropped out of the Jewish community of Philadelphia. [10] The socially prominent Gratz family followed the same pattern—acculturation, acceptance by the "Philadelphia Gentlemen," intermarriage, and formal conversion to Christianity. Without the mid-nineteenth-century influx of German Jews and the subsequent larger influx of Polish and Russian Jews, it is quite possible that the Philadelphia and New York communities might have gone the way of the Newport congregation.[11]

The creation of Charleston's Reformed Society of Israelites was, in the words of sociologist Nathan Glazer, a "harbinger of Reform," [12] but the establishment of Reform Judaism in America was very largely the work of Ashkenazic Jews from Germany. The Jews of Germany had been among the first to enjoy the benefits and suffer the problems of *Emanzipation*. "We have no principles which are contrary to or beyond reason," wrote the philosopher Moses Mendelssohn in 1771.[13] Despite his rationalism, he continued to think of himself as a Jew and stoutly resisted attempts to bring him to the baptismal font; but his sons and daughters were typical of many of their generation when they converted to Christianity and plunged into the dark forest of German Romanticism. Although thousands converted to Christianity, the majority of German Jews contented themselves with the rejection of dietary laws, the adoption of "modern" dress, and, in general, the creation of a rationalized faith in tune with the *Aufklärung* (which, ironically, was soon abandoned by German Christians influenced by Romantic doctrines).

Although Emancipation was slower in Germany than in America and Jews suffered longer from various legal disabilities, German Jews more quickly developed a philosophical justification for their modern version of the ancient faith. When economic conditions in the 1830s sent thousands of Ashkenazim across the Atlantic, they found it relatively easy to establish themselves in conditions to which their ideas were, in a sense, already adapted. The degree of adaptation can, of course, be exaggerated. Isaac Mayer Wise, the greatest nineteenth-century leader of the Reform movement in America, complained frequently of the ignorance and backwardness of American Jews. Nonetheless, Wise was able to lead the German-American Jews to their first national organization, the Central Conference of American Rabbis, in 1889. Four years earlier, Wise, with the help of David Einhorn and Kaufmann Kohler, had won acceptance of the Pittsburgh Platform, for fifty years the basic document of Reform Judaism in America.

The Pittsburgh Platform was a manifesto that might almost have won support from William Ellery Channing and Ralph Waldo Emerson: "We recognize in every religion an attempt to grasp the Infinite One, and in every mode, source or book of revelation held sacred in any religious system the consciousness of the indwelling of God in man." The Mosaic and rabbinical laws of diet and dress, and even of morals, were rejected insofar as they failed to conform to "the views and habits of modern civilization." [14]

From the perspective of Orthodoxy, the Pittsburgh Platform was heresy and the practices of Reform Judaism were abominations. The old Sephardic congregations, which had been numerically overwhelmed by the influx of German Jews, were no longer strictly Orthodox, but they were not ready to abandon Talmudic law to "the views and habits of modern civilization." Led by Sabato Morais of Philadelphia's Mikveh Israel and Henry Pereira Mendes of New York's Shearith Israel, the Sephardim established the Jewish Theological Seminary Association, which began classes in 1887. Their manifesto was obviously a response to that of the Reformers:

> The necessity has been made manifest for associated and organized effort on the part of the Jews of America faithful to Mosaic Law and ancestral traditions; in particular by the establishment of a seminary where the Bible shall be impartially taught and rabbinical literature faithfully expounded. . . .[15]

In their effort they were supported—often to a degree beyond their desire—by the approximately two million Jews of Eastern Europe who arrived in the years from 1882 to 1914.

Although forty thousand East European Jews came to the United States in the 1870s, the exodus from Russia and Russian-ruled Poland did not begin until 1881, when the assassination of Czar Alexander II was followed by the massacre of Jews in Elizavetgrad and other cities. The travail of this migration and the vicissitudes of life in the Promised Land were to become major themes of Jewish literature in America, but the pogroms of Russia had a more immediate literary effect. They shocked Emma Lazarus from her assimilationist assumptions; in 1882 she published *Songs of a Semite*, the first important work of Jewish poetry in America.

2   Songs of a Self-Conscious Semite: Emma Lazarus

Emma Lazarus, a descendant of Portuguese Jews and the daughter of
Moses Lazarus, a wealthy industrialist, was a friend of Ralph Waldo
Emerson. The Concord sage received her first, imitative book—
Poems and Translations (1867)—politely, but was enthusiastic about
"Heroes," a Civil War elegy that appeared in *Admetus and Other
Poems* (1871). His enthusiasm for her Tennysonian renditions of
Greek myths and German legends was excessive, but her poetry did
prove that a Sephardic Jewess was able to join Henry Wadsworth
Longfellow in making literary use of European lore. The resem-
blances to Longfellow are most remarkable in a poem entitled "In
the Jewish Synagogue at Newport." The verses are derivative:

> Here, where the noises of the busy town,
>   The ocean's plunge and roar can enter not,
> We stand and gaze around with tearful awe,
>   And muse upon the consecrated spot.

Like Longfellow in his poem on the Newport cemetery, Emma
Lazarus meditated on the ironic failure of the eternal people to survive their American exile:

> No signs of life are here: the very prayers
>   Inscribed around are in a language dead;
> The light of the 'perpetual lamp' is spent
>   That an undying radiance was to shed.[16]
>   (p. 160)

The speaker's attitude is one of reverence for what once was, but
the nostalgia is muted, which seems appropriate in a book dedicated
to "My Friend, Ralph Waldo Emerson." The novel *Alide* (1874) was
further proof of the artist's ability to domesticate alien experience, in
this case the life and loves of Johann Wolfgang von Goethe. Many
passages of the novel are taken directly from Goethe's autobiography,
Dichtung und Wahrheit.

   Had Emma Lazarus died in 1880, she might today be remembered
for her words on the Statue of Liberty and for her place, along with
Isaac Harby and Mordecai Noah, in the long line of Jewish writers
whose work bore little or no trace of their religious origins.[17] *Songs*

of a Semite was, however, perfectly explicit. Half the book is taken
up by a play, *The Dance of Death,* based on one of the hundreds of
massacres that accompanied the Black Death in its march through
fourteenth-century Europe. The scene is the German towns of Nordhausen and Eisenach on May 4–6, 1349. The play opens with a dialogue in which a certain Naphtali laments the Christian response to
the plague: the Jews have not suffered from the pest and are, therefore, thought responsible for it:

> Yet even His favor
> Our enemies would twist into a curse.
> Beholding the destroying angel smite
> The foul idolator and leave unscathed
> The gates of Israel—the old cry they raise—
> *We* have begotten the Black Death—*we* poison
> The well-springs of the towns.[18]
>
> (p. 6)

His friend Baruch is sure that the good relations of Christians and
Jews in Nordhausen will continue. Although aged Rabbi Cresselin
arrives from France with news of horrors, the Jews of the town remain confident that they have the good will of the Landgrave
Frederick, whose son Prince William is in love with blonde, blue-
eyed Liebhaid von Orb. Her father is ready to allow the marriage
despite the fact that Liebhaid is "to the heart's core a Jewess—prop
of my house, / Soul of my soul. . . ." (p. 15) Landgrave Frederick
is, however, horrified. He shuts William up in a tower. Meanwhile,
Henry Schnetzen, who hates Liebhaid's father, convinces the Landgrave that all the Jews must be executed. Although Liebhaid's father
dramatically announces what he had earlier made known to Prince
William—that Liebhaid is really Henry Schnetzen's daughter—the
revelation is scorned and the Jews dance forth to their death, "Even
as David danced before the Lord, / As Miriam danced and sang be-
side the sea." (p. 44) When William arrives and convinces Henry
Schnetzen that Liebhaid *is* his daughter, it is too late.

The play is unlike any of its author's earlier work, but the significance is curiously ambiguous. In order to win the sympathy of her
readers, Emma Lazarus tells of love for a Semite who is not a Semite.
Although much of the play is given to affirmation of Judaism and to
condemnation of anti-Semitism, the revelation of Liebhaid's Gentile

parentage seems too obvious an attempt to win over the sentimental reader. The language, moreover, is derivative—from English poetry. Prince William sighs,

> Oh that I were yon star
> That pricks the West's unbroken foil of gold,
> Bright as an eye, only to gaze on her!
> (p. 22)

Comparisons to *Romeo and Juliet* are inevitable:

> See! how she leans her cheek upon her hand:
> O! that I were a glove upon that hand,
> That I might touch that cheek.

The other poems are mostly translations from Heinrich Heine and from the medieval Jewish poets of Spain. The original poems are forthrightly anti-Christian. "The New Year," for instance, celebrates Rosh Hashanah and compares the Jewish and Christian calendars:

> Not while the snow-shroud round dead earth is rolled,
>   And naked branches point to frozen skies.—
> When orchards burn their lamps of fiery gold,
>   The grape glows like a jewel, and the corn
> A sea of beauty and abundance lies,
>   Then the new year is born.
> (p. 51)

Another poem, "The Crowing of the Red Cock," condemns the new massacres and suggests the irony of murders done in the name of Christ:

> When the long roll of Christian guilt
>   Against his sires and kin is known,
> The flood of tears, the life-blood spilt,
>   The agony of ages shown,
> What oceans can the stain remove,
> From Christian laws and Christian love?
> (p. 52)

There is also "The Banner of the Jew," in which frail Emma Lazarus calls for a Maccabean struggle:

> Oh deem not dead that martial fire,
>   Say not the mystic flame is spent!
> With Moses' law and David's lyre,
>   Your ancient strength remains unbent
> Let but an Ezra rise anew,
>   To lift the *Banner of the Jew!*
>   (p. 56)

The formal and thematic comparison must now be to Byron's "Isles of Greece":

> Must *we* but weep o'er days more blest?
>   Must *we* but blush?—Our fathers bled. ·
> Earth! render back from out thy breast
>   A remnant of our Spartan dead!
> Of the three hundred grant but three,
> To make a new Thermopylae!

Too derivative to be considered a major poet, Emma Lazarus has been ignored by literary historians and remembered by others simply for her famous invitation to the "huddled masses yearning to breathe free"; but her passionate return to an identification with her ancestors makes her a forerunner of others who responded similarly to similar pogroms and, of course, to the catastrophic exterminations of the 1940s.

She had, however, no immediate followers of note. The Ashkenazic Jews who metaphorically accepted the invitation inscribed on Frédéric Bartholdi's statue had little time for closet drama or for elegiac verse. Eventually, they found their own literary spokesmen in Mary Antin and Abraham Cahan.*

3   *The Rise of a Lucky Few: Mary Antin and Abraham Cahan*

Mary Antin was born into the long since vanished world of the *shtetl. The Promised Land,* the autobiography she published in 1912, begins with a description of Jewish-Gentile relations. "When I was a

---

* Although Emma Lazarus died in 1887, when Mary Antin was a child, the older woman became an important influence on the younger by way of Josephine Lazarus, who expounded on her sister's early Transcendentalist work and befriended Mary Antin.

little girl, the world was divided into two parts; namely, Polotzk, the place where I lived, and a strange land called Russia." [19] (p. 1) The town was in Russia but not of it. She learned as a child to accept "ill-usage from the Gentiles as one accepts the weather. The world was made in a certain way, and I had to live in it." (p. 5) She learned also to accept the rigidly prescribed rituals and customs of the Jews of Polotzk.[20] Orthodox Judaism honors males above females. Mary Antin learned, therefore, to accept her own inferiority, to watch her brother trudge to the *cheder* (the religious school), and to listen to his recitations:

> When the rebbe (teacher) came on Sabbath afternoon, to examine the boy in the hearing of the family, everybody sat around the table and nodded with satisfaction, if he read his portion well; and he was given a great saucerful of preserves, and was praised, and blessed, and made much of. No wonder he said, in his [ritually prescribed] morning prayer, "I thank Thee, Lord, for not having created me a female." It was not much to be a girl. . . . Girls could not be scholars. . . . (p. 33)

Fortunately for Mary Antin, her family had already begun to break with tradition. She received Hebrew lessons and the beginnings of religious instruction. Like the characters of countless novels, she questioned the religious dicta that were offered to her as unquestionable: "Reb' Lebe," she asked, *"who made God?"* (p. 115) No more than the heroes of novels did she receive a satisfactory answer. (Reb' Lebe resembled the hypocritical characters in novels in another way: Mary Antin observed him one day about to steal a slice from a momentarily abandoned sausage. He sank in her estimation.) Before long, she was tempted to experiment with God. She ventured into the street with a handkerchief in her pocket, and thus deliberately violated the injunction against carrying objects on the Sabbath. No more than Reb' Lebe did God respond to her enacted question. Shortly thereafter, she witnessed her father's extinction of a lamp despite the Sabbath prohibitions against labor. The spiritual departure from Polotzk preceded the physical one.

Despite poverty, the restrictions of custom, and the constant threat of pogrom, there were also moments of idyllic happiness, as recounted in Chapter 5, "I Remember," which describes her grandfather's house by the River Dvina; but the life of Polotzk began to seem mean and circumscribed when Mary visited relatives in the city of Vitebsk and when the village's reality was set against the imagined wonders of life in America. When the Jews were expelled from Moscow and spread tales of their woe throughout the Pale, Mary's father decided to emigrate. They celebrated Passover in tears.

> But what said some of us at the end of the long service? Not "May we be next year in Jerusalem," but "Next year—in America!" So there was our promised land, and many faces were turned towards the West. And if the waters of the Atlantic did not part for them, the wanderers rode its bitter flood by a miracle as great as any the rod of Moses ever wrought. (p. 141)

When her father's letters called for the family to follow him to the New World, "A million suns shone out for every star. The winds rushed in from outer space, roaring in my ears, 'America! America!'" (p. 162) After a journey of six weeks, she reached "the Promised Land." The chapter in which she describes her passage is, of course, called "The Exodus."

America lived up to her expectations. Her teachers encouraged her. She found the Boston Public Library to be a "child's paradise." [21] She thrilled to the thought that she and George Washington were both citizens of the United States. She graduated from Barnard College and (subsequent to the period described in *The Promised Land*) married the son of a Lutheran minister.

Although she wrote that she doubted "if the conversion of the Jew to any alien belief or disbelief is ever thoroughly accomplished," she described her own conversion to America as a death and rebirth:

> I was born [she wrote in the Introduction], I have lived, and I have been made over. Is it not time to write my life's story? I am just as much out of the way as if I were dead, for I am absolutely other than the person whose story I have to tell. . . . My second birth was no less a birth because there was no distinct incarnation. (p. xi)

She ended her story with a burst of optimistic rhetoric:

No! it is not I that belong to the past, but the past that belongs
to me. America is the youngest of the nations, and inherits all
that went before in history. And I am the youngest of America's children, and into my hands is given all her priceless heritage, to the last white star espied through the telescope, to the
last great thought of the philosopher. Mine is the whole ma-
jestic past, and mine is the shining future. (p. 364)

Mary Antin lived to 1949 and was moved by Adolf Hitler to acknowledge her kinship with the people of Israel, but she never repudiated
the witness borne in *The Promised Land*.

Gratitude for her own success had, of course, led her to considerable underestimation of the difficulties faced by less gifted immigrants. The religious freedom celebrated by the leaders of Reform
Judaism was far more important to her than the crowded misery of
urban industrialism, but she must have known, as indeed the reformers must have when they extended the "hand of fellowship to all
who cooperate with us in the establishment of the reign of truth and
righteousness among men," [22] that the Promised Land was no Eden.
Historians and sociologists have shown that Jews converted to the
Age of Enterprise as well as to the ideals of the Enlightenment. At
their best, American Jews contributed immensely to the institutionalization of a liberty and an equality not available to them elsewhere.
At their worst, American Jews were latecomers to the "great barbe-
cue" of American capitalism, disadvantaged scramblers after the
scraps left by Carnegie and Rockefeller and Vanderbilt, greedy
greenhorns of the Gilded Age. Many an immigrant lapsed from traditional Judaism must have wondered, in the din of the marketplace,
if the baggage left behind at Ellis Island wasn't better stuff than the
shoddy goods bought and sold in Brookline and in Brownsville.

The gains and the losses were dramatized in the writings of Abraham Cahan, who fled from Vilna to Philadelphia in 1882. His novels
and stories are classic accounts of the crisis of ethnic identity confronted by the East European Jews as they poured into New York in
the 1880s and 1890s. As recently as 1958 it was possible for a major
Jewish critic to dismiss Cahan's work as "irrelevant to the main lines
of development of fiction in the United States," [23] but a new sense of
American fiction can lead to a new canon in which Cahan's name
finds its rightful place.

Yekl: A Tale of the New York Ghetto (1896) is the story of Yekl Podkovnik, who has changed his name to Jake and become an admirer of prizefighters and baseball players. "Once I am in America," he insists to the other employees of a New York cloak shop, "I want to know that I live in America." [24] (p. 9) Although Jake is supposed to save money to bring his wife and son to America, he spends time and money at a dance hall, where he flirts with other women, especially with a certain Mamie. ". . . his Russian past appeared to him a dream and his wife and child, together with his former self, fellow-characters in a charming tale, which he was neither willing to banish from his memory nor able to reconcile with the actualities of his American present." (p. 54) When Gitl, his wife, actually arrives in New York, Jake is horrified by her slovenly dress and by the "voluminous wig of a pitch-black hue" (p. 71) with which she conceals her hair—as every pious Jewish matron did and, in the most Orthodox homes, still does. Although Jake is fond of little Yossele (soon transformed into Joey), he and Gitl grow to hate each other. She weeps and curses her fate with the proverbial ghetto curse: "America *has* made a mountain of ashes out of me. Really, a curse upon Columbus!" (p. 139) Mamie's money persuades Gitl to accept a divorce and to marry again. (With Mamie's savings, Gitl and her new husband open a grocery.) Meanwhile, Jake goes reluctantly to marry his "American" floozy. "Each time the [trolley] car came to a halt he wished the pause could be prolonged indefinitely; and when it resumed its progress, the violent lurch it gave was accompanied by a corresponding sensation in his heart." (p. 190) Poor Yekl is caught —has caught himself—in the American machine.

Cahan's collection of stories, published in 1898, contains more subtle characterizations than the somewhat awkward *Yekl*, which failed commercially despite the praise of William Dean Howells, who reviewed the book in conjunction with Stephen Crane's *Red Badge of Courage*.[25] Flora Stroon, heroine of the title story of *The Imported Bridegroom and Other Stories of the New York Ghetto*, is a modern miss who prefers to read Dickens while her father and his housekeeper pray. Since her father has already departed further than he realizes from tradition, Flora is "the irremovable consequence of his former error." [26] Her desire to marry a cultivated man —a doctor, perhaps—receives a shock when her father returns from a visit to the old country. He offers her an "imported" bridegroom, a prodigy of Talmudic lore. Although religious scholarship enhanced a young man's marital eligibility in the old country, Flora is not impressed. "Mister," she tells the bewildered youth, "you had better go. If you think you are going to be my bridegroom, you are sadly mistaken." [27] (p. 53) The mistake, however, turns out to be her father's. The pious young scholar soon becomes an *appikoros* ("Epicurean," or atheist), takes to cigarettes, marries Flora in a secular ceremony, and falls in with a group of radical intellectuals from whose excited concerns Flora feels completely excluded. Her father's pathetic lament sums up the situation: "America has done it all." (p. 111)

A similar fate is encountered by David Levinsky, the hero of Cahan's partially autobiographical novel, *The Rise of David Levinsky* (1917). The village of Antomir is a *shtetl* like a thousand others, with its synagogue, its *cheder,* its run-down houses, its poor Jews, and its dangerous Cossacks. Antomir's claim to fame is its *yeshiva,* its Talmudic seminary, which attracts Jews from several provinces. David's mother points to the multivolumed Talmud and tells him, "This is the trade I am going to have you learn, and let our enemies grow green with envy." [28] (p. 23) Tragedy enters in Book III, when David's mother foolishly rushes out into the street to attack a crowd of Gentiles who had turned from the mild sport of "rolling brightly colored Easter eggs" (p. 51) to the more exciting game of Jew-baiting. Instead of avenging her son, whom the Gentiles had beaten, she is herself killed. This shock is quickly followed by the apostasy of David's closest friend, Naphtali, who now laughs at Talmudic study. David's faith is challenged also by the "modern" Minsker family, with whom he stays after his mother's death.[29]

The outbreak of the pogroms of 1881–82 and the mysterious attractions of America combine to influence David's decision to leave Antomir. Matilda Minsker, with whom David is in love, gives him the money for passage. When Reb Sender learns of David's intentions, "he was thunderstruck. 'To America!' he said. 'Lord of the World! But one becomes a Gentile there.'" David reassures him that "there are lots of good Jews there, and they don't neglect their Talmud, either," (p. 61) but the rabbi proves to have been right.*

* Cahan may have had in mind the famous speech of Rabbi David Wilowsky in New York in 1900: "It was not only home that the Jews left behind in

David shears off his earlocks and abandons the 613 commandments by which the truly pious Jew regulates his life. The transition has been prepared for by subtle psychological shifts in Antomir and in New York, but the fall into apostasy is swift:

> If you are a Jew of the type to which I belonged when I came to New York and you attempt to bend your religion to the spirit of your new surroundings, it breaks. It falls to pieces. The very clothes I wore and the very food I ate had a fatal effect on my religious habits. A whole book could be written on the influence of a starched collar and a necktie on a man who was brought up as I was. It was inevitable that, sooner or later, I should let a barber shave my sprouting beard. (p. 110)

The day of decision comes when a peddler remarks that David Levinsky's beard makes him look like a "green one." David's actions fulfill the requirements stated by a popular handbook of the day: "Forget your past, your customs, and your ideals. Select a goal and pursue it with all your might." [31]

More successfully than Yekl and the heroes of Cahan's short stories, David Levinsky learns to be "a greenhorn no longer." [32] His greatest ambition is to attend City College, which he refers to as his "Temple," but he continues instead in the garment industry and rises—in the course of many years whose events are recorded in detail—to the ranks of the millionaires. Like many of his generation, he becomes a freethinker for whom Herbert Spencer's Unknowable replaces the God of Abraham and Isaac. His ethics are those of Social Darwinism; they establish his title "as one of the victors of Existence." [33] (p. 283)

David Levinsky's deepest loyalty is to America. He describes a concert at which the audience sits apathetically, unmoved by operatic themes or Yiddish songs. The national anthem brings the Jews enthusiastically to their feet: "It was as if they were saying: 'We are not persecuted under this flag. At last we have found a home.'" (p. 424) David Levinsky's enthusiasm is perhaps less unbounded than

---

Europe; it was their Torah, their Talmud, their *yeshivot* [seminaries]—in a word, their *Yiddishkeit,* their entire Jewish way of life." [30] Cahan's own experience was, of course, sufficient, but Wilowsky's castigation upset many who thought they had achieved a compromise between old and new.

Mary Antin's, but he too might have been cited by Melvin M. Tumin in his study of American Jews and the "cult of gratitude." [34]

But David Levinsky, unlike Mary Antin, remembers his past with considerable ambivalence. He begins his story with comments on the miraculous metamorphosis that transformed a boy with four cents in his pocket to a man worth two million dollars, but he concludes with serious doubts about his career, and about his identity:

> I can never forget the days of my misery. I cannot escape from my old self. My past and my present do not comport well. David, the poor lad swinging over a Talmud volume at the Preacher's Synagogue, seems to have more in common with my inner identity than David Levinsky, the well-known cloak-manufacturer. (p. 530)

Isaac Rosenfeld's commentary on this passage has the insight one expects from a writer whose own novel, written before Rosenfeld read Cahan, ponders what it means to be an American Jew: David Levinsky's nostalgia for his past, argues Rosenfeld, is purely Jewish, but the novel is,

> at the same time, an exemplary treatment of one of the dominant myths of American capitalism—that the millionaire finds nothing but emptiness at the top of the heap. It is not by accident that Cahan, for forty years and until his death the editor of the *Jewish Daily Forward,* and identified all his life with Jewish affairs and the Yiddish language, wrote this novel in English. . . . He was writing an American novel par excellence in the very center of the Jewish genre.[35]

Another way to put the matter is to argue that this story of assimilation and nostalgia, of success and regret, is typical of American Jewish writers of the first generation. The difficulty with Cahan's conclusion is that Cahan has done little to prepare the reader for it. Although the *shtetl* was poor, cramped, dangerous, and provincial, it seemed in retrospect to many an immigrant to have been all of a piece, a community, an island of tradition in a sea of uncertainty. It was certainly possible for Yiddish writers like Sholom Aleichem, Mendele Mocher Sforim, and Isaac Bashevis Singer to make literature from the *shtetl's* dirt and superstition and ritual and religious ecstasy, but Cahan has allowed his narrator to write matter-of-factly of Antomir and of his alienation from the role of Talmudic scholar. To announce on the last page that the Talmudic student may have represented a truer identity than the manufacturer is to sacrifice verisimilitude and consistency on the altar of nostalgia.*

4 *Interlude: Anzia Yezierska and Samuel Ornitz*

Abraham Cahan's contributions to American literature have been undervalued, especially in the era of the hegemony of the New Critics, who esteemed a subtly poetic prose quite unlike the frequently awkward language of Cahan's fiction. The contributions of Anzia Yezierska and Samuel Ornitz have been almost completely forgotten. Although neither writer can be termed major, except perhaps within the realm of Jewish writing, both deserve to be read for their insights into the 1920s, into the period between *The Rise of David Levinsky* (1917) and Meyer Levin's *The Old Bunch* (1937).

Anzia Yezierska was a more fluent but less profound writer than Abraham Cahan. Like him, she wrote essentially of the first generation. Her collection of stories, *Hungry Hearts,* came out in 1920. The first, allegorical story sets the pattern for the entire book. Shenah Pessah, a twenty-two-year-old dowryless girl, works as a janitor, lives in an almost sunless basement apartment, and bewails her outcast fate: "My heart chokes in me like a prison!" [37] (p. 1) Into her life, like the prince of the fairy tales, steps the handsome stranger, an instructor in sociology busy with field work on "Educational Problems of the Russian Jews." He rents an apartment in Shenah's building and is soon charmed by her innocence and by her untutored desire for an education. (Of a book, she says, "It lifts me on wings with high thoughts." [p. 7]) He seems to Shenah to be, quite literally, a God-sent alternative to the wife-seeking Motkeh, an illiterate fish peddler. The sociologist takes her to the Boston Public Library,

* *The Rise of David Levinsky* set a pattern for the novel of regretful success. Twenty years later, Beatrice Bisno writes of her wealthy protagonist: "Throughout these later years of creature comforts, the tragic picture of tattered Yossel, his paternal grandfather, lived on with him. Yossel, a lifelong serf tailor to a feudal lord and landowner, had worn the same black coat at seventy years of age that he had donned at seventeen, the day he became a bridegroom under the canopy." [36] Norman Bogner's *Seventh Avenue* (1967) is a more subtle rendition of the same theme.

where Mary Antin found what *she* hungered for, and begins to fall in love with her. But America is no fairyland. He moves from the apartment and leaves Cinderella (Shenah) to console herself with the possibility of escape through education. Sociological princes know that love seldom survives the movement across class and religious lines.

Shenah appears in the second story, "Hunger," to tell sympathetic Sam Arkin of her love for the village she left to come to loveless America: "I love the houses and the straw roofs, the mud streets, the cows, the chickens and the goats. My heart always hurts me for what is no more." (p. 56) But when Sam Arkin proposes marriage, Shenah reveals that she still loves her lost sociology instructor and the wider world that he symbolizes: "This fire in me, it's not just the hunger of a woman for a man—it's the hunger of all my people back of me, from all ages, for light for the life higher!" (p. 63)

The reader never learns whether or not Shenah's hungry heart is to be satisfied, but the characters of other stories suggest that she had better settle for minimal satisfactions. In one story, the narrator feels that a single act of kindness is compensation for years of disappointed struggle. In another, the effort to create "beautifulness" in the form of a newly painted kitchen is thwarted by the greed of the landlord (also a Jew), who raises the rent beyond his desperate tenant's ability to pay. Still another story ends with the night-school teacher's declaration of love for his hungry-hearted student, but this story is appropriately entitled "The Miracle."

The best story moves beyond the first generation and anticipates the novels of generational conflict that appeared in the 1930s and 1940s. The irony of "The Fat of the Land" is that fulfillment is also disappointment. Hannah Breineh is introduced in her crowded tenement, where she knocks across an air shaft to borrow a wash boiler from kindly Mrs. Pelz. While she gossips, her youngest child topples over with the chair he had been strapped into. "For what did I need yet the sixth one?" (p. 185) The children fight over their food, except for Benny, who is delivered by the police who picked him up for truancy. From this squalor, the scene shifts to the opulence into which Mrs. Breineh's grown-up children have placed her. The trouble is, of course, that the "successful" children are ashamed of their mother and want to Americanize her. She finds her plight unbearable, flings groceries all over her Persian rug, and rushes off to live with Mrs. Pelz. But she is too old and pampered to live in poverty and must return to the hateful elegance of Riverside Drive. What does it profit a woman to have her wishes granted when they were not what she wanted after all? *

Only three years separated the publication of Anzia Yezierska's poignant stories from the appearance of *Haunch Paunch and Jowl: An Autobiography* (1923) by Samuel Ornitz, but the books can be taken as representative of two different generations. *Hungry Hearts* belongs with Mary Antin's autobiography and with Abraham Cahan's novels and stories of the first generation; *Haunch Paunch and Jowl* suggests by its very title the irreverent Americanization of the second generation. The style is brash, and the sentiments are appropriate to the "tough-guy" literature of the 1930s.

The "autobiography" is that of Meyer Hirsch, nicknamed "Ziegelle" because his wet nurse was a goat. The name is suggestive because goats are both unpleasant and tough. Yoshke the lamblike peddler was clubbed by the police and moans in his sleep, from which one of Meyer's friends draws a lesson: "I think, Meyer, I think a goat has got a better chance in this world." [39] (p. 21) There is no doubt that Meyer will make his way in the world. Goats are good at climbing.

The conflict between old and new is symbolized by the *cheder* (Hebrew school) and the street gang. The narrator's rejection of the first takes two forms. The ideological: "Little wonder we rebelled against our daylong studies of Biblical lore with emphasis on the raw curses and chastisements, the subtle Apocryphal enlargement of the portrait of the God of Vengeance; the endless Rabbinical rules and rites and fasts and laments to appease that insatiable monster—God of Vengeance." (pp. 62–63) The personal: ". . . I can't swallow that bunk: I puke it right back." (p. 63) The boys long for the moment of release: "At last we are free. It is the riot of a jail delivery. And now for the real business of life." (p. 35) The "real business" is done by the gang: "I long, passionately, to be part of it and hear

---

* The story can be read as prophecy. Anzia Yezierska's first book won her an invitation to Hollywood, which she long after described as "a glass-house with crooked mirrors." [38] Of her later novels, *Bread Givers* (1925) is sometimes admired.

the grave and grim pow-wow of the chieftains, and share the pungent promise of potatoes baking in the embers." (p. 18) It is obvious that Indian pow-wows are no more a part of the children's experience than the vengeance of God, but the call of an imagined, and partly realized, wild is far stronger than the appeals of "rules and rites and fasts and laments."

When the boys grow older, the "real business" of life includes a system of petty extortion ("protection money"), fights against the Irish boys, and sexual initiation. Meyer Hirsch becomes a "runner" for the local courts, an aid to dishonest lawyers, a student of the law who studies from stolen textbooks. For entertainment, there is song and dance at Levelle's bar, where posters announce a sacrilegious picnic to be given on Yom Kippur, the most holy day of the Jewish year, where one of the boys shouts "in glee that he can twist a blareful, stirring Wagnerian fugue into nigger jazbo stuff." (p. 160)

Meyer becomes a politician and discovers a new role, that of the "Professional Jew." (The role does not keep him from his Gentile mistress Gretel.) An alternative to political chicanery is set forth in the appeal of Lionel Crane, born Lazarus Cohen and reborn as a Harvard-educated doctor. Crane calls for complete assimilation: "The Jews will create a Jewish Question in America as long as they cling to their bizarre Jewishness . . ." Crane condemns the immigrant Jew's "slovenly, baggy clothes," "his overdressed, bejewelled, flashy appearance; his blatancy and vulgarity," "his maddening infallible belief in himself as being better, wiser, cleaner, more moral, shrewder, greater." Crane is especially vehement against the "Professional Jew" who panders to his people's prejudices and plays on their ignorance and prefers to manipulate rather than to lead them. The "Professional Jews" are "the jailors of their people, keeping them from enlightenment and self-liberation." Crane then announces, "I will take the sick ego of my people to the clinic." (pp. 198–200) Meyer Hirsch listens but is not moved (although he later follows Crane's advice and marries exogamously). He forms the firm of Hirsch and Freund. "I split fees with court clerks, attendants, keepers, detectives, policemen, their superiors, saloonkeepers—anybody who will bring us cases." (p. 206) Dishonesty pays. Accepting the ways of the world, ready to switch sides in an instant, adept at conspiracy, bribery, and the management of a limited amount of violence, Meyer

Hirsch rises to the point where he can quash a case at the request of a governor and win appointment to the Superior Criminal Court. No trouble at all. He is a superior sort of criminal. He ends his career on Riverside Drive, in the fat and flashy vulgarity of "Allrightniks Row." He has married his mistress and found another, an actress.

But he too is nostalgic. David Levinsky remembers the Talmudic scholar that he had once been; Meyer Hirsch remembers Esther, the romantic symbol of peoplehood, whom he had loved as a youth. He had turned from her in order to court Josephine Rauch Munsterkase (i.e. "smoked Munster cheese"), daughter of socially prominent German-Americans, but Esther ruled his fantasy life: he imagined her asleep with "a moonbeam upon her shoulders, and she moved . . . the coverlet turned down and you saw the whiteness of a marble bust, a Grecian bust . . . and a cat rankled over the cans in the backyard and you fled . . . Oh, the sheer beauty of the Grecian bust." (p. 264) Symbolically, American reality—or Meyer Hirsch's ambitions—keeps him from the Greek body of his Jewish love. The book ends with Gretel's call to a typically "Jewish" dinner—potted breast and potato pancakes.

5 *How Some of Us Made it: Meyer Levin and Daniel Fuchs*

Looking back from what has proved to be the middle of his long literary career, Meyer Levin wrote in 1950 that he was "a peculiar mixture of Chicago and Chassidism." [40] The central questions of his autobiography—"Was I an American, or a Jew? Could one be both?" [41]—were also the questions of his most significant work. Assimilation, radical protest, and Zionism have all attracted him and have all become a part of his fiction, so that the disadvantages of a book-by-book approach are more evident in his case than in that of any other writer discussed in this present study. I have, therefore, chosen to follow one strand of Levin's career through 1937, when he published *The Old Bunch,* and to deal separately with his other work.

A Chicago-born contemporary of James T. Farrell, Levin attended the University of Chicago and, while still an undergraduate, became a reporter for the *Chicago Daily News.* The Leopold-Loeb

murder of Bobby Franks was then *the* news item of the day; that
Levin was strongly affected is evident in the novel *Compulsion*
(1956), the most popular of his works. After his graduation from
the University in 1924, Levin journeyed to Paris. Rather than linger
with Ernest Hemingway, F. Scott Fitzgerald, and the other expatri-
ates of the 1920s, he went on to what was then the Mandate of
Palestine. His first novels were almost totally unrelated attempts to
dramatize first one, then another aspect of his still uncertain identity.

The first to be written was *Reporter,* published in 1929. The influence of John Dos Passos is evident in the use of headlines at the top
of every page, in the words run together into unconventional coin-
ages (for example, "cityed" for "city editor"), and in the self-
conscious modernity of the prose. The plot is inconsequential ("Who
murdered Vittorio Manfredi?"); the language is typically Jazz Age:
"Chickie was Dinky's pet mulatto, fiery as hot tamales, and peppy as
pluto water. When Chickie did the Charleston, naked on that table.
. . . Owow." [42] (p. 372) One assumes the book was typed with shirt-
sleeves rolled, with tie loosened, with cigarette at the side of the
mouth, and with Ernest Hemingway of the *Toronto Star* clearly in
mind.

The influence of Hemingway is still more obvious in Levin's second novel, *Frankie and Johnnie* (1930). The title characters are star-
crossed lovers in Chicago, where only the names of shops and cine-
mas suggest the possibility of romance: "After that Johnnie took
Frankie to the Tivoli every Wednesday and they went to the Athens
Confectionery after the show, except sometimes they went downtown to the Chicago instead of going to the Tivoli or else they went
on Wednesday to the Tivoli and on Saturday to see Paul Ash." [43]
(p. 109) Even the ironies are Hemingwayesque: Johnnie imagines
Frankie on the elevated railway, but "all the time Johnnie was think-
ing these things Frankie wasn't riding home on the L at all. All that
time, Frankie was riding home on the bus." (p. 212) Frankie and
Johnnie will never meet again, not even in the mind.

There is nothing about these two early novels to distinguish them
from the imitative early works of other young men who grew up in
Protestant rather than Jewish homes, but Levin's third and fourth
books—*Yehuda* (1931) and *The Golden Mountain* (1932)—represented an attempt to articulate his other self, Chassidism rather than

Chicago. These books, and Levin's "proletarian" novel, will be discussed in later chapters. Relevant to the present moment is *The Old Bunch* (1937), the book for which Levin ought to be remembered.

Although Levin was familiar with the Yiddish literature of the Chassidic tradition, as evidenced in his fourth book, the standard American influences are present in *The Old Bunch*—Dos Passos, Fitzgerald, Hemingway, perhaps Farrell. The book is certainly not stylistically innovative, but Levin's conception of the form was a departure from convention:

> I felt that I had a fundamental observation to make on a form of society in our time in America. While novelists emphasized the individual in the family unit as the determining human relationship, I saw the surrounding group, the bunch, as perhaps even more important than the family in the formative years. Particularly in the children of immigrants, the life-values were determined largely through these group relationships.[44]

Levin concentrated, that is, upon what Herbert Gans, in *The Urban Villagers* (1962), called "peer-group society."

The "old bunch" is a group of twenty boys and girls whom the reader encounters all at once, through the device of a club for teenagers along Roosevelt Road on Chicago's West Side. Together for a moment in time and space, and in their shared perception of their urban environment, they grow apart, as every group does. In the language of Louis Wirth's sociological study of the Chicago ghetto of those years, the group experiences diversification, differentiation, and disintegration.[45] The fascination of the novel is less in individual characters and specific actions than in Levin's evocation of an entire social system which he marked off as his novelistic domain. Marcus Klein has remarked on the obvious comparison between Dos Passos and Levin: "With all its devices of topicality and with all its great efficiency in narrative, and with all its anger, *U.S.A.* does not have the sense of *The Old Bunch* that history is something that happens to *me* and to *my* friends and *my* family." [46]

It was a time and place that Meyer Levin knew. *The Old Bunch*, 964 pages long, moves from 1921 to 1934—the years of *The Jazz Singer* and *Show Boat* and Leopold and Loeb and the Lindbergh flight, of Samuel Insull and Al Capone and the Great Crash of

1929 and the magnificent mid-Depression symbol of hope, Chicago's
Century of Progress World's Fair. In those years the second-generation Jews of Chicago's West Side divested themselves of what they
deemed to be their ancestral encumbrances and eagerly scrambled
upward into the middle class. Doctors, lawyers, dentists, artists,
teachers, dry cleaners, realtors, gangsters, and part-time bicycle
racers, yes; rabbis and Talmudic scholars, no.

Although the parents of the old bunch are all first-generation
Americans, they have already begun to differ among themselves
in wealth, status, and attitude. Rube Moscowitz, father of Celia, has
grown rich in the scrap-iron business (a typical first-generation
enterprise). He has political influence and a pleasant *modus vivendi*
with the Irish alderman who still represents the district. Levin's
narrator describes the Moscowitz house, which characterizes the
family just as Huckleberry Finn's description of the Grangerford
House characterizes the *nouveau riche* of the 1840s:

> The apartment was swell, too, with a full-width sunparlor and
> French doors. Near the gas log fireplace was a grand piano—
> not a baby grand. A great red and yellow Spanish shawl was
> slung over its propped-up top. There were at least a dozen
> lamps, floor lamps and table lamps, and Celia's mother was
> always buying marvelous new lamp shades at Field's. Yellow
> silk shades with domes growing out of domes, and pagoda
> shapes with gorgeous long bead fringes. There was a big ori-
> ental vase that was always full of flowers.

Mrs. Moscowitz has pretension, which means that "you would
never see a Yiddish newspaper in her hands." [47] (p. 13) Celia's friend
Estelle Green bears a name that indicates Americanization, but her
mother—Mrs. Greenstein—is still faithful to the past. Mrs. Greenstein is convinced that bobbed hair means bad morals, and she is
outraged when her daughter adopts the hairstyle of a prostitute.
(The hint of F. Scott Fitzgerald's "Berenice Bobs Her Hair" is no
surprise; the first chapter is entitled "Flappers and Jellybeans.")
When the club has a dance, complete with Enrico Caruso on the
Gramophone, it is Mrs. Greenstein who rushes in to break it up.

But there are no Mrs. Greensteins in the younger generation, from
whose perspective the narrator tells the story. The old bunch goes

many ways, but only one of them has a career that can be called religious in the conventional sense, which is no wonder when one considers that their parents have already scanted tradition and left *their* parents to uphold Orthodoxy.

For the second-generation Jews, as for the Italians who followed them to America, crime was one avenue where prejudice placed no roadblocks. Runt Plotkin, son of a cigar maker, attempts as a youth to peddle fake cigars. It is he who becomes the youthful sophisticate: he rents a cottage at Benton Harbor and "makes out" with a girl. When he fails an examination in the moderately dishonest law course that many of the boys take, he manages to avoid paying the two-dollar fee for a make-up (which was the reason the teacher failed twenty-four of thirty boys). Runt eventually becomes a lawyer rather than a gangster, but he keeps in touch with the underworld. When the union tries to close down Epstein's Cleaners, Runt Plotkin hires a Jewish gunman to ride the truck and protect it.

Crime was one traditional route out of the ghetto. Sports were another. One charm of *The Old Bunch* is that the athlete is a bicycle racer rather than a boxer (as in Clifford Odets' *Golden Boy*) or a baseball player (as in Bernard Malamud's *The Natural*). Why not? Sol Meisel's races seem as appropriate as Joe Freedman's art. His scenes are, in fact, among the most memorable in the novel.

Although the visual arts were never a part of Jewish tradition, painting and music were also avenues open to ambitious Jews. Joe Freedman voyages to Paris, meets a sculptor who depicts Biblical scenes in hammered copper, talks of Zionism and of the founder of Chassidism, returns to his grandfather's village of Kovno, makes his way to Safed in Palestine, and falls in love with a *sabra* (a girl born in the Holy Land). Although his path is remarkably similar to Meyer Levin's own, he is by no means the author's spokesman. Graven images are one possibility, and one only, for the secular Jew.

Two idealists of the group are Mitch Wilner, who becomes a doctor, and Sam Eisen, a lawyer. (The names suggest the necessary determination.) The latter is in love with Lil Klein but breaks off when he discovers that she "pets" with Mort Abramson, youthful driver of an Oakland automobile, eager seeker of pleasure from Polish girls. At the University of Illinois, Sam agitates against compulsory R.O.T.C. and is expelled. He makes reluctant compromises, marries Lil Klein after all, and accepts Runt Plotkin as a law partner. The compromises are painful ones, and domestic quarrels reach a crisis. In one of the first of these scenes, Levin describes a Passover *seder* (ritual supper) that Sam Eisen's friends turn into a drunkenly sacrilegious brawl:

> The place cards were the cleverest things! Each card was a cut-out of a biblical character, only Ev had fixed devilish little short skirts over the long gowns of the women characters, and put derby hats on the men. But the most comical thing she had done was to get pictures of movie stars and paste their faces on the biblical figures.

Adolphe Menjou "in a silk hat, on the body of an Egyptian taskmaster" (p. 481) brings shrieks of pleasure. Groucho Marx appears as Adam, and Lillian Gish as Queen Esther. The *Haggada*—the book of procedure for Passover—is passed around as a curiosity, after which the maid "brought in an immense, sugar-baked ham." (p. 484) She is greeted by squeals and titters. The layer cake is topped with an effigy of Moses. Sam Eisen had hoped to go to his parents' home for the *seder*, but Lil had refused: "Oh, mygod, do I have to sit like a prisoner till twelve o'clock while your grandfather mumbles the whatyacall it through his beard?" (p. 477) Now Sam finds it all too much to bear, especially when Manny blows red crepe paper across the table where it settles on Sam's ear. At length, he excuses himself and rushes out. Lil asks if he's sick and then wonders if he's crazy, thus to disgrace her before her best friends. No one present can imagine why an atheist should make such fuss about a little Passover fun. Sam Eisen eventually obtains a divorce, through deceitful proceedings, from a judge who keeps a mistress in Lil's building.

Judge Horowitz figures more than once. Sam Eisen brings suit on behalf of a client whom the police had beaten (at the request of Mort Abramson), but the jury is made up of the policemen's relatives and the case is thrown out of court. Sam is not, of course, a paragon. When Joe Freedman's statue is stolen from an exhibition, Sam sues the exhibitor for the value of the statue as calculated by the time invested in its manufacture. When his divorced wife wants to evict a tenant from an apartment, he defends her action. His education is, however, accelerated by the Great Depression. He is hired to defend a group of Communist-led rent strikers. The police, once again, have been brutal. Some of them have been especially brutal because they are black and therefore anxious to prove their loyalty to the Establishment. Judge Horowitz refuses to let Sam speak in court: "You ain't got no rights! Reds and radicals got no rights!" (p. 814) Judge Julius Hoffman of "Chicago Seven" fame was clearly not the first to lose patience with dissenters. Judge Horowitz does, at least, turn first offenders free. Sam Eisen is now, in the term currently popular, radicalized.

Among careers open to Jews of Meyer Levin's generation, medicine was as important as law and far more important, numerically, than the academy. Rudy Stone and Mitch Wilner both determine upon medicine. The "Judge Horowitz" of the medical profession is a certain Dr. Feldner. At Israel Hospital, Dr. Feldner operates at unfavorable odds in order to earn a $5,000 fee. Mitch Wilner does medical research and reads a paper on a successful experiment, but Rochester refuses him, despite his rank among his group. Mitch's story is continued in Levin's next book, *Citizens* (1940), but the present focus is upon Rudy, who leads a group of dissident doctors into group practice in a clinic. Dr. Feldner leads the opposition within the local medical association. The group practitioners are expelled from the association and shut out of the hospitals (just as their real-life counterparts have been in similar situations then and now). The clinic falls apart, dramatically, when the doctors discover amoebic dysentery at the Del Roi Hotel. Why doesn't the Health Department announce a quarantine? The answer is obvious to the worldly-wise: Chicago's World's Fair has opened. Dr. Orr, director of the group, wants to "play ball" with the Health Department, but he is ousted from leadership by the others, who then send a statement to the press and wait naïvely for the news to be published. The papers print "a cute story about a rift in the 'cafeteria medicine' clinic," (p. 904) but they refuse to say a word about the danger of an epidemic. The Fair goes on.

The Fair that Chicago celebrated in 1933 metaphorically dominates the last section of the novel. The book ends with everybody at the Fair, with a kaleidoscopic succession of short scenes, with snatches

of popular songs, with suggestions of *Walpurgisnacht*. The Fair
ends with a scene comparable to the final, apocalyptic moments of
Nathanael West's *The Day of the Locust* (1939):

> The huge mob that had jammed the streets of the Fair slowly
> contracted, congealed, until only the night-hunters, the bloody-
> eyed remained. In the Black Forest, incendiary flames arose.
> In the Streets of Paris there was a free-for-all; tables were
> smashed on backs and heads, a grabbing hand ripped Estelle's
> gown, and the cold air met her breasts; a mob got hold of a fire
> hose and doused a squad of cops; the free-for-all was carried
> from the Streets of Paris to the Bowery; Runt pushed through
> crowds, grabbed girls, got socked. . . . Lou Green was yanked
> awake by a cop, and found that he had passed out against the
> imitation log palisades of Old Fort Dearborn. (pp. 963–64)

Meanwhile, Mitch Wilner goes home to his wife, Mort Abramson
races down Sheridan Road at sixty-five in the new airflow DeSoto,
and Harry Perlin listens to the cowboy tune that ends the novel,
"Git along, little dogie, git along . . ." There is no reason to believe that Chicago's "Century of Progress" has brought the millennium, but there is good reason to think that the old bunch will
continue to get along.

In the year that Meyer Levin published *The Old Bunch*, Daniel
Fuchs completed what is now commonly referred to as his Williamsburg Trilogy. Although the three novels do form a unity, *Summer
in Williamsburg* (1934), *Homage to Blenholt* (1936), and *Low
Company* (1937) constitute a triptych rather than a trilogy. Although each of the novels contains an action, in the literary sense,
the actions seem pretexts around which Fuchs was able to place his
characters in a landscape.*

Each of the three novels has a hero of sorts, but minor characters
continually usurp attention, like colorful figures scattered through a
picture by Brueghel. Like Brueghel's peasants, they are mostly "low

---

* Irving Howe has written well on the trilogy. The novels "are dominated
by a sense of place—the sense of place as it grasps a man's life and breaks
him to its limits." [48] For those unfamiliar with New York and its history, it
is perhaps worthwhile to note that Williamsburg is a section of Brooklyn
into which the East European Jews began to move in large numbers in the
1890s, when the Lower East Side of Manhattan seemed too crowded to
contain any increase in population.

company," first- or second-generation East European immigrants hard put to survive despite the ingenuity of their adjustments. Although the rest of America occasionally intrudes, in the form of Joan Crawford movies or in the person of a thug named Gilhooley, the world of Williamsburg is relatively isolated. Insiders compete with insiders for minor advantages, for the wherewithal to make it through another day. Nonetheless, as the allusion to Brueghel suggests, the result is comedy rather than tragedy.

This in itself is noteworthy. Philip Roth, Bruce Jay Friedman, and the "Black Humorists" of the 1960s have often been compared to Sholom Aleichem and other Yiddish writers of comedy. Much has been written about "Jewish humor" and about the comic styles of Jewish entertainers. There is, therefore, a tendency to imagine that all Jewish writers create characters typified by ironic self-mockery or by the tone and gestures of Gimpel the Fool and Tevye the Dairyman, but none of the writers hitherto discussed, not even Meyer Levin, can be characterized as comic. Daniel Fuchs was the first to take apart the world of Sholom Aleichem's Kasrilevka and to reconstruct it on the sidewalks of New York.*

Although *Summer in Williamsburg* opens with a suicide and includes murder and accidental immolation, the grim comedy of those who *must* laugh predominates. The same sense of life as a ridiculous ordeal informs *Homage to Blenholt* (organized around a funeral) and *Low Company* (organized around gangland struggles and later filmed as *The Gangster*). Incongruity of speech is one form of humor; Mrs. Wohl tells of the birth of her son: "When I was her age I had my first baby already. Yankele. Born black, without a breath. I thought I lost him for sure, good-by Charlie." [49] But the incongruity of language is merely the superficial evidence of deeper disparities.

There is the gap between old and new customs, the strain of Americanization, which is a recurrent theme of Jewish writers. Mrs. Wohl, for instance, continues to operate by the folkways of the past, without regard to newer forms. She breaks in upon a young couple:

* In his recent study, *The Schlemiel As Metaphor* (1971), Sanford Pinsker concentrates on Yiddish writers until he reaches Bernard Malamud. He ignores Fuchs.

The door opened and Mrs. Wohl marched in with her mop and dust cloths. Munves and Rita stopped.

"Dancing?" Mrs. Wohl asked, beaming at the sight. "Dance, dance, children. Don't let me stop you."

"Mrs. Wohl," Rita said severely, "you got a door in your house?"

"Sure, I have a door. What a question. Who hasn't a door in America?"

"Do people walk in without knocking in your house too?"

Mrs. Wohl turned and rapped on the door with her mop. "All right," she said pleasantly. "Now I knocked." [50]

Similarly, widowed Mrs. Sussman writes to her sister in Montana and receives the following reply:

> You write, dear little sister, what can you do now? From us, as you already can imagine, you can not expect great things. Sam is still unwell and the grocery store pays a poor living. Nevertheless, if you wish to come here, to be with your own flesh and blood in a world of strangers, it will be a burden, but come, you will be always welcome. [51]

It is clear that middle-class roles fit like hand-me-down suits. It will be another generation before new patterns are learned (and old completely forgotten).

Adaptation is made more difficult by the familiar fact that American capitalism has always included, at every level, a measure of illegality. The businessmen of Williamsburg and Neptune Beach operate on a less grand scale than the Robber Barons of the 1890s, the collusionists of contemporary corporations, or the Mafia, but they are a hardened group, prepared perhaps in the old country for the survival of the fittest. A major element in *Summer in Williamsburg* consists of the struggle over a transit monopoly. Sabotage and even murder are a part of the game. The efforts of Morand (born Pomerantz) to set up a rival bus line are beaten back by Uncle Papravel's moderate use of just the right amount of violence. Uncle Papravel celebrates with his "boys":

> Tonight we celebrate because all that comes, knock wood, is good news. Morantz [Papravel's coinage], he's quit not only in Williamsburg but in the mountains altogether. . . . And just this morning the railroad company sent out an announce-

ment they take no more passengers, only freight. And it is only
a beginning, because, remember, there is still a God over
America. (pp. 379–80)

When Mrs. Van Curen weeps to think that unbaptized Uncle
Papravel will never enter heaven, he urges her to leave that problem to him. America is, indeed, the *goldene Medineh* (the golden
land). All will be well. One world at a time.

A similar struggle is central to *Low Company*. Shubunka, opera-
tor of a chain of brothels, is ruined when a larger organization
negotiates a better arrangement with the police. (One is reminded
of the situation in *Haunch Paunch and Jowl,* where Meyer Hirsch
divides up the area among groups of pickpockets and has the
police keep out the interlopers.) Louis Spitzbergen, owner of a
store at Neptune Beach, is caught up in Shubunka's troubles and
killed. The other businessmen are not greatly disturbed:

> It was too bad about Spitzbergen, but after all, business was
> business and a man had to make a living. It was a blazing sun,
> pouring thickly over the atmosphere which was heavy with
> dampness. It was like a steamy blanket. Their clothes were
> damp and chafing on their bodies. Going inside the stores, they
> scratched their chins thoughtfully and said it was a pity the
> soda man wasn't alive to enjoy the wonderful weather.* [52] (pp.
> 313–14)

Better gangsters than Cossacks. There is still a God over America.

But what of Judaism in this world where businessmen and gangsters exchange roles, where enterprise and crime are scarcely to be
distinguished, where adaptability is the key to survival? The
representatives of Orthodoxy are rudely satirized:

> In the synagogue a dozen old men leaned on their elbows
> over a bare board table studying the Talmud like a bunch of
> college boys working on Kant. An old man read three or four
> lines aloud.
> "Rabbi ben Onz said this is to mean this, Rabbi ben Twoz,
> of a later generation, said it is to mean that, while here, nearer

---

* The same sense of the fated ends *Homage to Blenholt:* ". . . it seemed to
the old man that this death of youth was among the greatest tragedies in
experience and that all the tears in America were not enough to bewail it.
But all the same the evening sun that day went down on time." (p. 302)

to our own time, Rabbi ben Threez said that in spite of the opinions of these venerated rabbis, it means neither this nor that, but, if the word 'fourz' is properly understood, the passage clearly means part of this and part of that together but neither this nor that in themselves, but in part, together, and also the other thing added. All these have been the words of the learned, and what say you now?"

One of the old men says "Hichle," another says "Pichle," and the third says "Schmichle," but the "ultimate sage, the man who contained within his skinny body all the cold, clinical wisdom," opines differently: "Let us go again to the Talmud, the Good Book. It says, 'Va-cha-choo-loo, va-cha-choo-loo.' And this means, when the wind will blow, the cradle will rock." [53] Youth has seldom been less favorably impressed by the wisdom of its elders.*

6 Fathers and Sons: Henry Roth and Isaac Rosenfeld

Meyer Levin and Daniel Fuchs photographed their scenes with a wide lens. Other novelists chose to focus on the family, rather than on the city or the section. But the "family" is a complex institution. It can, for instance, be a "line" that extends through time for as many generations as genealogy can account for, or a conjugal unit limited to a man, a woman, and their children. With the exception of Nathaniel Hawthorne and William Faulkner, major American writers have tended to write of families in the second sense—or, more likely still, of individuals. Jewish writers have not been an exception. Some have followed families through several generations, but these writers have often been critical of the Americanization of the Jews (and are, therefore, taken up in the next chapter). Writers who take a more affirmative view of assimilation are likely to focus on the conjugal family and, within that family, upon the father-son relationship.

The sociological situation, the literary conventions dominant at the time, and the regnant psychological theory all encouraged second-generation writers to center their work on the conflict of fathers and sons—if autobiography were not motive enough.

---

* It ought, however, to be noted that the epigraph to *Low Company* is from the prayer said on Yom Kippur, the Day of Atonement.

Generational conflict was probably inevitable as the children of immigrants found themselves caught between the ideals of their parents and the realities of American conditions. Although Oscar Handlin's famous history of immigration, *The Uprooted* (1952), has been faulted for its idyllic evocations of peasant life in the Old World, his account of domestic strains in the New World has withstood critical scrutiny. In Biblical and Talmudic tradition, sons are submissive to their fathers; the ideal is a patriarchal one. But, as Irving Malin has noted, traditional concepts of the father-son relationship have not survived transplantation to American soil. The seven writers he discusses in *Jews and Americans* (1965)*

> deal with imperfect father-son relationships in which rebellion supplants acceptance; violence replaces tenderness; and fragmentation defeats wholeness. Thus the father-son relationship mirrors the moment of exile: the Jewish-American family is no longer holy.[54]

What the writers of the second generation experienced in the ghetto they also read about in the books held up to them as models of modernism. James Joyce was, of course, the most influential figure of all; the relation of Stephen Dedalus to Simon Dedalus and Leopold Bloom, his actual and his metaphoric fathers, became a paradigm for many American writers. Joyce's *Ulysses* was certainly a central fact of Henry Roth's literary consciousness when he sat down to write his classic study of second-generation childhood, *Call It Sleep* (1934).

Henry Roth and Isaac Rosenfeld were, like most of the writers of their generation, strongly influenced by Sigmund Freud and by the psychoanalytical tradition. In Freudian theory they found a third reason to stress the uneasy relationship between fathers and sons. Although the search for instances of Oedipal conflict in the literature (and biography) of earlier times can lead to reductionist conclusions, Freudian patterns are now—that is, since the development of psychoanalysis—a part of literature if for no other reason than that authors write them into their books. It well may be that this third factor, the psychoanalytical tradition, is genetically related

---

* The seven writers are Karl Shapiro, Delmore Schwartz, Isaac Rosenfeld, Leslie Fiedler, Saul Bellow, Bernard Malamud, and Philip Roth.

to the sociological factor; Sigmund Freud himself was an assimilated
Jew who had consciously broken with the traditions of his parents
and grandparents. No wonder then that *Call It Sleep* is the most
Freudian of the great American novels.

The Prologue is devoted to the arrival in New York, in May of
1907, of Genya Schearl and her baby, David. Although she is dressed
in clothes that her husband Albert had sent her from America,
little David wears an "odd, outlandish, blue straw hat" with "polka
dot ribbons of the same color." [55] (p. 5) Genya says gently, "And
this is the Golden Land," (p. 6) but Albert is angered, in no mood
to rejoice, because she has failed to recognize him, changed as he
is by American conditions. In his anger, Albert flings away David's
symbolically foreign cap—his son will be an American. Above the
boat is the Statue of Liberty, the "New Colossus" of the poem by
Emma Lazarus. The scene is subtly symbolic:

> Behind the ship the white wake that stretched to Ellis Island
> grew longer, raveling wanly into melon-green. On one side
> curved the low drab Jersey coast-line, the spars and masts on
> the waterfront fringing the sky; on the other side was Brook-
> lyn, flat, water-towered; the horns of the harbor. And before
> them, rising on her high pedestal from the scaling swarmy
> brilliance of sunlit water to west, Liberty. The spinning disk
> of the late afternoon sun slanted behind her, and to those on
> board who gazed, her features were charred with shadow, her
> depths exhausted, her masses ironed to one single plane. Against
> the luminous sky the rays of her halo were spikes of darkness
> roweling the air; shadow flattened the torch she bore to a black
> cross against flawless light—the blackened hilt of a broken
> sword. (p. 10)

The golden door is also a darkened portal. Black cross suggests an
alien faith; broken sword foreshadows Albert Schearl's sexual im-
potence. The promise of American life seems as ominous as Albert's cruel greeting. No wonder the boat seems to drift slowly,
"as if reluctant," to her dock.

Book I is set four years later, when David is almost six. The
book is named "The Cellar" and dominated by the image of that
black unknown. Although the image is female, David's fears of
the cellar, which "bulged with darkness," (p. 19) are associated

with his fear of his father, who is given to fits of unrestrained rage.
When Albert is fired from a job for having threatened another
worker with a hammer, David is haunted by the vision of masculine
anger: "David could almost see him, the hammer raised over his
head, his face contorted in terrific wrath, the rest cringing away.
He shuddered at the image in his mind." (p. 28) The sexual associations of the hammer are obvious. In David's dreams, his father
becomes a fearful God, a combination of Yaweh and Thor.

David's life is complicated by a boarder whom his father brings
home, a boarder who subsequently attempts to seduce his mother,
thus acting to separate David from his only security. Another complication is introduced by a neighbor's daughter who wants him
to "play bad."

> "Yuh know w'ea babies comm from?"
> "N-no."
> "From de knish."
> *"Knish?"*
> "Between de legs. Who puts id in is de poppa. De poppa's
> god de petzel. Yaw de poppa." (p. 64)

The girl attempts to place his hand in her "knish," but David
manages to escape to his mother.

It is his mother who comforts him when the vision of a coffin
brings a new form of terror into his life. It is also she who is the
keeper of the Sabbath:

> With a little, deprecating laugh, his mother stood before the
> candles, and bowing her head before them, murmured through
> the hands she spread before her face the ancient prayer for the
> Sabbath. . . .
> The hushed hour, the hour of tawny beatitude . . . (p. 88)

She is, however, unable to protect him from his father's wrath.
When David loses some pennies on an errand, Albert is angry; when
David bloodies another child's nose in retaliation for a blow, Albert
comes after him in rage, inspires terror, seems about to strike with
the symbolic hammer.

> Suddenly he cringed. His eyelids blotted out the light like
> a shutter. The open hand struck him full against the cheek

and temple, splintering the brain into fragments of light. Spheres, mercuric, splattered, condensed and roared. He fell to the floor. (p. 105)

The scene foreshadows the conclusion of the novel, where Albert's ungoverned wrath sends David out to his symbolic death and rebirth.

Scene follows scene for almost two hundred pages, and each episode adds its fear to the basic terror of the rat-filled cellar that David must pass whenever he leaves or re-enters the apartment. The rhythm of the narration is skillfully handled. It is only when the reader feels that the tension is too much for *him* that Book I ends and Book II begins.

"The Picture" opens with a new job for Albert, who becomes a milkman, and a new neighborhood, the Lower East Side rather than the Brownsville section of Brooklyn. The tone changes with the scene. Now there are moments of comedy, in which Genya's newly arrived younger sister plays a major part. Bertha is merry, tart, ready-tongued, red-haired, stoutly built, and quite able to hold her own in verbal bouts with her brother-in-law. She and David go off together to the Metropolitan Museum of Art and have a series of hilariously funny, probably allegorical experiences. A peanut vender queried for directions predicts the outcome:

"Is dat a museum?"
"Dotsa duh musee," he flickered his eyebrows at her while he spoke. "You go inna straight," he pushed out his chest and hips, "you come out all tire." (p. 194)

In they go, to explore the labyrinth of culture, to emerge sweat-stained and exhausted. Bertha is also the butt of one of Albert's rare moments of humor. Back from the dentist's office, Bertha asks about dental bridges:

"Britches, he called them, no?" Aunt Bertha cheered up ruefully. "Pritchig, he ought to call them, a hearth in other words, there's such a fire in my mouth. But I will look handsomer soon, won't I?"
"What else!" Her brother-in-law's cheek scrolled into a sour smile. (p. 213)

Bertha's curiosity is also the means by which we come to understand the significance of the emblematic picture after which the entire book is named. Genya buys a picture of a field of green stalks and tiny blue flowers because they remind her of her Austrian home. It is revealed, when Bertha presses her for her long-kept secret, that the flowers in the picture are like the blue cornflowers that Genya had looked at when deserted by her Gentile lover. The blue flowers are also associated with the blue straw hat that David wore when he arrived at Ellis Island. David eavesdrops and begins inarticulately to feel that the vengeful father whom he fears may not be his father after all. The Oedipal fantasy may have in this instance a basis in fact, somewhere among the cornflowers of Austria.

Book III, "The Coal," introduces the *cheder,* where Reb Yidel Pankower, dressed in the baggy, stained, rumpled clothes that seem to have been the *melamud*'s uniform, attempts to teach Hebrew, largely through blows to the head, to an unruly group of restless boys. In this unlikely place, David learns to imagine salvation. Reb Pankower tells the story of the vision of Isaiah:

> "But just when Isaiah let out this cry—I am unclean—one of the angels flew to the altar and with tongs drew out a fiery coal. Understand? With tongs. And with that coal, down he flew to Isaiah and with that coal touched his lips—Here!" The rabbi's fingers stabbed the air. "You are clean! And the instant that coal touched Isaiah's lips, then he heard God's voice say, Whom shall I send? Who will go for us? And Isaiah spoke and—" (p. 305)

And the squabbling urchins rush back into the room. David is left to wonder what follows, to wonder how fiery coals can cleanse. Soon after, on the bank of the East River, David is dazzled by a sense of light and of mystical transfiguration. In the very next chapter, David discovers the trolley tracks that will be the dominant symbol of the fourth and final book. Two boys catch him on the way back from the dock and force him to thrust a sheet-zinc sword into the slotted rail, into the source of electrical power.

> Like a paw ripping through all the stable fibres of the earth, power, gigantic, fetterless, thudded into day! And light, un-

leashed, terrific light bellowed out of iron lips. The street quaked and roared, and like a tortured thing, the sheet zinc sword leapt writhing, fell back, consumed with radiance. (p. 340)

In the blaze of light, Roth fuses the phallic and the divine, and prepares the reader for the more complicated fusion at the novel's conclusion.

Book IV, "The Rail," brings a renewal of terror. David is victimized again by his father's anger. He is also humiliated and horrified when he realizes that the naked woman seen by a gang of boys was his mother. In a pair of bull's horns purchased by his father he sees a threat and a challenge. Book IV also introduces the forbidden faith, in the form of a Polish boy with a "scapiller" and a "pitcher o' de holy Mudder an' Chil'." (p. 413) By introducing his Polish friend to one of his female cousins, David obtains a rosary, symbol of the strange religion of the vast America that looms beyond the ghetto. His cousin's outraged parents arrive with their complaints just as Albert Schearl spills forth his resentment and his suspicions against Genya. He had always hated David because he thought him the child of another man. When he begins savagely to whip the boy, out tumbles the rosary, and pandemonium takes over.

David rushes into the night, secures a milk dipper for his sword, and goes to the rail to worship the God of Power. At this point Roth changes his fictional technique and most displays the influence of James Joyce. Against the background of many scattered conversations, David plunges his phallic dipper-sword into the source of power and, presumably, of manhood. His father's hammer, the cellar, Isaiah's fiery coal—all the images are brought together symphonically into a crescendo of significance. The electrical power that blasts and sears him is also the magical coal that grants redemption from sins. Too long to quote, the twenty-two pages of Chapter XXI are among the most remarkable in American literature, comparable perhaps to Captain Ahab's defiant worship of the fiery God who torments him.

When it is over, David's foot is burned—no doubt a further allusion to club-footed King Oedipus. Nonetheless, he has survived the challenge and overcome the threat. On the other side of his experience, David realizes that his father has been defeated, and a "vague, remote pity stirred within his breast like a wreathing, raveling smoke." (p. 598) While his imagination plays over his extraordinary initiation, his mother asks if he is sleepy:

> He might as well call it sleep. It was only toward sleep that every wink of the eyelids could strike a spark into the cloudy tinder of the dark, kindle out of shadowy corners of the bedroom such myriad and such vivid jets of images. . . . It was only toward sleep one knew himself still lying on the cobbles, felt the cobbles under him. . . . (pp. 598–99)

He felt "not pain, not terror, but strangest triumph, strangest aquiescence. One might as well call it sleep. He shut his eyes." (p. 599) Perhaps it was not ignorance that let *Call It Sleep* drop into oblivion from its publication in 1934 to its reissue in 1960. Perhaps David Schearl's pain and terror and triumph came *too* close to the experience of the young men and women of the second generation as they moved from childhood to adulthood and from one culture to another. Perhaps Henry Roth had to wait for another generation to recognize that he wrote for every generation. He found himself, in any event, unable to write another novel.

The highest compliment that one can pay to Isaac Rosenfeld's single novel, *Passage from Home* (1946), is to say that it is comparable to *Call It Sleep*. Bernard Miller, the narrator, is older than David Schearl, but his situation is similar. His father has remarried and deprived him of the comfort given David by Genya, but Bernard finds a kind of substitute in Aunt Minna, his mother's sister. In his Oedipal conflict with his father, he can look—as David could not—to his grandparents' generation.

At his grandfather's Passover *seder*, which Rosenfeld describes in rich detail, Bernard is happy, but even at the *seder* there is the strong suggestion that old ways are doomed. Minna's Gentile boyfriend Willy interrupts the service to sing his own song:

> I believe in the good old Bible,
> I believe in the good old Bible,
> I believe in the good old Bible,
> And it's good enough for me.

He sings of "that old time religion," and all cry "Amen." [56] (p. 20) Grandmother knows she ought to disapprove of such behavior, but even she smiles an unconscious approval.

Bernard's stepmother urges him to "take more of an interest in Jewish life," (p. 79) but she herself is more in love with her own body than with the God of Abraham and Isaac. "I don't know," comments Bernard,

> what women in the old country would do of a Friday toward nightfall; whether they went to *mikvah,* the ritual bath, for purposes of purification. We, however, had none of the usual concomitants of an orthodox Sabbath. My stepmother baked no *chalah,* traditional woven loaves, billowy or braided like wigs and covered with a glossy patina of egg; nor, covering her head and cupping her hands, did she light candles after sundown. All this was left to my grandmother. Stepmother's tabernacle was the toilet, and the tub was *mikvah* enough; she braided her hair in place of dough, and as for the gleaming of candles, she found an equivalent in cold cream. (pp. 77–78)

To provide her stepson with a Jewish life, she packs him off to his grandfather's house, but Bernard has no real rapport with "this poor, overdone figure of an old man" (p. 86) nor with his friend Reb Feldman—until Reb Feldman begins to snap his fingers, until the old men gathered at Feldman's house begin to clap their hands, weave on bent knees, and dance their Chassidic dance. "Though unable to understand, I had shared the experience of that ecstasy, and I, too, felt grateful for it." (p. 94) But Bernard cannot participate, cannot be a part of his own past.

Bernard returns to family quarrels. Like David Schearl, he has good reason to be suspicious. Was it possible that Bernard's father had an affair with his sister-in-law Minna in the short period between Bernard's mother's death and his own remarriage? Bernard pursues the truth because its knowledge is in itself "a kind of ecstasy." (p. 101) He runs off to stay with Minna after she is ordered out of his father's house (where she had come for a surprise party). Minna's life is characterized by the freedom of Bohemianism, but her house is filthy and Bernard discovers that he has no patience with bedbugs:

> The welts on my body were long and swollen, bleeding at several places where my nails had dug in. Under a fold of the

sheet I saw a small, flat brown insect running. I crushed it
with my nail and for a long time sat staring at the bloody
mark and regretting the rain, which, I thought, had brought
on the bedbugs. (p. 195)

The bugs become the insistent symbol of the impossibility—for Bernard—of Minna's way of life. Bernard decides eventually to return
to his father and to get the truth from him. Thus will they be reconciled. He actually dreams that he "had become my father. I had
reached his age, my hair was gray, my eyes were his shape and color,
and when I looked through his eyes I saw the world, not differently,
but yet altered as if it were by his own perception." (p. 241) He feels
loss, bereavement, the need to bridge the gulf that separates them, but
his father is cold, accusing. Bernard blurts out that he went off to live
with Minna "because of the way you treated her!" (p. 274) But
Harry Miller brusquely leaves the room, returns, attempts to explain
away his actions, fobs off his son with a smile and a pat on the head.

> I felt myself suspended over the unmade declaration, the
> postponed scene of final understanding. I had been ready to
> follow my father into the peril of intimacy where we speak
> clearly and know one another all too well. . . . Now, I thought,
> it was too late. (p. 280)

If Bernard will not be a Job who bows his head in repentance before
God or an Isaac who trusts his father unto death, then he had better
prepare himself to be another Stephen Dedalus as he goes forth, not
to become "the uncreated conscience of my race," but simply to be
himself.*

7 *Marriage with a* Shikse

Although Bernard Miller leaves home, he does not formally renounce
his grandfather's religion. There is always the possibility—if we
choose to let our fancy run freely—that Bernard will grow older and

* This theme of generational conflict is nearly ubiquitous. Herbert Gold,
for instance, has written eight novels over the past twenty years and peopled
them with carnival grifters, Wall Street stockbrokers, and university professors, but his most memorable story is his sentimental exploration of the
conflict between a grocer and his son. "The Heart of the Artichoke" (1957)
will probably outlast *Fathers* (1966) and all the rest of Gold's fiction.

wiser and, eventually, decide to take his place in the long line of prodigal sons that dates from the Biblical past. Perhaps. But when passage from home is a conversion to Christianity and not simply to secularism, then the problem is serious. Even more serious is the problem of intermarriage. The Talmudic ban on exogamy is based largely on two Biblical passages. In the twenty-fourth chapter of Genesis, Abraham sends a servant to find a wife for his son Isaac:

> Put your hand under my thigh, and I will make you swear by the Lord, the God of heaven and of the earth, that you will not take a wife for my son from the daughters of the Canaanites, among whom I dwell, but will go to my country and to my kindred, and take a wife for my son, Isaac.

In the seventh chapter of Deuteronomy, Moses—whose first wife was Zipporah the Midianite—urges his followers not to marry among the Hittites, the Canaanites, and the other peoples of the Promised Land:

> You shall not make marriages with them, giving your daughters to their sons or taking their daughters for your sons. For they would turn away your sons from following me, to serve other gods; then the anger of the Lord would be kindled against you, and he would destroy you quickly.

It is uncertain whether or not the anger of the Lord has been turned against American Jews, but large numbers of them have, indeed, made marriages with the people among whom they live.

The behavior of unusual men and women is by definition atypical, but it is at least suggestive that Bernard Baruch, Louis Brandeis, Fiorello LaGuardia (whose mother was Jewish), and Jacob Schiff all married Gentiles and that the Guggenheim and Seligman families became predominantly Episcopalians (as the Gratz family had before them). The arrival of two million East European Jews caused the rate of intermarriage, calculated for the entire Jewish population, to plummet, but the figures began to climb again when the children of the new immigrants began to marry. In New York in the period from 1908 to 1912, mixed marriages accounted for only 1.17 per cent of the total,[57] but figures in the neighborhood of 5 per cent began to appear in the 1930s. Relying largely on the statistics and the theory of Ruby Jo Reeves Kennedy, who found that Protestants, Catholics, and Jews in New Haven tended to marry within their religious groups, Nathan Glazer and other sociologists asserted that an intermarriage rate of 5 per cent was a "natural limit" and that the Jewish community's leaders need not be panicky about "losses" to Judaism.[58] By 1957, however, the Bureau of the Census found that 7.2 per cent of married Jews had non-Jewish partners.[59] A study of Greater Washington, published the same year, found a rate of 11.3 per cent.[60] In the San Francisco area in 1959 the rate was 37 per cent.[61] Rural figures were a greater shock. In the state of Iowa, from 1953 through 1959, 42.2 per cent of all marriages involving Jews were exogamous.[62] With these statistics in mind and with occasional glances at European cities—like Amsterdam in 1933, where 70 per cent of the Jewish population was intermarried [63]—secular Jews wishing for the survival of the Jews as a people have begun to respond to the threat of intermarriage with almost the same intensity as Orthodox Jews, for whom marriage to a *shikse* is the religious equivalent of death.

If intermarried couples were composed of Jews married to *converts*, there would be far less anxiety in the Jewish community, but the Christian or agnostic partner rarely converts to Judaism. Since the children of a mixed marriage generally follow the mother's faith and since Jewish males are far more likely to marry exogamously than are Jewish females, approximately three-fourths of the children of mixed marriages are reared as Christians or agnostics.[64] In the literary treatment of intermarriage, there is often tension between fathers and sons, but sociological and psychological evidence indicates that intermarriage is rarely the result of Oedipal conflict and rarely opposed with determination by the parents if the children insist on their own preferences.[65] For the son or daughter reared as a "real American" and thrown among non-Jews in the classroom and at the office, nothing seems more obvious than that every person has an inalienable right to marry according to the dictates of the heart. Marriages arranged by the *shadchan* (marriage broker) take place in the Chassidic community of Williamsburg and in the stories of Bernard Malamud but not in middle-class America; youth will be served. And youth assumes that love transcends all difference, that Montagu and Capulet are simply names. The dilemma has its comic elements, as evidenced in the popular success of that simple-minded theatrical heart-warmer, *Abie's Irish Rose*. But the conflict can be a desperate one.

Of the many novels written to dramatize the dilemmas of "marital assimilation," Myron Kaufmann's *Remember Me to God* (1957), Barbara Probst Solomon's *The Beat of Life* (1960), and Neal Oxenhandler's *A Change of Gods* (1962) are exemplary. Although Kaufmann's book was praised by Norman Mailer and commended by more than one sociologist, it remains little known. The father of the novel's errant son is appropriately named Adam Amsterdam. The name brings together the Edenic myth and the memory of the first Jews to arrive in America. An immigrant who worked as a butcher, Adam Amsterdam has made himself into a lawyer and become a judge in Boston. His family attends Temple Abraham, where Rabbi Budapester earns prestige through his ostentatious inability to speak Yiddish. Adam Amsterdam, however, finds Temple Abraham too cold for his religious instincts. He takes his son Richard to visit an Orthodox synagogue and tells him, "This is our heritage." But Richard is rude: "And we're stuck with it." Adam's answer is typically latitudinarian (typical of him, not of Orthodoxy): "I don't want you sneering at any religious faith, not even your own." [66] (pp. 255-56)

The difficulty is that Adam Amsterdam has already lost the core of the faith that he wants his son to respect. When Richard in a subsequent argument accuses him of neurosis, he confesses his confusions: ". . . I may not know *what* I believe, but I know I believe." This belief is really an inarticulate sense of inherited identity: "I can't explain it. I just feel as if to be anything else but a Jew is terribly wrong. . . . It's sort of as if that word is me. When I hear that word 'Jew,' I know it means me." * (pp. 427-28) Although Adam Amsterdam is not a reader of the Talmud (as every pious Jew must be), he knows that he is the descendant of Talmudic scholars and of martyred believers in the God whom Moses confronted on Sinai:

> Why should I make a bum out of my ancestors? All those generations that went to the trouble to keep on staying Jewish, so I could know I'm descended from Abraham, Isaac and Jacob,

---

* Hagar, the heroine of Miriam Bruce's *Linden Road* (1951), shuns assimilation with similar remarks: "I guess I'm a Jew because I feel like one. . . . I only know it's what I am." [67] (p. 279)

and if I were to turn Christian now, it seems to me I'd be making a monkey out of all those generations. If the Jewish religion in our family is going to die out with me, then our ancestors might just as well have saved themselves the trouble.

Richard has no patience with this line of argument: "So what am I supposed to do? Devote my life to being a propaganda poster?" (p. 426) This argument ends when Adam desperately reverts to the primitive basis of authority and strikes his son. Much later in the novel, Adam returns to the argument based on continuity and survival, but his language betrays him: "All those generations and now I'm the Last of the Mohicans." (p. 502) Had he called upon the "last of the Just," upon the thirty-seven just men whom God sends for each generation, he might at least have had a Jewish alternative to his son's ambitions, but James-Fenimore-Cooper-quoting Adam Amsterdam has gone too far along the path of assimilation to prevent his son from going further.

He is more dignified, however, even when striking his son and weeping in despair, than Rabbi Budapester, who tells Richard, "It's fun to be a Jew." (p. 529) Budapester borrows from those literary critics and existential theologians who have turned away from the revelation at Mount Sinai in order to marvel at the Jew as archetypal victim or Marginal Man. "Jews are Man in the extreme," Budapester declaims; they "have been at once the most magnificent and the most wretched of peoples, and this is the essence of Man." Richard is unmoved: "I don't want to be anybody's legend. . . . The trouble with you guys is that you want me to act out your fairy-tale." (pp. 538, 540) Rabbi Budapester leaves in a huff—in a Cadillac.*

Richard goes to Harvard College, minds his manners, and becomes an unscrupulous, scheming aspirant to Hasty Pudding. He scorns a lovely Jewish girl in order to whore indecently after a Jezebel from Beacon Hill. Wilma Talbot, suggestively nicknamed "Wimsy," is the blonde Yankee of Richard's dreams, but Richard is the dark stranger of her father's nightmares. He is not eager to see her mar-

* Up-to-date Rabbi Budapester may be compared to Rabbi Robert Schechtman of Springfield, Massachusetts, whose 1966 Mustang, the "Heavenly Hauler," can accelerate to 100 m.p.h. in 14 seconds. "To be religious," he avows, "doesn't mean that one must be withdrawn" (N.Y. Times, Oct. 14, 1967).

ried to young Mr. Amsterdam: "Damn it, Wims, I didn't send you over to Radcliffe to run around with Jews and gypsies." (p. 389) Since unwed mothers are definitely included among Mr. Talbot's exclusions, the plot becomes even more complicated when Richard's sister Dorothy is made pregnant (out of wedlock) and attempts suicide. Wimsy's father coldly announces, "There are no whores in my family." (p. 603) Richard's induction into the Army is still another complication, but the implication of the novel is that Richard's desire was certain to be frustrated. Richard is sent off to the Army for the same reason that Huckleberry Finn is sent off to the Territory—because no other conclusion seems plausible.

More tragic still is the outcome of the affair in Barbara Probst Solomon's unfortunately neglected novel, *The Beat of Life*. The author's contribution to a symposium on "Jewishness and the Younger Intellectuals" suggests that her heroine, Natasha Thompson, is to some degree autobiographical:

> I have a memory of a noble religion in which I no longer believe, nor was taught to believe, and of a heroic struggle in which I have never participated. . . . When one gives up a belief in God, one ought to have the strength to give up the forms associated with religious observance.[68]

Natasha Thompson's family indulges itself in a Passover similar to that celebrated in Meyer Levin's *The Old Bunch*. Natasha's agnostic father gobbles shrimp and explains to Natasha's Roman Catholic boyfriend, Timothy Lanahan, "This isn't exactly traditional." [69] (p. 10) The second chapter, narrated by Timothy rather than by Natasha, tells of his thrice-married political-scientist mother and of the domestic chaos that resulted from her unusual marital choices. The young lovers feel cut off from the past, but the past is the political events of the 1930s rather than Judaism or Catholicism. They go to old films at the Thalia on 95th Street because synagogue and church no longer make sense. "What happens to people like me," asks Natasha, "who would like to be mystics but can't, who can't go to churches or temples or take mescaline? Where do we go?" (p. 65)

Her questions became more pointed when they discover that she is pregnant. Timothy wants the unborn child to be reared as a Jew, but Natasha is filled with doubts: "But what right have we to our gentle Passovers, our conscience tithe of Bonds for Israel? How do we get off so easily? Why do we call ourselves Jews?" (p. 110) That she cannot answer the question still contested by the most learned scholars is no surprise.

She decides on an abortion and then, when it is too late, broods on the beat of life that she had felt within her. She decides to give a life for a life, and takes her own. Timothy goes about his routines, registers for Columbia, buys texts, and realizes that the beat of life will never be the same again, not for him. Although the novel falls into the well-worn "star-crossed lovers" category, it is also a remarkable, deft—and poignant—treatment of the theme.

The theme of intermarriage is taken up and carried through to apostasy by Neal Oxenhandler, whose novel *A Change of Gods* opens in Nice on the Riviera, where Paul Shiel courts Candida Martin. The relations of *The Beat of Life* are reversed. He's a secular Jew and she's a lapsed Roman Catholic. Her religious commitment is not strong: ". . . if you want to learn about the Church," she tells him, "I suggest you write the Knights of Columbus." [70] (p. 17) They tour the Midi together and, by the time they reach Rapallo, register as man and wife. When this honeymoon of sorts is over, he puts a wine-foil ring on her finger and she comments, "I hope you mean it, I think I'm pregnant." (p. 22) They marry in Florence.

But motor scooter and hotel room are false symbols of mobility and freedom. Behind the facade of liberation is the reality of family ties. The voyage back to America is the transition. Candy's mother is given to writing letters to her senator about the menace of Communism. Her aged grandfather—a philologist—is austere, devout, and determined. He urges Paul's conversion to Catholicism, while Paul's father, under additional strain from an investigation for income-tax evasion, is enraged at the very thought of a *shikse* in the family. When he behaves abusively, his son defends him and his wife shouts at Candy, "You better get used to it! We're not so hoity-toity polite in this family!" (p. 68) Christmas Eve brings the in-laws together—physically. The occasion is a disaster comparable to the Passover riot in *The Old Bunch*:

> At Lilian's [Mrs. Shiel's] Christmas Eve party, Grandfather suffered a mild heart attack, followed by a stroke, that paralyzed his right side. Sam [Shiel] blamed it on the flowers,

three hundred dollars' worth. He told Lilian later that even he had got a little sick from the smell. She was distressed, not because she felt guilty, but because it spoiled her party to have him collapse onto the table, right in a plate of lobster salad. (p. 86)

Candy nurses her grandfather until his death, at which moment he renews his request that Paul convert to Christianity.

Crises multiply. The trial of Sam Shiel begins just as Candy bears his granddaughter Sarah. To save his distraught father, Paul perjures himself in court, whereupon his father becomes his jaunty self again, until he hears that Paul intends to convert to Catholicism. Sam and Lilian Shiel scream with rage and Paul screams back in phrases similar to Richard Amsterdam's: "You never sent me to *shul* [synagogue]. I was never even bar mitzvah [confirmed into Jewish manhood]. Why should I feel like a Jew?" Lacking answers to his question, Sam Shiel cries out, "You—you Eichmann!" (p. 180) The group must survive; exogamy is genocide. To punish Paul, Sam confesses in court. To punish Paul or herself, or both of them, Candy returns to devout Catholicism and adopts the rhythm method of contraception and, predictably, become pregnant again. She loses the baby. Paul disappears, drifts, returns, and is sentenced to three months in jail (for perjury). The book ends with father and son reconciled, with the marriage in ruins. The conversion to Christianity is, however, apparently for keeps. Paul—like his Damascus-bound namesake—has joined the ranks of those who pray on Good Friday, until some Vatican Council deems otherwise, for the conversion of the Jews.*

8 *Philip Roth and the Rabbis*

It is no surprise that the most famous of the stories of conversion is by Philip Roth. Of Jewish writers a generation younger than Saul Bellow and Norman Mailer, he is the most talented, the most con-

* Among others who have dealt with the theme of intermarriage, Norman Katkov and Samuel Yellen merit a note. Although a long list of publications suggests that Katkov has had a mildly successful career as a writer, he has never won any kind of recognition from those literary critics who establish reputations. Nonetheless, his novel *Eagle at My Eyes* (1948) deserves mention as an early, optimistic dramatization of intermarriage. Yellen's *The Wedding Band* (1961) is an excellent novel dealing with intermarriage and its results from the point of view of the children.

troversial, and the most sensitive to the complexities of assimilation and the question of identity. Roth's first collection of a novella and five stories, *Goodbye, Columbus* (1960), received the National Book Award, the praises of those writers generally associated with *Partisan Review* and *Commentary,* and considerable abuse from men institutionally involved in the Jewish community.[71] Two stories were the focus of resentment: "The Conversion of the Jews" and "The Defender of the Faith."

Ozzie Freedman, the inquisitive hero of "The Conversion of the Jews," asks the questions that any intelligent boy wants to ask, questions like those young Mary Antin put to her teachers. How can Jews be the Chosen People if the Declaration of Independence affirms that all men are created equal? How can an omnipotent God who made the heavens and the earth be *unable* to "let a woman have a baby without having intercourse"? [72] (p. 141) Rabbi Marvin Binder cannot handle questions of this sort. He sends for Mrs. Freedman. When Rabbi Binder attempts to explain to Ozzie why it is that "some of his relations" consider airplane crashes tragic in proportion to the number of Jews killed in them, Ozzie shouts "that he wished all fifty-eight were Jews." (p. 142) Mrs. Freedman is summoned again.

Ozzie is punished and becomes prudent, but Rabbi Binder feels an unacknowledged urge to force another confrontation with his recalcitrant pupil. Forced by Binder's nagging demands, Ozzie drops his reticence and re-asks his question: "Why can't He make anything He wants to make!" While Rabbi Binder prepares his answer, another child causes a disturbance and Ozzie takes advantage of the commotion:

> "You don't know! You don't know anything about God!"
> The rabbi spun back towards Ozzie. "What?"
> "You don't know—you don't—"
> "Apologize, Oscar, apologize!" It was a threat.
> "You don't—"
> Rabbi Binder's hand flicked out at Ozzie's cheek. Perhaps it had only been meant to clamp the boy's mouth shut, but Ozzie ducked and the palm caught him squarely on the nose.
> (p. 146)

Ozzie flees from the room and climbs to the building's roof and locks the door. The crowd gathers, the rabbi begs him from the street not to be a martyr, and his schoolmates—eager for sensation—urge him, "Be a Martin, be a Martin!" (p. 155) His mother comes and the child becomes the teacher. Ozzie catechizes from the rooftop:

> "Do you believe God can do Anything?" Ozzie leaned his head out into the darkness. "Anything?"
> "Oscar, I think—"
> "Tell me you believe God can do Anything."
> There was a second's hesitation. Then: "God can do Anything."
> "Tell me you believe God can make a child without intercourse."
> "He can."
> "Tell me!"
> "God," Rabbi Binder admitted, "can make a child without intercourse." (p. 157)

Mrs. Freedman agrees and Ozzie leaps into a safety net. Although one critic has assured us that Ozzie's leap "becomes paradoxically a moral symbol of his conversion to Judaism and to life," [73] the form of the catechism and the imagery are unmistakably Christian: ". . . right into the center of the yellow net that glowed in the evening's edge like an overgrown halo." (p. 158) It is a doubly parabolic descent. The economy of characterization and the simplicity of the fable make the allegorical implications unavoidable. Was it not written that a child shall teach them?

In Roth's collection, Ozzie's story was followed by "The Defender of the Faith," in which the protagonists are Sergeant Nathan Marx, a veteran of World War II, and Sheldon Grossbart, a trainee under Sergeant Marx's care. Sheldon Grossbart, ironically named "Big Beard," begs cravenly for special treatment on the basis of the ethnic bond between him and the sergeant. Although military tradition sanctifies Friday nights to "G.I. parties" (i.e. everyone scrubs the barracks and prepares for Saturday morning inspection), Sheldon points out that Jews must attend religious services. Sergeant Marx allows the request and goes, another night, to attend the services he hasn't gone to for years. Then he thinks he hears Sheldon cackle, "Let the goyim clean the floors!" (p. 172) The sergeant begins to worry. When the captain in charge of the company informs him that Sheldon's congressman has called the general to complain about the

Army's non-kosher foods, Sergeant Marx's ambivalence increases. The captain's outrage is deftly captured:

> Look, Grossbart, Marx here is a good man, a goddam *hero*. When you were sitting on your sweet ass in high school, Sergeant Marx was killing Germans. Who does more for the Jews, you by throwing up over a lousy piece of sausage, a piece of firstcut meat—or Marx by killing those Nazi bastards? If I was a Jew, Grossbart, I'd kiss this man's feet. He's a goddam hero, you know that? And *he* eats what we give him. (pp. 180–81)

It turns out that Sheldon himself, not his father, wrote the letter to the congressman, that Sheldon will use his Jewishness to draw advantage for himself from the persecutions of others, that Sheldon does not even have the excuse of sincerely held faith. Given a chance to go to town for Passover, he heads for a Chinese restaurant. The penultimate turn of the screw comes when Sheldon arranges, with a Jewish acquaintance at headquarters, to be removed from orders that send him to the Pacific, where the war has not yet ended. At this moment, Sergeant Marx decides to defend the faith; he has the orders changed so that Sheldon Grossbart goes with the rest. Sheldon shrieks, "There's no limit to your anti-Semitism, is there!" (p. 199) Sergeant Marx calls himself vindictive, but he may also be seen as the defender of a democratic theory by which the accidents of birth give no exemption from our common fate. He acts from a sense of justice that is, finally, humanistic in its universality.

Given only these two stories, an unsympathetic reader might suspect that Roth holds a wholly negative view of Jewishness and of Judaism, but the first and final stories of *Goodbye, Columbus* and Roth's first novel, *Letting Go* (1962), are longer and more complex. The long title story plays with names. Although the story is certainly about the country discovered by the Genoese explorer, the words are from a phonograph record dedicated to memories of Ohio State University, located at Columbus, Ohio. The record is owned and utilized as a devotional aid by Ronald Patimkin, an athletic young man who is about to enter his father's business, where he will "start at two hundred a week and then work himself up." (p. 61) Through sales of kitchen sinks, phenomenally good during the war years, the Patimkins have risen to suburban wealth. Is not cleanliness more profitable than godliness?

The Patimkin family has whatever goods the world calls good. Their refrigerators burst with fruit; their trees are hung with sporting goods. Beefy Ronald Patimkin is a type unrelated to the pale scholar of the *shtetl* and the exploited needle-trades worker of the ghetto. Harvey Swados has noted this with characteristic acuteness:

> We might measure the distance that has been traveled by contrasting Hemingway's Jewish athlete of the Twenties, Robert Cohn, the boxer, forever attempting with fists or flattery to join the club, the expatriate Americans who exclude him, to Philip Roth's Jewish athlete of the Fifties, Ronald Patimkin, who hangs his jockstrap from the shower faucet while he sings the latest pop tunes, and is so completely the self-satisfied musclebound numskull that notions of Jewish alienation are entirely "foreign" to him.[74]

Brenda Patimkin, the family's older daughter, is a paragon of Olympic virtues; she plays tennis, she runs, she rides, she swims. In the pool, she is a far cry from the *Yiddishe Momma* of yesteryear. "I went," says her boy friend,

> to pull her towards me just as she started fluttering up; my hand hooked on to the front of her suit and the cloth pulled away from her. Her breasts swam towards me like two pink-nosed fish and she let me hold them. Then, in a moment, it was the sun who kissed us both, and we were out of the water, too pleased with each other to smile. (p. 17)

And, as Leonard Baskin lamented in a recent symposium, "For every poor and huddled *mikvah* [ritual bath], there is a tenhundred of swimming pools." [75] In this suburban world, the past seems passé indeed.

Brenda Patimkin stands on the magic casement of a world sharply contrasted to that of Neil Klugman's Aunt Gladys, a woman of the immigrant generation. Immediately after the first poolside scene, Roth shows us the milieu from which Neil Klugman (i.e. "wise man") wants to rise:

> That night, before dinner, I called her.
> "Who are you calling?" my Aunt Gladys asked.

"Some girl I met today."

"Doris introduced you?"

"Doris wouldn't introduce me to the guy who drains the pool, Aunt Gladys."

"Don't criticize all the time. A cousin's a cousin. How did you meet her?"

"I didn't really meet her. I saw her."

"Who is she?"

"Her last name is Patimkin."

"Patimkin, I don't know," Aunt Gladys said . . . (pp. 3-4)

Aunt Gladys does know that a growing boy should eat. But Neil is not about to be satisfied with the food she makes the center of her life.

Neil has his chance. He dates Brenda, watches her at tennis, runs around a track (that may or may not symbolize the final futility of his efforts), basks in the hard sunshine of her father's wealth. He is accepted as her fiancé, as a future worker in the porcelain vineyard of Patimkin sinks.

The marvels of money, and simple physical beauty, are counterpointed by the vision of Gauguin's Tahiti. In the downtown library where Neil works, a little Negro boy comes daily to stare at a book of reproductions of Gauguin. His moan of pleasure is poignant: "Man, that's the fuckin life. . . . *Look, look,* look here at this one. Ain't that the fuckin *life?*" (p. 37) But the breadfruit-and-wildflower life is unobtainable for the little Negro boy, except in fantasy; Neil's dream of classless, creedless hedonism turns out to be equally unobtainable. He bullies Brenda until she purchases a contraceptive diaphragm, but when he goes up to Boston to spend the Jewish holidays in unholy union with her, he learns that she has left the diaphragm behind, where her mother discovers it. The affair is over. Neil is convinced that the discovery was intentional, Brenda's way out. He goes off and stares into the glass that walls Harvard's Lamont Library and asks himself questions that Roth leaves to the reader's imagination. Then he takes "a train that got me into Newark just as the sun was rising on the first day of the Jewish New Year. I was back in plenty of time for work." (p. 136) The days he meant to spend in carnival he spends at work. He cannot join the Patimkins, cannot use Brenda to rise up "those lousy hundred and eighty feet that make summer nights so much cooler in Short Hills than they are in Newark," (p. 14) but he cannot remain in the world of Aunt Gladys either.

The suburbs that Neil Klugman aspires to are the ones that Eli Peck, inhabitant of Woodenton, lives in. The last story of *Goodbye, Columbus,* "Eli, the Fanatic," is the most complex and difficult to interpret. (It has certainly drawn the most contradictory interpretations.) The contrasts in this story are extreme, for the highly assimilated "successful" Jews of Woodenton are suddenly confronted by a group of Jews more strange and Orthodox than Neil's Aunt Gladys. The newcomers are from Eastern Europe, refugees from unnamed but clearly suggested persecutions; they open a *yeshiva* in pastoral Woodenton, whose name indicates both its forested environment and its hardness of heart.

Eli is the tragic go-between. Standard critical opinion holds that the "demarcation [in the story] between good and evil is absolutely clear," [76] but this is simplification. In truth, both sides in the suburban dispute are equally rigid. With a comedy painfully true to life, Roth demonstrates how far the nominal Jews of Woodenton are from their ancestral faith. One of Eli's friends argues with him on the telephone:

> Sunday mornings I have to drive my kid all the way to Scarsdale to learn Bible stories? And you know what she comes up with, Eli—that this Abraham in the Bible was going to kill his own kid for a *sacrifice!* You call that religion, Eli? I call it sick. Today a guy like that they'd lock him up. (pp. 276–77)

From this position, an Orthodox *yeshiva* is simply incomprehensible. But the caftan-clad Jews of the *yeshiva* are equally unable to understand the Americans or to realize why Eli and his neighbors are upset. Eli's desperation is intensified by his pregnant wife's devotion to the dogma of the followers of Sigmund Freud. Eli pats his wife's belly and says, "You know what your mother brought to this marriage— . . . a sling chair, three months to go on a *New Yorker* subscription, and *An Introduction to Psychoanalysis*." His wife answers, "Eli, must you be aggressive?" (p. 259) There is no comfort for him.

When *Weltanschauungen* collide, it is Orthodoxy that yields. Although Eli prevails on Mr. Tzuref (i.e. troubles) to dress his assistant in one of Eli's greenish tweed suits, Eli cannot stand the sight of the "greenie" dressed in his clothing, like a vision of another self. Tormented, guilty, unable to withstand the pressures from every side, torn apart by conflicts of identity, Eli breaks down, dons the black clothing deposited by the Orthodox at his door, and wanders through the town like the Last of the Just. He goes to the hospital to see his newborn son and tells him,

> . . . I'll keep the suit at home, and I'll wear it again. I promise. Every year on the nineteenth of May, I'll wear it. I promise. All day. I won't work, I won't talk, I won't do anything but walk around with this black suit. And when you're old enough, I'll get you one, and you'll walk with me. . . . (pp. 297–98)

Eli is interrupted by the men in white with needles in their hands.

It has been argued that Eli's transformation is a "conversion into the essential Jew," whose essence is to suffer for the truth;[77] it has also been argued that Eli has been touched by "the strange power of an authentic religion." [78] A third view is that

> Eli's grotesque attempt at atonement is doomed to failure: it cannot be understood or accepted by his neighbors, for it is private and also dishonest in the sense that Eli can no more own the experiences that make orthodox dress a truthful expression of the Greenie's identity, than he can disown that part of himself which belongs to Woodenton.[79]

The third version seems closer to the truth, but Eli's fanatical act is pathetic rather than dishonest. There is only one path across the psychic abyss that separates Woodenton from the *yeshiva*—madness. Eli's fate is truly a tragedy and not an expiatory aberration. He has been driven to insanity, at least for the moment, by the hardness of the zealots who have treated him as a fanatic.

Support for this interpretation can be found in an extraordinary response made by Roth to a symposium conducted by *Commentary*: asked about his sense of identity, he answered with a statement and a question serious almost to solemnity:

> I cannot find a true and honest place in the history of believers that begins with Abraham, Isaac, and Jacob on the basis of the heroism of these believers, or of their humiliations and anguish. I can only connect with them . . . as I apprehend their God.

> And until such time as I do apprehend him, there will con-
> tinue to exist between myself and those others who seek his
> presence, a question . . . which for all the pain and longing it
> may engender, for all the disappointment and bewilderment it
> may produce, cannot be swept away by nostalgia or sentimen-
> tality or even by blind and valiant effort of the will: how are
> you connected to me as another man is not? [80]

To put the matter more abstractly, martyrdom proves the martyr's
commitment to his beliefs but cannot validate them. It seems improbable that Roth intended Eli Peck to affirm an apprehension that he
himself was unable to achieve.

Like Neil Klugman and Eli Peck, like Ozzie Freedman and Sergeant Marx, the hero of Roth's first (and best) novel is caught in the
middle, but the dilemmas confronted by Gabe Wallach are less spe-
cifically Jewish and more easily universalized. *Letting Go* (1962) is a
series of episodes in which Gabe Wallach becomes increasingly involved with people to whom he is not emotionally committed.

While doing graduate work at the University of Iowa, Gabe receives the impetuous embraces of Marjorie Howells, a *shikse* from
Kenosha, Wisconsin, who revolts "against Kenosha as though Caligula himself were city manager." [81] (p. 27) In her eyes he is the
exotic outsider; to please her, he proclaims himself her Trotsky, her
Einstein, her Moses Maimonides, but he knows that he's none of
these and was not meant to be. In Chicago, where he takes a job in
the university, he becomes involved with Martha Regenhart, a di-
vorcée with two children, but the affair has an air of impermanence,
and Gabe's admiration for his departmental chairman is, to speak
mildly, limited:

> Spigliano is a member of that great horde of young anagram-
> ists and manure-spreaders who, finding a good deal more
> ambiguity in letters than in their own ambiguous lives, each
> year walk through classroom doors and lay siege to the minds
> of the young, revealing to them Zoroaster in Sam Clemens and
> the hidden phallus in the lines of our most timid lady poets.
> (p. 63)

And Christ in the work of every Jewish writer?

Gabe's rootlessness has tragic consequences for others. In a grotesque and horrible disaster, one of Martha Regenhart's children kills

the other. The moment is followed by the climax of a crazy situation in which Gabe acts as go-between for a couple who attempt illegally to adopt the baby of a girl whom Martha had encountered at work. The girl turns out to be married to a brutal and stupid man appropriately named Harry Bigoness. Gabe rushes back and forth until, at last, he decisively seizes the baby and brings it to his childless friends.

In contrast to Gabe, Roth sets forth a circle of characters committed to adjustment. Claire Herz, once known as "hot Claire Herz," has become "an outstanding mother." (p. 96) Dora and Maury Horvitz lead lives dictated by the *New Yorker*. Of him she says, "Maury is a very Jewish fella." (p. 186) The one possible affirmative contrast to Gabe and Martha is the intermarried couple, Paul and Libby Herz.

The Herzes are almost as important within the structure of the novel as narrator-hero Gabe Wallach. They had married against the will of their parents: Libby's conversion to Judaism, she explains to Gabe, was "switching loyalties": it

> somehow proved to them [the Herz family] I didn't have any to begin with. I read six thick books on the plights and flights of the Jews, I met with this cerebral rabbi in Ann Arbor once a week and finally there was a laying on of hands. I was a daughter of Ruth, the rabbi told me. In Brooklyn . . . no one was much moved by the news. Paul called and they hung up. I might be Ruth's daughter—that didn't make me theirs. . . . And my father wrote us a little note to say that he had obligations to a daughter in school, but none to Jewish housewives in Detroit. (pp. 21–22)

Nonetheless, their marriage, economic difficulties, quarrels and reconciliations, suggest a way of life that is neither aimless nor complacent. It is for them that Gabe secures the illegitimate baby—for the intermarried couple, an adopted girl.

From this book, Roth went on to write a novel without Jews, almost without urban scenes, a novel that rivals and perhaps surpasses *Main Street* and *Winesburg, Ohio* as portraits of small-town America, but *When She Was Good* (1967) falls outside the bounds of this study—except insofar as it proves what everyone should have known: Philip Roth is a thoroughly assimilated American writer. Roth's next book was quite another matter.

Alexander Portnoy, the desperately comic narrator of *Portnoy's Complaint* (1969), is derived from the same sociological sources as Neil Klugman and Eli Peck and Gabe Wallach, but the literary mode in which he grotesquely lives and suffers is the novelized joke, the night-club gagster's ethnic line drawn out to nearly three hundred pages. In the hot pursuit of the blonde *shikse* by the Jewish libertine, Leslie Fiedler has seen the myth of Samson and Delilah, which allegedly underlies American Jewish fiction to the end of the 1920s.[82] Whether or not the argument holds for Abraham Cahan and Ludwig Lewisohn, none can doubt that Alexander Portnoy's sexual adventure is freighted with social significance:

> I don't seem to stick my dick up these girls, as much as I stick it up their backgrounds. . . . Columbus, Captain Smith, Governor Winthrop, General Washington—now Portnoy. As though my manifest destiny is to seduce a girl from each of the forty-eight states. As for Alaskan and Hawaiian women, I really have no feeling either way, no scores to settle, no coupons to cash in, no dreams to put to rest. . . . .[83] (p. 235)

His conquests are a series of *shikses* (preceded by a series of *shikses* whom he failed to conquer). Kay Campbell of Iowa, "The Pumpkin," is a ludicrous version of Gabe Wallach's Marjorie Howells. With her family, among the "real" Americans who live on farms and never raise their voices in argument, Portnoy celebrates Thanksgiving. Finally, *he* rejects *her,* looks higher in the social system: "Another gentile heart broken by me belonged to The Pilgrim, Sarah Abbott Maulsby—New Canaan, Foxcroft, and Vassar . . ." (p. 232) And lower in the system too. His most serious affair is with an illiterate from West Virginia, Mary Jane Reed, nicknamed "The Monkey," for whom he represents the exotically Hebraic, just as Gabe Wallach did for Marjorie. Miss Reed is outrageously vulgar; en route to a party given by Mayor John Lindsay, Portnoy appeals to her, "Don't make a grab for Big John's *shlong* until we've been there at least half an hour, okay?" (p. 211) Portnoy abandons her in Athens, after sexually intricate escapades in New England and in Rome. In Israel, however, he is impotent. Exhilarated by a world in which everyone, even the longshoremen, is a Jew, Portnoy picks up a female lieutenant and is sexually helpless. He listens to her idealistic

lectures on the superiority of Israeli socialism to American capitalism
and then attempts to rape her. She is strong but he is stronger—and
impotent. She tells him in a fine exchange of insults ("Tomboy,"
"Shlemiel") that he is a victim of the Diaspora, another Jew who
hates himself.

There is no doubt that he does. There is no doubt that his childhood is an Oedipal joke: "She was so deeply imbedded in my consciousness that for the first year of school I seem to have believed that
each of my teachers was my mother in disguise." (p. 3) Her over-
protective, overabundant love and her vindictive demands for love in
return combine to drown him in guilt. Portnoy's father is, of course,
a failure, Freud's anal type write large, writ grotesquely, a consumer
of All-Bran and Ex-Lax and prune juice, a salesman of insurance to
Negroes in the slums of Newark. His rage is related to the Boston-
based insurance company that gives him stationery with his name
printed beneath a picture of the *Mayflower* but makes it clear that
he is forever on his way to America and can never arrive. Portnoy's
own secret rebellion is a denial of Judaism; he claims to be an atheist
and not a Jew.

Now, at the age of thirty-three, he is Assistant Commissioner on
Mayor Lindsay's Commission on Human Opportunity, but still an
undutiful child in the eyes of his ever-watchful parents. He can turn
upon them and imitate their transparent nag into one of the classic
parodies of the excesses of assimilation: he mimics Mother on Seymour Schmuck:

> I met his mother on the street today, and she told me that
> Seymour is now the biggest brain surgeon in the entire West-
> ern Hemisphere. He owns six different split-level ranch-type
> houses . . . and belongs to the boards of eleven synagogues,
> all brand-new and designed by Marc Kugel, and last year with
> his wife and his two little daughters, who are so beautiful that
> they are already under contract to Metro, and so brilliant that
> they should be in college—he took them all to Europe for an
> eighty-million-dollar tour of seven thousand countries, some
> of them you never even heard of, that they made them just
> to honor Seymour, and . . . in every single city . . . he was
> asked by the mayor himself to stop and do an impossible oper-
> ation on a brain in hospitals that they also built for him right
> on the spot. . . . (pp. 99–100)

Et cetera, et cetera. But what of poor Portnoy? He lies on Dr. Spiel-vogel's couch while the doctor, presumably, takes notes for the essay that is cited in the epigraph-in-the-form-of-an-encyclopedia-entry. He, Portnoy, is the "Puzzled Penis."

What are we to make of his puzzlement? Is the book a Jewish joke or is it a joke about Jewish jokes? If the latter, which seems more probable, then it is—like Black Humor—a kind of terminus, a suggestion that the satirist of assimilation has grown tired of the harvest he himself desired. A good place for a satirist to stop.

9 The Black Humorists

It is not likely, however, that the writers of Black Humor will stop their savage satire of American customs. Burt Blechman and Bruce Jay Friedman are prolific writers, skillful combatants in a literary guerrilla war.* Although the specific targets of their verbal fire are Jews, these fictional Jews are grotesque caricatures meant to repre-sent *Homo Americanus,* the mindless, frenzied consumer on the make. The ambivalence of the first generation has become disgust.

In his excoriation of the all-too-assimilated Jews, Blechman is with-out mercy, but his victims are a remarkably thick-skinned and un-sympathetic lot, at least as he portrays them. *How Much?* (1961), Blechman's first novel, is based on the broad humor of mother-in-law jokes. Rona Halpern asks her mother, Jenny Stern, to move in with her and her husband Berney (who, at twenty-six, wants a new career as folksong singer). Mama is jammed into a closet, but she manages to aggravate a situation already deranged. Rona is a mad-woman who buys "bargains" at any price, who goes through the novel screaming "How much? how much?" When her mother runs off, Rona indulges herself in compensatory extravagance. She bids $200 for a pair of candlesticks her mother had sold for $20 (to buy a radio as a present). Mama dies while her son-in-law sketches a car-

---

* In addition to the three men discussed, the list of nominally Jewish Black Humorists might be extended to include Joseph Heller, Wallace Markfield, Irvin Faust, Mark Mirsky, Richard G. Stern, L. S. Simckes, and Jerome Charyn. Leslie Fiedler's novels and stories are similar to Black Humor in tempo and in a tendency to the grotesque, but Fiedler's fiction reveals an uncommon delight in the wild variety of American ethnicity. He is more celebrator than satirist.

toon of her. Rona hears of her mother's death and rushes immediately to a sale.

Almost as if he wanted to be sure that all his readers realized that Americanized Jews are no worse than anyone else, Blechman decided in his third and fourth books to satirize the *goyim*. *Stations* (1964) is a thoroughly obscene allegory in which subway stops are analogues for Stations of the Cross. The central figure is Dominick Wright (Dominus), whose daughter Tina is engaged to a certain Rosso. Since the dust jacket, as well as each chapter opening, has a cross, the allegorical intent is hard to miss. In a dream of power and pornography, Dominick is elected our leader. Whether the peroration shocks, disgusts, entertains, or bores the reader is probably a function of the reader's own sensibility. *Maybe* (1967) returns to the themes of *How Much?*

The most openly "Jewish" of Blechman's books is also the most interesting. Randy Levine, the child hero of *The War of Camp Omongo* (1963), is a version of the American Adam. His experiences are like those encountered by Huck Finn but without the moments of serenity and communion. Instead of the banks of the Mississippi, Randy stares out on the urban landscape, on the "corpse-strewn, stench-filled, fossil-lined shore," [84] (p. 4) on the junk and garbage and the filth of millions of people crowded together in a polluted parody of civilized life. Like Huck Finn and Holden Caulfield, Randy Levine sees ugly words scrawled on walls where no janitor can get them off again. His parents send him to Camp Omongo for the summer.

Steiner, the camp's owner, hustles the ceremonial rabbi through his role, raises the American flag, and lectures his charges on the merits of "total victory or total defeat." He points to the rotting eagle above the flag and shouts, "America and Omongo are one and the same." (pp. 17–18) The counselors systematically favor the children of wealthy parents: "You know Levine here lives in the cheapest part of the Bronx?" (p. 20) Religious services are merely a repetition of the opening ceremony. The rabbi, whose synagogue in the city has been turned into a supermarket, attempts to pray, but Steiner interrupts him with a tape of the Marine Corps Band's rendition of "The Stars and Stripes Forever." Omongo's credo is appropriate to the age: "Nobody believes in God. But you still gotta have a religion."

(p. 77) Omongo's religion is set forth in its Decalogue; Commandments III, VI, VII, and IX read:

> All graven images shall be as follows: Gold for first; Silver for second; Bronze for third; and Strontium 90 for the rest.

> Thou shalt kill for God and country on demand.

> Thou shalt adulterate the water, pollute the land, and poison the air for the sake of our fathers' pride.

> Thou shalt witness falseness and smile. (p. 182)

There is clearly little need for Aaron's Golden Calf.

The camp features violence as well as blasphemy. Seeing a film in which Japanese are burned alive, the boys cheer. There is, moreover, animality rather than the study of animals. The counselors seduce, or are seduced by, Sylvia Steiner, the owner's wife. Their charges are prematurely worldly-wise. The summer draws to an appropriately violent end with a treasure hunt, which Randy ruthlessly wins, and with the camp destroyed by a conflagration, which Randy starts. The fire, like that which consumed Sodom and Gomorrah, is purgatorial, but the book is not one to inspire boundless confidence in the future.

Bruce Jay Friedman seems to have approached the Black Humor camp more slowly than Burt Blechman did. His first novel, _Stern_ (1962), was by no means in the realistic tradition, but it was distinctly related to novelistic conventions, which Friedman has since rejected. Although it is not entirely clear whether Stern discovers or creates anti-Semitism in the suburbs, he certainly has a hard time of it. When a neighbor pushes Stern's wife and tells his son not to play with "kikes," Stern is paralyzed by fear. His bravery consists of plans to send his wife to ask the man not to torment him and make his ulcer worse. In a friendly Negro, Stern sees stereotypes about fighters. Eventually, Stern goes to a rest home, where he finds companionship and sexual adventures with an unlikely group of people. Stern is released, finds his wife tan and perky, goes to see the nasty neighbor, and talks back to him despite a punch on the ear. He now seems to have the prospect of moderate happiness. The moral seems to be that one can make things worse than they are.

Friedman's second novel is filled with the sort of people whom

Stern found at the rest home. *A Mother's Kisses* (1964) tells of Meg, a "Mom" who can hold her own with Mrs. Portnoy or with D.J.'s mother (in Norman Mailer's *Why Are We in Vietnam?*). Joseph's father is a nonentity: "His father stopped at the corner to buy a newspaper and said, 'I buy a paper here.' In the subway car he said, 'I usually stand at this end and hold on to the strap.' " [85] (p. 14) Meg is all entity: " 'Did your mother ever let you down?' She gave him an ear kiss that seemed overly wet and said, 'Will you please learn to put your last buck down on this baby?' " (p. 86) When Joseph is of an age for college, Meg arranges it (Kansas Land Grant Agricultural) and accompanies him to the campus. The humorous adventures eventually conclude when Joseph persuades reluctant Meg to go home. His "resolution" of the Oedipal conflict—almost miraculous given Meg's thunderous presence—is a victory comparable to Stern's final triumph over his exaggerated fears of anti-Semitism.

Friedman's most recent novelistic effort, *The Dick* (1970), is topical, repetitive, and tiresome. Kenneth Sussman changes his name to Kenneth LePeters and finds employment as a public-relations expert for a police department that seems to have recruited its detectives from some of the nation's least plausible psychiatric wards. Sussman-LePeters is timidly deranged, a retouched portrait of Friedman's first hero. Like Stern, he eventually asserts himself. After a series of mildly comic adulteries, including an affair with a girl who took the name of Ellen Rosenberg because someone said she looked Jewish (she isn't), Sussman-LePeters humiliates his faithless wife's Latin lover, rejects the now repentant wife, rescues his daughter from an improbable elementary school, and promises to take her and her pet fish upon some unspecified adventure. The terminal bravado seems excessive.

The most gifted practitioner of the genre, however, transcends its limitations through a seriousness that has sometimes gone unnoticed among the marvelously comic effects. It is high time that Stanley Elkin's high jinks are adequately noticed.

Typical of Elkin's characters is Ed Wolfe, who appears in the second story of *Criers and Kibitzers, Kibitzers and Criers* (1966). Fired from his job as telephone collector for Cornucopia Finance Corporation, Ed Wolfe cashes his pay check, clears out his bank account, sells his car, his furniture, his books, and his records, pawns the rest of his impediments, and seeks, like Henry David Thoreau, to live deliberately and Spartanlike. The whole world, proclaims another of Elkin's seekers after simplicity, "was a Walden if you knew how to look at it." [86] Ed Wolfe determines "to drive life into a corner, and reduce it to its lowest terms, and, if it proved to be mean, why then to get the whole and genuine meanness of it, and publish its meanness to the world; or, if it were sublime, to know it by experience, and be able to give a true account of it. . . ." [87] Amidst the meanness of a Negro club, Ed Wolfe finds a girl who is sublime; but he leaves her, and as he leaves he sees her "luxuriant brown hand" holds his pale one, "lifeless and serene, still and infinitely free." [88] (p. 66)

The association of freedom and death is dramatized, savagely, in another story, "In the Alley," wherein the protagonist rises splendidly to heroism while he lives out the last month of his life in freedom from every responsibility (other than his debt to mortality). But the doctor was wrong. Feldman outlives his heroism, finds himself alone with the malignancy inside him, attempts pathetically to seduce a vicious woman he meets in a bar, is beaten, and dies in an alley, too weak to remove the sign pinned to his jacket: STAY AWAY FROM WHITE WOMEN.

Ed Wolfe is literally an orphan. Feldman is metaphorically one, like all the kibitzers (who live to put each other on) and all the criers (who exist only to bemoan the world they never made).

Stanley Elkin is both kibitzer and crier. Fantastically comic characters people his world: a well-dressed unemployed Negro who sits in a hotel lobby reading *The Wall Street Journal* because it "looks good for the race," [89] a Nobel Prize winner in anthropology who took up his profession because of "the color photographs of the bare-breasted native girls in *The National Geographic*," [90] a piano player (Mussolini's son) whose "riff on 'Deutschland, Deutschland Über Alles' makes strong men weep," [91] a nymphomaniacal princess who is one of the "five unmarried women in Roman Catholic Italy fitted for her own diaphragm." [92] But the comedy is always within a tragic context. Greenspahn, stricken by the death of his son, is told to busy himself in his store: "What was he, a kid, that because he was making up somebody's lousy order everything would fly out of his mind? The bottom dropped out of his life and he was supposed to go along as though nothing had happened. . . . Like in the movies after the horse kicks your head in you're supposed to get up and ride him so he can throw you off and finish the job." [93] What's funny? A boy is dead. We are all bereft.

James Boswell, the hero of Elkin's novel *Boswell: A Modern Comedy* (1964), is an orphan himself and the father of an orphan. "My parents are dead. . . . I am thirty-five years old, but I have a son twenty. He was born out of wedlock to a fifteen-year-old girl who died bearing him. Her parents took my child in exchange for their own. He knows me and who I am." (p. 10)

Boswell, as an adolescent, was counseled by the famous Leon Herlitz, the man who turned Freud to psychology and told Lindbergh to fly the Atlantic, the man whose correct placement of German officers prolonged the duration of World War I. (The name suggests Hertz car rentals and the Berlitz schools.) Herlitz sees in Boswell a fable. The emperor had no clothes; Boswell has no self. He will be, therefore, a guest, a go-between, a voyeur, a collector of celebrities seen, heard, touched, slept with. But how will he support himself in this expensive occupation? "Become a strong man." (p. 19)

He does. He works out.

> We moved with steamy abandon inside our glazy bodies, our muscles smoothly piling and meshing like tumblers in a lock. There was in the atmosphere a sort of spermy power, but a power queerly delicate, controlled, something not virginal but prudish, held back. Everywhere the taped wrist, the hygienically bandaged knee joint, the puckered, cottony whiteness of jockstrap gently balancing our straining balls.

The gym is a church, a bank, "a cautious, planned development of the body part, a sort of TVA of the flesh." (p. 20) Boswell's identity disappears into his swelling body, and his adventures begin.

He meets the Great Sandusky, a quondam strong man named for the noted turn-of-the-century weightlifter, Eugene Sandow. ("Hercules could probably take care of himself, but your general run-of-the-mill Greek was a guy with lousy force. So don't tell me about Hercules!" [p. 57]) Sandusky is old and sick, but Boswell rejoices in the photographs Sandusky shows him and takes Sandusky's advice.

He becomes a wrestler. Matched against Joe Sallow, The Grim Reaper, Boswell forgets the counsel Herlitz gave him and tries to win. He is badly beaten, nearly killed. His bout with death instructs him.

> It was stupid to struggle, stupider still to struggle in vain—and that's all struggle ever amounted to in a universe like ours, in bodies like our own. From now on I would be the guest. I would haunt the captain's table, sweating over an etiquette of guesthood as others did over right and wrong. Herlitz knew his man, who only gradually, and after great pain, knew himself. (p. 119)

This decision, this flight from the self, ends Part I. Part II is a preposterous picaresque in which Boswell chases after millionaires, whisks guests from crashed parties ("I am a Nobel Prize winner winner" [p. 187]), advises a mad revolutionary during the world's first truly international revolution, and courts the wealthy, well-connected, and beautifully shaped Principessa dei Medici. His escapades are comic and futile. No one is related to anyone else.

> All genuinely great men were martyrs whose characters and purposes were like those double ramps in architecture which wound and climbed and never touched in a concrete illusion of strand. . . . It was the barber-pole condition of life, and we assumed in good faith some matrix common to all. But *isolate, isolate*—that was the real lesson. Hecuba was nothing to any of us. (p. 154)

The "isolate, isolate" is an ironic reply to E. M. Forster's famous "connect." The reference to Hecuba is a sorrowful extension of Hamlet's painful lament.

The moment Boswell actually begins to care for the Principessa, his strength fails him. "Hairless as Samson, like some gross fairy, I sweated outside the Colosseum in the moonlight, in the soft air." (p. 272) When he tells himself that the princess is only a means to an end, when he convinces himself that he wants her only for her money, his strength returns.

He marries the girl and realizes his ambition (but not until he casts her off again, and spurns his teenage son, and gives up the desire for further children). Boswell, free again, plans The Club, the world's innermost group. At The Club the great can gather, under his sponsorship, under his gaze.

Before the grand opening of The Club, Boswell dreams of the great event and imagines himself beginning to grow, expanding, ballooning, crushing everyone in the room, filling, finally, the entire world with his bulk. All other life is blotted out by his own. " 'Ah,' I said, my voice like thunder in the surrounding silence, 'a way had to be found, and a way *was* found.' " (p. 380) The flight from self has led to the ego's apocalypse.

When Boswell actually arrives at The Club, he refuses to give his name and is denied admission. He chooses now to remain nameless, a part of the crowd. "So I watched. Peacefully, with the others. The self at rest, the ego sleeping, death unremembered for once." He is cured at last of the disease, of "this gluttony of the ego . . . that baffled our chances and wasted our hope and used up our lives." (pp. 386–87) The myth of selflessness is the worst egotism of all. Boswell accepts himself as a person, as the creator of The Club, from which he can now detach himself. He joins the others at the barricades. "Hey, hey, down with The Club. Down with The Club. *Down with The Club!*" (p. 387) Orphaned Boswell is redeemed.

All men are not orphans in Stanley Elkin's world; some are parents bereft of their sons. Greenspahn, whose son is dead, is alone with his grocer's grief in a mercantile world where Mrs. Frimkin pokes her finger through the wrapper on the bread ("Can I have it for ten cents?" [94]), where Siggie delivers cheese that has been returned by other stores ("Do you think a customer wants a cheese it goes off like a bomb two days after she gets it home?" [95]), where customers come three times a day to purchase, unrecognized if possible, the loss leader and nothing more ("Lady, don't you ever eat? Is that all you do is drink coffee?" [96]). Worst of all, it is a world where Frank, a mildly dishonest employee caught in petty extortion, shouts to Greenspahn that his dead son Harold stole from the cash register. That night, after his return from the synagogue, Greenspahn dreams of his son's face in the coffin, "his expression at the very moment of death itself, before the undertakers had had time to tamper with it." The rabbi and the *minyan* (the ten men necessary for services) stare at Greenspahn.

He saw it now. They all saw it. The helpless face, the sly wink, the embarrassed, slow smug smile of guilt that must, volitionless as the palpitation of a nerve, have crossed Harold's face when he had turned, his hand in the register, to see Frank watching him.[97]

Elkin's second novel, *A Bad Man* (1967), returns thematically to the concerns of *Boswell*. Leo Feldman, the "bad man" of the novel's title, carries within him a mysterious homunculus, a "little stunted brother of his heart," a "fossilized potential" undeveloped because of a freak of the genes.[98] (p. 140) The homunculus berates Feldman: "I *know* your heart. I've been there. I've been lying on it for years. It's a rack, buddy, a desert, some pre-historic potholed thing. It's a moon of a heart. It will not support life, Leo. So don't start up." (p. 141) These harsh words come at a bad time, for the novel opens with Feldman sentenced to a year in the penitentiary, where he suffers from the persecutions of the warden and his Kafkaesque regulations.

Feldman is assigned to the canteen and dismissed with hard words: "Glutton. Pig. Sedentary piece of shit. . . . We've got your number, and it's zero." (p. 58) The prison is filled with grotesques, like Ed Slipper, who watches obituaries because he longs to be the oldest prisoner in the nation. Among them Feldman is too inexperienced to flourish. One climax comes when Feldman is invited to one of the warden's parties and seduced by a woman who may or may not be the warden's wife. After the seduction, Feldman is placed in a dark room, through which he wanders like a character from Edgar Allan Poe until he finds a light: "Across the room—it was enormous—thrust out from the wall, was a narrow wooden platform like a low stage. On it, stiff, its rigid form and strict ninety-degree angles already suggesting the function, was the electric chair." (p. 176) Feldman's attempt at suicide is, however, a fiasco. He falls asleep in the electric chair. "Soon he was dead to the world." (p. 181)

Eventually, Feldman is elected to the prison's Crime Club, where he boasts of his misdeeds. At the very end, just before his year is up, Feldman is summoned to testify before Warden Fisher. He tells of his alter-ego friend, Leonard Dedman, whom he had sadistically victimized in a dozen imaginatively bizarre ways, but he still expects to be found innocent, to survive the threat of homunculus within and Warden Fisher without. He imagines that he may be fated to fill up the world, "all its desert places and each of its precipices, all its surfaces and everywhere under its seas," because God was not ready to call an end to the Diaspora of the Jews. "Why I *am* innocent, he thought, even as they beat him. And indeed, he felt so." (p. 336) Is it because wickedness always believes in its own innocence? Interpretation of Elkin's fantasy is not a simple matter in which one can have complete confidence, but the egoism of bad man Feldman seems analogous to that of strong man Boswell. It seems, for that matter, the contemporary comic counterpart to the fearful egoism that afflicts the villains of Nathaniel Hawthorne's stories. Seeing himself portrayed in Elkin's fictions, the American reader—*hypocrite lecteur*—must admit to a resemblance.*

10 *Back to Brownsville: Alfred Kazin*

It is grammatically convenient to refer, as I have just done, to "the American reader," but it is common knowledge that not many Americans read serious fiction and even fewer read poems. It is quite unlikely that even one per cent of the adult population has read a reasonably popular author like Stanley Elkin, and many of the older writers felt themselves fortunate to have sold two or three thousand copies of their books. The audience for most serious books not assigned in classrooms is located largely within twenty-five miles of Times Square. No one knows the precise sociological composition of this audience or the characteristics of the other readers scattered across the nation (frequently in an academic environment), but it is generally assumed that many are secular and Reform Jews (but not Orthodox, for whom *all* secular works are anathema). A certain resonance between Jewish reader and Jewish writer is, therefore, no surprise.

But this is only part of the situation. Impressionistic evidence— the only kind available—indicates that the Gentile reader of serious fiction does indeed feel himself involved in the stories told by contemporary Jewish writers. Assimilated Jews are scarcely numerous

* The theme of egoism is ingeniously manipulated in Elkin's newest novel, *The Dick Gibson Show* (1971).

enough, as readers, to secure Book-of-the-Month-Club adoption and best-seller status for books that they alone admire, not even with the help of an alleged critical Establishment that they allegedly control. There is, in other words, a case to be made for the day-of-doom assertions of critics like Leslie Fiedler; the dilemmas of the modern Jew are imaginatively shared by others.

> . . . in this apocalyptic period of atomization and uprooting, of a catholic terror and a universal alienation, the image of the Jew tends to become the image of everyone; and we are perhaps approaching the day when the Jew will come to seem the central symbol, the essential myth of the whole Western world.[99]

In an age of anxiety, the victim's lot becomes the common fate. There is, at any rate, no dearth of argumentation to this effect.

But this, too, is only part of the situation. One factor in the current popularity of Jewish authors is that many of them are only nominally Jewish and present fictional worlds all but indistinguishable from those presented by other writers of their generation. Although Mark Harris is nominally a Jew, his marvelous book about baseball, *The Southpaw* (1953), has simply been accepted as a fine novel, while Bernard Malamud's *The Natural* (1952) has been worked over for evidence of its author's Jewish sensibility. Had his name been Horowitz, Harris would long since have been discussed as a Jewish writer. Now that Harris has published a novel blatantly entitled *The Goy* (1970), we can expect critics to be more attentive. It is, of course, easy to detect differences between the milieu of Philip Roth's Gabe Wallach or Stanley Elkin's Leo Feldman and the invented environments inhabited by the characters of John Updike and Gore Vidal, but there is also a similarity that was not to be found fifty years ago. In the already quoted words of Herbert Gold, "Chicken soup and Yiddish jokes will tarry awhile, but the history of the Jews from now on will be one with the history of everybody else." Gold's comment is half a lament, half a sigh of relief. Do we really want the Jews to be like everyone else?

The literary evidence that suggests the acculturation of most American Jews to the larger society is corroborated by the data of the social sciences. Orthodoxy has all but disappeared in three generations; its distinctive practices are almost gone. In Milwaukee, for instance, 67 per cent of the first generation kept the Jewish sabbath; 12 per cent of the second generation and only 2 per cent of the married sons of the third generation keep *Shabbes*.[100] In Providence, Rhode Island, 41 per cent of the first generation was classified as Orthodox and only 6 per cent of the third generation.[101] In Minneapolis and St. Paul, only 1.2 per cent of the third generation can be classified as Orthodox.[102] Detailed studies of the "Lakeville" community have led the investigators to conclude that the third generation is "minimally" observant. In Lakeville, only 5 per cent of the second generation attend weekly services, but 68 per cent light Chanukkah candles—once a year.[103] Even Jews denominated "observant" by the investigators emphasized "moralism" over "sacramentalism." In other words, the main difference between Judaism and Christianity has been disavowed by contemporary Jews. When 56 per cent of the members of a Jewish country club in the Twin Cities area send Christmas cards *to each other*,[104] when a rabbi announces that he is an "ignostic" who doesn't know what is meant by the term "God," [105] there is something new under the sun.* "There cannot be the least doubt that what the immigrant loses quickest in this country is his Judaism." [107] This judgment by Solomon Schechter, one of the great leaders of Conservative Judaism, is quoted by Marshall Sklare and Joseph Greenbaum, who question on the basis of their studies the "long-range viability" of the contemporary pattern of Jewish adjustment.[108] Irving Greenberg, writing as one committed to *Chalacha,* is even gloomier about the "terminal Jews" living on the residue of the past.[109]

Prophecies of gloom cannot be silenced by discussions of "Jewish education" or by references to the increased attendance at Hillel meetings. Third-generation Jews are attentive when their elders can

---

* Grace Paley's story "The Loudest Voice" seems realistic in this remarkable age. In the story, Shirley Abramowitz has an important part in her school's Christmas celebration and feels sorry that the Christian children did not play important roles. "They got very small parts or no part at all," says Mrs. Kornbluh. "In very bad taste, it seemed to me. After all, it's their religion." The parents, after some debate, accept the situation, except for the rabbi's wife. But she is suspect: "Under the narrow sky of God's great wisdom she wore a strawberry-blond wig." After the pageant, Shirley goes to sleep—with a prayer for the "lonesome Christians." [106]

point to a heritage that reinforces democratic values; they lose interest when urged to avow "those *tangible* elements of traditional ethnicity to which they had been directly exposed in their parental homes." [110] It is easier to admire the heroism of the Jews who died at Masada than to maintain in a modern society the folkways of the *shtetl*. The "formative experiences and the dominant environments of most immigrant fathers and sons," argue two of the most astute scholars of ethnicity, "rendered the family ineffective as an agency for the transmission of traditional ethnicity." [111] It is easier to light a candle than to live by the Law.

The Americanization of the second and third generations is manifest in more ways than in the decline of traditional religious observance and the appearance of an "apathetic identification" [112] with Jewishness. Numerous sociologists have documented the economic patterns of American Jews and concluded that their occupations and incomes—and even their religious lives—correspond closely to those of Episcopalians and Presbyterians. [113] Long before higher education was deemed a middle-class necessity, Jewish parents sent their children off to college, to the environment wherein ethnic ties are most quickly loosened. [114] Although Jews continue to vote more often than others for liberal candidates, electoral returns and preference polls show a gradual convergence; on most political issues, Jews are now likely to divide as others do. [115] In the world of *haute couture*, statistical precision is hardly *à la mode*, but the foremost historian of American immigration has commented that the "ladies gathered for Hadassah's tea stepped out of the pages of *Vogue*." [116] The wigs they wear on Fifth Avenue are a far cry from Gitl Podkovnik's *sheitl*.

There is every reason to believe that most American Jews are pleased by their remarkable adaptation to modernity, but artists like Leonard Baskin, critics like Irving Howe, and novelists like Norman Fruchter and Arthur Granit have been moved to nostalgia. Once the mythic voyage from Antomir to New York was successfully completed, David Levinsky was able to look back upon his youth and articulate his doubts. Once the children and grandchildren of the immigrant generation had moved from the urban *shtetls* of Chicago and New York to America's wider world, they too were able to indulge themselves in memories of community and in moments of regret. The most poignant and complex literary statement of these second thoughts is probably Alfred Kazin's memoir, *A Walker in the City* (1951). Irving Howe's historical account of the "New York Intellectuals" is a tough-minded memoir and a precise analytic model of the milieu he shared with Kazin and a dozen others whose names are now (academic) household words,* but Howe is less prone to nostalgia's retrospective ambivalence.

The frontispiece for Kazin's book is Alfred Stieglitz's famous photograph, "The Steerage," the group portrait of an immigrant era. The title page has for its epigraph lines from Walt Whitman's poem, "Crossing Brooklyn Ferry": "The glories strung like beads on my smallest sights and hearings—on the walk in the street, and the passage over the river." In the contrast between the photograph and the poem lies the tension of the book. The memoir is about those anonymous immigrants whom Stieglitz fixed forever at the moment of their arrival in the Promised Land and about Kazin's own passage from the Brownsville of the immigrants to the "great world" beyond the ghetto, the world that he, like Whitman, was to claim as native ground.

The first chapter, "From the Subway to the Synagogue," has its own epigraph, from William Blake's "London":

> In every cry of every man,
> In every infant's cry of fear,
> In every voice, in every ban,
> The mind-forg'd manacles I hear.

How does this statement of universal imprisonment relate to the opening words of *A Walker in the City*?

> Every time I go back to Brownsville it is as if I had never been away. From the moment I step off the train at Rockaway Avenue and smell the leak out of the men's room, then the pickles from the stand just below the subway steps, an instant rage comes over me, mixed with dread and some unexpected tenderness. . . . I am back where I began. . . . I miss all those ratty little wooden tenements, born with the smell of damp in them, in which there grew up how many school-

---

* Howe mentions, among others, Philip Rahv, William Phillips, Lionel Trilling, Harold Rosenberg, Lionel Abel, Sidney Hook, Delmore Schwartz, Saul Bellow, Paul Goodman, Meyer Schapiro, and Alfred Kazin.

teachers, city accountants, rabbis, cancer specialists, function-
aries of the revolution, and strong-arm men for Murder, Inc.;
I miss that affected squirt who always wore a paste diamond
on his left pinky and one unforgotten day, taught me to say
children for kids; I miss the sinister "Coney Island" dives
where before, during, and after the school day we all anxiously
gobbled down hot dogs soggy in sauerkraut and mus-
tard. . . .[117] (pp. 5–6, 13)

It is as if Kazin had paraphrased another Romantic author, Lord
Byron: "And even I regained my freedom with a sigh." There is in
the specificity of his descriptions an almost obsessive desire to see in
the present a past that was.

The title's chapter indicates its organization. On his walk from
the subway stop, whose physical distance from Manhattan symbolized the cultural and psychic separation between Brownsville and the
"real" America, Kazin passes his private landmarks, especially the
school that was both agony and opportunity and the synagogue
where he encountered a god who was his burden, his misfortune, and
his fascination.

The second chapter, "The Kitchen," evokes the solidarity of the
family and of the ethnic group. Each member of the family—except
his sister, who never appears—is characterized, but the whole is obviously greater than the sum of its parts and the peoplehood of Israel
more important still:

> So it was: we had always to be together: believers and non-
> believers, we were a people; I was of that people. Unthinkable
> to go one's own way, to doubt or to escape the fact that I was
> a Jew. I had heard of Jews who pretended they were not, but
> could not understand them. We had all of us lived together
> so long that we would not have known how to separate even
> if we had wanted to. The most terrible word was *aleyn*, alone.
> (p. 60)

Although Kazin's father and many others were Socialists, he imagined then that Socialism "would be one long Friday evening around
the samovar and the cut-glass bowl laden with nuts and fruits, all of
us singing *Tsuzamen, tsuzamen, ale tsuzamen!*" (p. 61)

"The Block and Beyond" tells of Kazin's neighborhood and of his
gradual exploration of the larger city. In this chapter, the tensions

symbolized in the confrontation of Whitman and Stieglitz recur and intensify. "I wanted," he writes, "nothing so much as to be a 'good Jew,' as they said in the Talmud Torah on Stone Avenue," but he realized even as a child, even on the Day of Atonement, that the worshippers neither believed nor disbelived. "They never thought about it." (pp. 103–4) In contrast to their indifference was Kazin's excited discovery of the American past, of the pictures of Albert Pinkham Ryder and Winslow Homer and, especially, of Thomas Eakins.

Kazin's discovery of America dominates the last chapter, "Summer: the Way to Highland Park," in which he describes his ecstatic response to English and American literature. Like Mary Antin at the Boston Public Library, he knew that he had found the path:

> And though I knew somewhere in myself that a Ryder, an Emily Dickinson, an Eakins, a Whitman, even that fierce-browed old German immigrant Roebling, with his flute and his metaphysics and his passionate love of suspension bridges, were alien, too, alien in the deepest way, like my beloved Blake, my Yeshua [i.e. Jesus in the Hebrew form], my Beethoven, my Newman—nevertheless I still thought of myself then as standing outside America. I read as if books would fill my every gap, legitimize my strange quest for the American past, remedy my every flaw, let me in at last into the great world that was anything just out of Brownsville. (p. 172)

Reading this passage, one begins to imagine how fiercely the young man sought to escape the world that the autobiographer lovingly reconstructs.

It was by way of American literature that Kazin did escape Brownsville. His first book, *On Native Grounds* (1942), interpreted prose fiction from William Dean Howells to Hemingway and Faulkner. From there, Kazin went on to become a major critic of all modern literature, an "alienated" intellectual with only tenuous ties to his Jewish past. Contributing to a symposium in the *Contemporary Jewish Record,* in February of 1944, Kazin wrote:

> I learned long ago to accept the fact that I was Jewish without being a part of any meaningful Jewish life or culture. . . . The writing I have been deeply influenced by—Blake, Melville, Emerson, the seventeenth-century English religious poets, and the Russian novelists—has no direct associations in my mind with Jewish culture.[118]

A little more than a year later, on a rainy afternoon in London in 1945, he heard a radio broadcast of the rescued prisoners of Bergen-Belsen reciting their prayers of thanksgiving and felt himself carried back to Friday nights in Brownsville. From there, it was but a single emotional step to *A Walker in the City,* but the city in which Kazin and a million others walked is gone for good, ironic victim of America's partially fulfilled promise.*

---

* It is instructive to compare *Making It* (1967), the autobiography of Norman Podhoretz, with *A Walker in the City.* There are almost endless points of comparison. Like Kazin, Podhoretz emphasizes the cultural distance between Brownsville and Manhattan: "One of the longest journeys in the world is the journey from Brooklyn to Manhattan—or at least from certain neighborhoods in Brooklyn to certain parts of Manhattan." [119] (p. 3) Like Kazin, Podhoretz sought a world wider than the ghetto. He too came in middle age to recognize that not even radicalism was able to eradicate his ethnic roots, but this recognition is *not* the central theme of the autobiography. Central is the celebration of "success." Of himself as a young man, Podhoretz writes, "What I wanted was to see my name in print, to be praised, and above all to attract attention." (p. 146) *Making It* is the story of a proudly brash man who made it; the literary convention is that of Rousseau's *Confessions* rather than Kazin's nostalgic memoir.

III

One's Own People

1   *The Arguments for Peoplehood*

The God of Abraham and Isaac has faded from the consciousness of many American Jews, but others have withstood the temptations of *de goldene Medineh*, "the golden land," have resisted the lure of assimilation. American Jews who have remained true to Torah and Talmud have, moreover, struggled to win converts, not from the Gentiles but from those nominal Jews who have converted to secularism and shrugged off the faith of their fathers. The establishment of the Jewish Theological Seminary in 1886 and of the Rabbi Isaac Elchanan Theological Seminary (now Yeshiva University) in 1896 provided centers from which Conservative and Orthodox Jews were able to mount their counterattacks on the heresies of Reform Judaism. The rapidity with which secularized Jews severed the bonds that tied them to their tradition brought the leaders of Reform to sober second thoughts. They met, therefore, in Columbus, Ohio, in 1937, in order to restore to their creed the centrality of Torah and a belief in the peoplehood of Israel.

In the philosophy of cultural pluralism, first articulated by Horace Kallen in 1915, secular Jews anxious to avoid assimilation discovered a rationale to justify their instincts. Against the metaphor of the "melting pot," popularized by Israel Zangwill's 1914 play of that name, Kallen set the metaphor of the orchestra in which each ethnic group plays its distinctive part:

> As in an orchestra every type of instrument has its specific
> *timbre* and *tonality,* founded in its substance and form; as
> every type has its appropriate theme and melody in the whole
> symphony, so in society, each ethnic group may be the . . .
> instrument, its temper and culture may be its theme and
> melody and the harmony and dissonances and discords of them
> all may make the symphony of civilization.[1]

Refusal of an individual—like Mary Antin—to carry forth the traditions of the group, refusal to play the assigned part—this was a form
of betrayal. Against Emersonian notions of self-reliance and the popular myth of the self-made man, Kallen posited the theory of ancestral determinism:

> Men may change their clothes, their politics, their wives, their
> religions, their philosophies, to a greater or lesser extent: they
> cannot change their grandfathers. Jews or Poles or Anglo-
> Saxons, in order to cease being Jews or Poles or Anglo-Saxons,
> would have to cease to be . . . The selfhood which is inalien-
> able in them, and for the realization of which they require
> "inalienable" liberty is ancestrally determined, and the happi-
> ness which they pursue has its form implied in ancestral en-
> dowment. This is what, actually, democracy in operation as-
> sumes.[2]

Identity is inherited; the self is determined by the ethnic group into
which one is born.* Mary Antin and others who write of rebirth are
the heretical prophets of a naive miscomprehension of social reality.
A variation on Kallen's theme was offered by Morris R. Cohen,
whose *Reason and Nature* (1931) is one of the classics of American
philosophy. In *Reflections of a Wondering Jew* (1950), Cohen, too,
argued for cultural pluralism: "No change of ideology—no matter
how radical—can make a man cease to be the son of his parents. It
is not only vain but also incompatible with self-respect to try to appear other than what we are." [4] (p. 4) Neither Kallen nor Cohen
asked if a man can become a replica of his parents and grandparents.
Their lack of logic is less important, for my present purposes, than
their passionate judgments.

In the social and religious thought of Mordecai Kaplan, who

---

* A more recent writer has gone beyond Kallen and likened Jews to trees
that must accept their species.[3]

founded the Reconstructionist movement in 1935, many Jews have found an extension of the theory of cultural pluralism. In his most important book, *Judaism as a Civilization* (1934), Kaplan noted that faith in God once sustained the solidarity of the Jewish people but that faith has since waned. "In fact," he remarked, "the majority of Jews seem to have completely forgotten that it was the belief in exclusive eligibility for salvation that formerly held their people together." [5] (p. 48) Kaplan's scorn for Reform Jews was almost unmitigated; they seem to him to have committed "a new kind of suicide" when they departed from the concept of peoplehood. (p. 120) (This was written three years before Reform Judaism reversed itself and reaffirmed the principle.) The Reformers had traded the richly embroidered cloth of traditional custom for a threadbare conception of divinity. "Only in Wonderland," argued Kaplan, "can there be a cat which leaves its grin behind it." (p. 125) In short, "The assumption that a religion can be made the aim of a group of individuals that have only religion in common is altogether untenable." (p. 202) What Kaplan proposed, in order to achieve "a maximum of Jewishness," was a "complete Jewish civilization" based upon the Torah but adjusted—like Reform theology—to modern conditions. He imagined a coherent civilization with its own language (Hebrew), land, social structure, *mores,* art, and, of course, religion. "Of all civilizations," he insisted, "Judaism can least afford to omit religion." (p. 305) But Kaplan no more meant the God of Abraham and Isaac than did Horace Kallen. He went on in *The Future of the American Jew* (1948) to explain that "belief in God is belief in the existence of a Power conducive to salvation which is the fulfillment of human destiny." [6] (p. 172) God is what God was in the pragmatic philosophy of William James—whatever makes for human progress. This, of course, returns one almost to the world of the Cheshire cat, but not quite, for Kaplan's plea is fundamentally that of Kallen: "It is a law of human nature that, when people are engaged in a common enterprise for any length of time, they develop a mutual attachment which persists, no matter what becomes of the enterprise." [7] Jews must go on together because they have gone on together; theirs is indeed a *Schicksalsgemeinschaft,* a community of fate to which one is born, from which one cannot depart.

In 1935, one year after Kaplan's *Judaism as a Civilization*, Abraham Heschel published his first book, a study of Moses Maimonides. Born in Warsaw and educated in Berlin, the descendant of the chief disciple of the founder of Chassidism and Martin Buber's follower at the Jüdische Lehrhaus in Frankfurt am Main, Heschel came to America in 1940. In his books *Man Is Not Alone* (1951) and *God in Search of Man* (1955) he provided American Jews with what Reinhold Niebuhr and Paul Tillich provided American Protestants, a new interpretation of an old god. Heschel's theology emphasizes the wonder, the mystery, the ineffability of God. Religion is an answer to ultimate questions about this God, questions that philosophers of nature (and modernizers of Judaism) can never answer because nature is merely the fulfillment of God's will, an allusion to rather than a revelation of divinity. Heschel calls upon modern Jews to make the "leap of action" and return to Jewish law, to observance of rituals testifying to the transcendent power of God. Although the third and fourth generations of American Jews contine to drift further and further from Mosaic law and even from any detailed knowledge of Judaism, their elders no longer encourage them to do so.

A sense of peoplehood has been institutionalized in the form of fraternal institutions like the B'nai B'rith (1845) and the Young Men's Hebrew Association (1854); charitable associations like the Hebrew Sheltering Society (1890) and the Hebrew Immigrant Aid Society (1902); hospitals; newspapers and magazines in Hebrew, Yiddish, and English; campus organizations like Hillel; a civil rights organization like the Anti-Defamation League (1913); a system of parochial schools; and a major university, Brandeis, founded in 1948. The net is wide and the mesh is small.

Within the world of literature, the effort to maintain a sense of peoplehood and to win back those who have converted to secularism or to Christianity has taken many forms, two of which are the condemnation of those who defect from or denigrate the Jewish community and the continued emphasis on the external dangers of anti-Semitism. Examples of each are abundant.

In 1937, at the time that he published *The Old Bunch*, Meyer Levin found himself highly unpopular with more religiously committed Jews. His attempt to write realistically of the second-generation Jews of Chicago's West Side was interpreted as an anti-Semitic outburst. Looking back, he remarked that his work was preached against in the temples and described in some of the Jewish press as a degradation of our people. I received a call from the secretary of the Anti-Defamation League, who invited me to lunch at one of the downtown Jewish clubs. . . . The general theme was: Why do you young Jewish writers feel impelled to describe your people in this disgraceful manner? [8]

In more recent years, many of those usually identified as Jewish writers—for example, Edward Adler, Jerome Charyn, Babette Deutsch, Leslie Fiedler, Norman Fruchter, Allen Ginsberg, Herbert Gold, Irving Howe, Alfred Kazin, Philip Roth, Muriel Rukeyser, L. S. Simckes, and Louis Untermeyer—have been denounced as anti-Semitic or abused for their aloofness from the Jewish community.[9] Norman Podhoretz, editor of *Commentary*, has described the difficulties he encountered in his attempts to combine the traditional and the modern: "Once . . . I nearly caused a riot when I attacked the prosody of a minor Israeli poet by invoking E. E. Cummings as a standard. I was howled down with talk of the blood shed by the six million [whom the Nazis killed]." [10] A rather extreme book review begins like this: "The renegade Jew in the limbo of lost identity is a sad phenomenon of the West. He is a self-hating, self-created, ectoplasmic figure who, having renounced his origins, realizes from time to time that he has also deprived his own children of a history." [11]

In referring to "self-hate," the polemicist has fired condemnation's most popular weapon. The theory holds that alienated Jews apparently committed to secularism or converted to Christianity are motivated not by any positive values but rather by a negative valuation of their inner selves. These Jews, it is asserted, seek neurotically to deny what they know to be their true identity. The most sophisticated spokesman for this theory was the German-American social psychologist Kurt Lewin.

> In an underprivileged group, many of these [disaffected] individuals are . . . forced to stay within the group. As a result, we find in every underprivileged group a number of persons ashamed of their membership. In the case of the Jews, such a Jew will try to move away as far as possible from things Jewish.

The disaffected Jew wants to distance himself from other Jews but

is frustrated by the anti-Semitism of the Gentiles who consider all
Jews to be alike:

> We know from experimental psychology and psychopathology
> that such frustration leads to an all-around state of high ten-
> sion with a generalized tendency to aggression. The aggression
> should, logically, be directed against the majority, which is
> what hinders the minority member from leaving his group.
> However, the majority has, in the eyes of these persons, higher
> status. And besides, the majority is much too powerful to be
> attacked. Experiments have shown that, under these condi-
> tions, aggression is likely to be turned against one's own group
> or against one's self.[12]

Lewin's conclusions have been widely applied.*

Recent writers and critics have found the self-hate theory as attractive as writers and critics of the 1920s and 1930s found the Oedipal
complex. In some cases it is difficult to remain skeptical. When the
novelist Ben Hecht wrote of the loathesome desire of the Jew for the
blonde and of "Jew faces in which race leers and burns like some
biologic disease," he seemed indeed to typify the "negative chauvin-
ism" on which Lewin speculated.[15] But the theory, which defies
either validation or invalidation, has since Lewin's day been used almost without restraint. The term is, in the words of one annoyed
novelist, "the Jewish community's great all-purpose putdown
word." [16] Meyer Levin has, for instance, accused Harold Robbins,
Budd Schulberg, and Jerome Weidman of self-hate. Like the rabbis
who urged him to write "positively," Levin has chastized young
writers and appealed for "integrity and responsibility on the part of
writers and publishers." [17] Levin has also written *Compulsion*
(1956), in which Leopold and Loeb murder Bobbie Frank because
of self-hate, and has suggested in *The Fanatic* (1964) that converts
from Judaism to Communism are exemplars of self-hate.

Sermons against the "self-hate" of Philip Roth were the mission-

---

* Another conclusion contained in the same essay has been less popular: "In
a minority group, individual members who are economically successful, or
who have distinguished themselves in their professions, usually gain a higher
degree of acceptance by the majority group. This places them culturally on
the periphery of the underprivileged group and makes them more likely to
be 'marginal' persons." [13] Sociologist Ralph Segalman is one of the few who
have studied the concept of "leadership from the periphery." [14]

ary's set piece long before the publication of *Portnoy's Complaint*. Like Meyer Levin, Roth has been telephoned and invited to lunch and advised to be more positive. He too has been denounced in the synagogues and vilified in print as one whose "criticisms, exaggerated by the self-hate of [his] alienation, cannot serve as an adequate guide to the true condition of the American Jewish community of today." [18] Unlike most writers, Roth has braved the fury and answered back. Goaded by accusations of anti-Semitism and by abusive sermons, Roth retaliated with a far from apologetic essay:

> The question really is, who is going to address men and women like men and women, and who like children. If there are Jews who have begun to find the stories the novelists tell more provocative and pertinent than the sermons of some of the rabbis, perhaps it is because there are regions of feeling and consciousness in them which cannot be reached by the oratory of self-congratulation and self-pity.[19]

It is ironic that *Portnoy's Complaint,* a parody of self-hate, is likely to be remembered when the work of those who have denounced Roth's alleged self-hate has been forgotten.

It is the threat of anti-Semitism and the memory of the fate of European Jews under Hitler that make understandable the fanaticism of the conventional novelistic exposés of self-hate. American novelists and poets have, however, tended to shy away from dramatizations of the almost unimaginable horror of the camps, a horror that no major American novelist or poet has experienced except in imagination. Although Edward Lewis Wallant's *The Pawnbroker* (1961) and Saul Bellow's *Mr. Sammler's Planet* (1970) have drawn upon their characters' memories of wartime atrocities, most American Jewish novelists have shied away from the concentration-camp situations taken up by European novelists, diarists, and documentary film-makers.

One discovers, therefore, that the novels concerned with anti-Semitism in America are usually trivial and, in the fashionable social-scientific term, perhaps even counterproductive. Consider, for instance, Arthur Miller's *Focus* (1945), Laura Z. Hobson's *Gentleman's Agreement* (1947), and Irwin Shaw's *The Young Lions* (1948). These novels imply that Jews and Gentiles are really indistinguishable in their behavior and in their basic values. Only names are different. But this argument weakens rather than strengthens the demand that Jews affirm their unique and distinctive identity. Ironically, the most impressive novels to deal with the theme of anti-Semitism have, like Bruce Jay Friedman's *Stern* (1962), suggested that the relations between Semite and anti-Semite are a great deal more complicated than those between victim and victimizer. While no sane observer can deny that instances of anti-Semitism continue to occur in the United States, there is no reason to doubt the moral implied in Ivan Gold's story "Taub East": the defense against anti-Semitism can become almost comically disproportionate in the United States of Arthur Goldberg, Harry Golden, and Barry Goldwater.[20] It is perhaps for this reason that young writers have tended to deal with "the comedy of Jewish dissolution in the midst of prosperity" rather than with the tragic themes of Franz Kafka and the chroniclers of catastrophe.[21]

2   The Forgotten Achievement of Ludwig Lewisohn

Another and more important form of conservative response to the conversion of millions of Jews to the "religion of Americanism" is the presentation in literary form of a positive view of Judaism and Jewish life. In many, but not in all instances, the positive commitment includes the espousal of Zionism. Cynthia Ozick, for instance, has written forcefully to warn the assimilationists that "the culture they buzz round like honeybees drops them." Jews of the Diaspora, she argues, are doomed to aridity if they do not emphasize their Jewishness. "If we blow into the narrow end of the *shofar* [ceremonial ram's horn], we will be heard far. But if we choose to be Mankind rather than Jewish and blow into the wider part, we will not be heard at all. . . ." [22] Time will test her judgment.

Of those many writers who have urged a return to a sense of peoplehood, none has been more eloquent or more persuasive than Ludwig Lewisohn. Time, Shakespeare's dealer of alms for oblivion, has been harsh to Lewisohn, who is now remembered only by specialists, but his most significant book, *The Island Within* (1928), has a claim upon every serious reader's attention, whether or not the claim is honored. In this and other books and in the pattern of his career as a writer, Lewisohn is the exemplar of at least one phase of the process of assimilation: he is, in a sense, the Jewish writer as Prodigal Son.

Fortunately, Lewisohn wrote autobiography as well as novels and criticism. In *Up Stream* (1922), he told the first part of his story. He was born in Berlin in 1882, the scion of a family that "seemed to feel that they were Germans first and Jews afterwards." [23] (p. 17) Christmas was more familiar to him, as a child, than the traditional holidays of Judaism. His mother's father was a rabbi, but one without a beard, with little regard for ritual, a modernist.

After a failure in business, Lewisohn's father migrated to America, to St. Marks, South Carolina. The town is described in the second chapter of *Up Stream* under a somewhat ironical title, "American Scene." (That Lewisohn was alluding to Henry James and to his unpleasant remarks about American Jews is quite probable.) Subsequent chapters, "The Making of an American" and "The Making of an Anglo-American," are devoted to the assimilation of the author, to his transformation first into a fundamentalist Christian and then into a teacher of literature, an intellectual. Like many another Southern boy, Lewisohn labored in the vineyards of the Epworth League under the auspices of the Methodist Church. In college, he grew skeptical of Christianity and turned to Thomas Henry Huxley, John Fiske, and other advocates of Darwinian evolution. Passionately in love with English literature, Lewisohn went to Columbia University for graduate work, did well, was refused a fellowship, left without his Ph.D., and discovered that a German-American Jew, even a secular one in love with Keats and Shelley, was not welcome in the English departments of American universities. His bitterness is understandable: "All the men who had refused me at the various universities were Anglo-Americans, pillars of the democracy, proclaimers of its mission to set the bond free and equalize life's opportunities for mankind." (p. 147)

Lewisohn found employment as a teacher of German literature and began to establish a reputation both as a literary historian and as a novelist. His highly Romantic temperament was manifested in his first novel, *The Broken Snare* (1908). In this quite conventional book, the heroine quotes Gautier and Swinburne "without feminine reticence and hesitation" [24] (p. 41) and is courted by a hero more

than a little tinted by the Yellow Decade: "I cannot render my love
for you official and Philistine; I cannot enter upon a round of hideous and vulgar domesticities." (p. 67) After numerous complications,
hero and heroine find bliss:

> She looked into his eyes, and then up unto the stars that began
> to gather in the fields of heaven, and it seemed to her that she
> had come at last from the weary plains of life, beaten upon
> by scorching suns, choked with blood and sand, and had
> emerged into some fair, wide upland region of cool waters
> and spacious winds, where love dwells, and blessedness, and
> a perennial peace. (pp. 288–89)

The author of *The Broken Snare* was not the man to respond
stoically and stubbornly to the crises encountered when war in
Europe divided the loyalties and allegiances of Americans, especially
of German-Americans. In 1916, Lewisohn published *The Spirit of
Modern German Literature* and reaped the wrath of a real-estate
broker who considered Lewisohn disloyal to American ideals. He
was called before the district attorney and, despite support from the
president and faculty of the university, driven to resign his position.
"Yet," he wrote, "this was a university and there they taught . . .
Plato and Kant, Montaigne and Voltaire, Goethe and Shelley and
even Walt Whitman who 'beat the gong of revolt and stopped with
them that plot and conspire.' " [25] No wonder that he turned in his disgust from the doctrines of assimilation, which he thought likely to
lead to "a race of unconscious spiritual helots," [26] a generation of
boobs equipped with baseballs and comic strips. Cultural pluralism
seemed the only answer.

Lewisohn's new sense of Jewish identity can be seen in *Roman
Summer,* the novel he published in 1927. John Austin, a journalist
who writes verse, goes to Rome, where he haunts the Forum, writes
a play about Catullus, and meets a beautiful young woman, Esther
Azancot. She is a Jew, a Zionist, a believer in peoplehood. He expects
her to give up her sense of the Jewish past while he luxuriates in his
own return to the origins of our civilization. Her scorn of assimilationists is unmistakably Lewisohn's scorn as well: "The Jews you
have known have probably all pretended to be Americans with just
a different religion." [27] (p. 120) She tells him of her Moroccan birth

and of her childhood in Metz, where her best friend, upon discovering that Esther was *une Juive,* struck her. John Austin proposes marriage despite the fact that she is a Jew, but she rejects him and leaves him to return to the empty life of middle-class America.

Roman Summer was a tryout for *The Island Within* (1928), the most eloquent statement of Lewisohn's conviction that the American dream was an illusion and that survival was possible only in Palestine. The novel begins with a Menckenesque assault upon the vacuities of American life in the 1920s: The United States had once had a "Golden Age, alloyed and faint, but golden, in the past," when democracy "lived a feeble life," but lived nonetheless.[28] (p. 4) The imperialist war of 1898 and the greater catastrophe of World War I destroyed the possibility:

> The state is an image—brazen, remote, implacable except by stealthy magnates; the augurs, fat-paunched, bellow at each other on the public roads; the gates of the land are sealed; the duped and stupefied populace—no more a people—dances about fundamentalist preachers, baseball pitchers and a Rumanian queen. . . . (p. 5)

But the past is real, whether the present notices it or not.

The past of Arthur Levy, the novel's protagonist, is introduced almost as if his story were being told in the tradition of Yiddish literature by Sholom Aleichem or I. L. Peretz: "In the year 1840 there lived in the city of Vilna a Jew whose full name was Reb Mendel ben Reb Jizchock, with his wife and his two children. The man's calling was that of a *melamed,* or teacher of little children, and he was, like all of his kind, indescribably poor." (p. 7) Encouraged by Shimen the Crooked, Mendel begins to read forbidden books, including the *Guide to the Perplexed,* by Moses Maimonides. He takes a job with Chaim Bratzlawer the distiller, a man who has ceased to observe Jewish customs. Mendel's son Efraim leaves the *yeshiva,* ceases to wear the caftan required of Orthodox Jews, and marries Hannah Bratzlawer. He opens a branch of the distillery in Germany. To smooth the way, he changes his name: "They arrived in Insterburg as Herr and Frau Efraim Levy and looked about them for a house in which to establish their business and bring their children into a fairer and a freer world." (p. 38)

Book II opens with a meditation on the identity of the Sephardim in distant Turkey, the Ashkenazim of Germany, the "Jewish gangsters" and modernist rabbis of Manhattan. Efraim and Hannah continue to think of themselves as Jews and to observe the Law and to attend the Orthodox synagogue of Insterburg: "Only into all their thoughts and observances there had stolen a laxness and a tinge of compromise." (p. 45) Their son Tobias has no doubts. Alone in the forest, he feels himself to be a German:

> He looked down a narrow forest path into the dim, half-green, half-golden glow. *"Deutscher Wald,"* he murmured to himself —"the German forest." He was a Jew. Yes. But he was not in *goles;* he felt no exile. This was his earth and sky and speech. (p. 55)

Against his father's will, Tobias volunteers for Bismarck's army in 1870 and receives an Iron Cross. When the war with France is over, he marries the daughter of a Jew converted to Christianity and becomes a Christian. He takes his father-in-law's name—Burghammer —and becomes immensely wealthy, but when his son is killed in the World War, he says, "Shmah Yisroel" ("Hear, O Israel!"). (p. 65) There is none to answer, as his father had answered at old Mendel's death, "Adonai Elohenu, Adonai echot!" ("The Lord, our God, the Lord is One!"). (p. 31) Book II ends with the arrival in America of Tobias's younger brother Jacob.

Book III opens with a discussion of "self-hate" followed by a demonstration of it—in the form of Judas Iscariot. In America, Jacob Levy works in a clothing and furniture store owned by an assimilated Jew and becomes himself the manufacturer of William Morris furniture. His children, Arthur and Hazel, are reared with no consciousness of their Jewish origins. The life of Arthur Levy, the central character of three-quarters of the novel, is unmistakably derived from Lewisohn's own experiences, just as much of Arthur Levy's past bears easily identifiable resemblances to the history of the Lewisohn family (whose very name might be construed to mean "Levy's sons").

Arthur Levy attends Columbia University and discovers the varieties of Jewishness in his generation. There are Marxists (like Joe Goldman) and "All-rightniks" (like Hollsworthy Brown). There are also anti-Semites, like drunken Dr. Duval, director of the hospital at which Arthur Levy studies medicine (after his tour of duty in the Army). The hospital is for mental patients, most of whom are Jewish, especially in the women's ward (by which Lewisohn seems to suggest that the falseness of assimilated Jews has a heavy price).

Arthur, like his creator, becomes a follower of Sigmund Freud.* He meets an attractive feminist, Elizabeth Knight, courts her, and sleeps with her. Discovering that she is pregnant, they marry, despite the hostile comments of Jacob Levy, who feels that the *goyim* are hopelessly ineducable. The marriage is also a question: "Couldn't one help to destroy all those remnants of man's barbarous past by living as though they had no real existence, by living in the light of reason?" (p. 237) The question has, of course, already been answered by Lewisohn's vivid documentation of the past that Arthur Levy naively imagines he can defy.

Ironically, the Freudian doctor has married a sexually repressed and unresponsive woman who writes psychological essays for popular magazines. The marriage is further threatened by the emergence of Arthur Levy's sense of his Jewish identity. He and Elizabeth quarrel over the education of their son John, over whether or not he should be reared as a Jew. Working for Beth Yehuda hospital, Arthur feels ever more strongly that Jews should live among Jews, Negroes among Negroes. The plot turns, at this point, with a creak. Thus far, Lewisohn's characters had behaved in probable ways; now, Arthur meets a distant cousin, a Chassidic Jew named Reb Moshe Hacohen, who tells him of a chest of documents left by Arthur's great-grandfather to his brother, Reb Moshe's great-grandfather. Elizabeth's departure, with their son John, removes the last impediment, the last barrier between Arthur and his identity. Divorce from Elizabeth is also separation from the false self of the assimilated Jew. Arthur is liberated to discover the past.

The documents go back nearly a thousand years, to the persecution of the Jews of medieval Speyer, Worms, and Mainz by the Crusaders in the year 1096. The fact that enlightened Christians have praised the Crusaders despite the atrocities they committed convinces

---

* *Don Juan* (1925) and *The Case of Mr. Crump* (1926) are fictional explorations of sexual repression and warped personality. Freudian theory is also evident in Lewisohn's literary history, e.g. *Expression in America* (1932).

Arthur that anti-Semitism is ineradicable. He decides to cast his lot with his own people. His father urges him to build up again the House of Israel which *his* generation had tried to tear down, and his former wife, who now rather magnanimously promises to give their son a Jewish education, wishes him well. Encouraged by the wisdom of Reb Moshe, he sets out to do charitable work among Jews living in the Balkans.

At the conclusion, Lewisohn has clearly become sentimental. Hollsworthy Brown ("Hell-worthy"?) sneers at Arthur Levy's decision, but the return to Judaism wins the ratification of Dr. Charles Dawson, an authentic Yankee: "I don't think that Jews who try not to be Jews do themselves any good in the eyes of intelligent people. There's something wrong with a man who betrays his own kind." (p. 349) In the face of this witless talk, the reader may want to ask if the moralistic Yankee intends to return to England, paint himself blue, and worship the pagan divinities of his Druid ancestors. Despite the stereotypes of the final pages of the book, *The Island Within* is a great achievement. The argument for peoplehood has never been more persuasively presented.

Lewisohn continued in later novels, stories, and essays to urge the moral of *The Island Within*. In the continuation of his autobiography, published in 1929, he asserted that assimilation does exactly the opposite of what the assimilated intend: "It is assimilation that excludes us from the civilizations amid which our lot is cast." [29] (This enigmatic statement is never clarified.) *The Last Days of Shylock* (1931) followed two other novels in which the theme of peoplehood was of minor importance or of none at all.* Shylock's story, as continued by Lewisohn, is a corrective sequel to Shakespeare's play in which the old man survives a series of pogroms and persecutions. *This People,* which followed in 1933, is a collection of variations on the theme: the saintly son of an assimilationist father finds his true identity in the home of a rabbi; a German Communist attains ecstasy in martyrdom because Nazi killers identify him as a Jew.

---

* *Stephen Escott* (1939) and *The Golden Vase* (1931) are not directly concerned with Jewish identity. *An Altar in the Fields* (1934), *For Ever Wilt Thou Love* (1939), and *Anniversary* (1948) are chiefly treatments of the theme of sexual repression and release.

Trumpet of Jubilee (1937), *Renegade* (1941), and *Breathe Upon These* (1944) are thinly polemical fictions addressed to the previously convinced. (The last title was published by the Jewish Publication Society rather than by a commercial press.) When assimilationists speak of "humanity," they are betrayed by an inner loss of conviction, revealed in a whine. They are dealt with sternly: "You have got a bad case of self-hatred." [30] From this diagnosis there can be no dissent.

Lewisohn was not content to work through the indirections of fictional forms. In 1939 he published *The Answer: The Jew and the World, Past, Present, and Future.* The experience of German Jews was very much on his mind. In his troubled mood, he repudiated the theory of cultural pluralism and indicated his loss of faith in American democracy. "The only Jew who can be loyal to the spirit of America," he asserted, "is the Zionist." [31] (p. 24) In *The American Jew* (1950), Lewisohn repeated that "authentic Jews are and must be Zionists." *[32] (p. 165) He heaped contempt upon the American Council for Judaism, an organization that considers Judaism as a religion among other religions and continues to reject Zionism and the concept of peoplehood. The Chassidic Jew, Lewisohn insisted, is the authentic Jew, while the member of the American Council for Judaism is "a slave in body and in soul, imprisoned in the cold and empty hell of a self-created *Galuth* [exile]." (pp. 47–48) Survival in America is possible only if Jews maintain a sense of peoplehood and observe the Mosaic laws, the *Mitzvoth* of traditional Judaism. "The Jew who has recovered his Jewish authenticity will spontaneously desire to practice the *Mitzvoth*." (p. 114) Whether or not God spoke at Mount Sinai, every prophecy of the Torah has been fulfilled. Lewisohn felt that the catastrophe of Hitler's *Endlösung* disproved forever the arguments for assimilation. Spurning the "old Hungarian assimilatory self-hatred" and the "sick-souled rage" of Arthur Koestler (pp. 17, 22), he marveled at Israel reborn and at the *sabras* of the new state, a new spiritual and physical type shaped by

---

* References to "authentic" and "inauthentic" Jews are derived from the polemics of Jean-Paul Sartre's *Anti-Semite and Jew*, translated and published in this country in 1948. Sartre's analysis adds little to that of Horace Kallen, except for these terms, which have become almost as popular as "self-hate."

a truly Jewish civilization. The shrill tone and the simplistic repetitions of Lewisohn's late work are unfortunate, but they should not diminish the extraordinary achievement of *The Island Within*.

3 Zionism and the Jewish Writer

Ludwig Lewisohn was by no means the only important writer among American Jews to dramatize the appeals of peoplehood or to advocate the necessity of Zionism. Meyer Levin, who had lived briefly in Palestine, published the first significant Zionist novel (in America) in 1931, at a time when American Jews were generally opposed to the establishment of an independent Jewish homeland in Palestine. Zionism itself, in its modern form, dates from 1895. In that year, a young Viennese journalist, an assimilated intellectual named Theodor Herzl, was stunned by the anti-Semitism stirred up in France by the Dreyfus Affair. He was stimulated to write *Der Judenstaat,* which called for a Jewish homeland, and to organize the first international Zionist conference at Basel, Switzerland, in 1897. Although the first *aliyah* (wave of immigration) had already begun in 1882 to flow from pogrom-ridden Russia to Palestine, Herzl's original conception did not specify Palestine (then under Turkish rule) as the only possible Jewish state. More religiously committed leaders, like Ashur Ginzberg, insisted that the territory actually inhabited by the ancient Hebrews was the only place suitable for the reconstructed State of Israel. Religious Zionists were successful in that Palestine was, finally, marked as the site for the Jewish homeland by the British government's Balfour Declaration of November 1917, but the leaders of the Zionist movement continued to be predominantly secular Jews. "The growing secularization of modern Jewry," writes Salo Wittmayer Baron, "made the transition from religious messianism to political Zionism appear as but another link in that long chain of evolution." [33] Orthodox Jews remained generally opposed to Zionism until after the establishment of the State of Israel in 1948, and a small number of very Orthodox Jews, known as Zealots, continue even today to oppose the State of Israel. By the time Meyer Levin came to Palestine, over 100,000 Jews lived in Jaffa, in Tel Aviv (founded in 1909), and in *kibbutzim* (communal settlements) scattered through the hinterland.

Meyer Levin's *Yehuda* (1931) is set in a *kibbutz*.* The hero is an improbable young man who practices the violin at night after a hard day in the fields of the commune and loves a girl from a nearby Chassidic village. The *kibbutz* has its internal dissensions, but the more serious threat comes from the Arabs, who look upon the Jews —then as now—as interlopers. After the usual complications, Levin brings his novel to a happy end:

> In the hot mid-afternoon Yehuda looked out over the plain. Never before had the clean air so joyously filled his body. He felt air vibrate within him, as it must vibrate in a songfilled violin. The whole plain danced in the white afternoon heat, wavered and beat under the glow of the sun.[34] (pp. 373–74)

Far more successful artistically was Levin's collection of Chassidic tales, *The Golden Mountain,* published in 1932. Far *less* successful was his second Zionist novel, *My Father's House* (1947), a tenuously allegorical book about a juvenile refugee sententiously welcomed home to Israel, the House of his Father.

Somewhat more plausible Zionist books have been written by Michael Blankfort, whose early works—for example, *The Brave and the Blind* (1940)—indicated a politically radical point of view. *The Juggler,* which came out in 1952, deals with Hans Muller's reluctant migration from Germany to Israel, where he eventually accepts his Jewishness. The climactic scene begins when Muller remarks to the lovely heroine, "I have grown fond of your *kibbutz*. . . . It has made being a Jew not so bad." To which she responds, not unexpectedly, "Is this the first time you have ever felt a little pride in our people—pride as a Jew?" [35] (p. 204) Like the juggler of medieval legend who performs for the Virgin because he has no other gift to offer, Hans Muller eventually wins salvation (and cinematic resurrection in the form of Kirk Douglas). Equally awkward but much more effective is Blankfort's more recent novel *Behold the Fire* (1965). The explanation for the novel's improvement over *The Juggler* may well be that Blankfort worked from the historical record of General Allenby's remarkable World War I campaign,

---

* For the purposes of this discussion, Zionist books by American authors are considered relevant whether they have American characters or not. Most do not.

which took him victoriously from Cairo to Damascus. At any rate, *Behold the Fire* ably commemorates the Jews who sacrificed their lives in support of Allenby's armies and thus helped to legitimize their claim to a homeland in the territory liberated from the Turks.

The most popular novel of the Zionist genre was, of course, Leon Uris's *Exodus* (1958), a book whose sentimentality was scarcely exaggerated when it was transformed into a melodramatic film. There is, one speculates, something about the American Zionist literature which suggests that the significance of the historical event is inaccessible to outsiders. It is not that subjects *determine* literary greatness; great literature can be made from the adventures of an aged Spanish knight bewildered by chivalric tales as well as from the momentous expedition of a thousand ships to recover the abducted wife of a Spartan king. It is simply that American writers, with one or two exceptions, have not yet demonstrated that Zionism is an important part of their literary imagination.[36]

If Meyer Levin is one exception to this generalization, Hugh Nissenson is another. Younger than Levin by two full generations, Nissenson graduated from Swarthmore College in 1955 and published a collection of stories, *A Pile of Stones,* in 1965. He was praised in *Commentary* by Robert Alter, who called him "the only genuinely religious writer in the whole American Jewish group."[37] Alter's judgment of the other writers is too harsh, but he is right to admire Nissenson's talent. The seven stories of the collection include tales of Poland and America as well as two set in Israel, but the Israeli stories are the most compelling. "The Blessing" tells of an immigrant from Germany whose eight-year-old son dies of Hodgkins disease. He will not be comforted by the rabbi who comes to console him. After the rabbi's departure, his wife's aunt speaks the traditional invocation upon hearing evil news: "Blessed art Thou O Lord our God who art the true judge in Israel." The bereaved man, however, will not go to the funeral and recite these words and accept the inscrutability of God as Job accepted it in not dissimilar circumstances. The story ends with the grieving man and the starry sky:

> He was weeping. With one hand, he gestured toward the sky. All the clouds had gone, and all motion had ceased. In its place, from horizon to horizon, countless stars were shining, arranged in a vast, quiescent and eternal order that Esther had

blessed, and from which he was excluded by the tumult in his rebellious heart.[38] (p. 82)

A recent story published in *Midstream* (a Zionist journal) is remarkably similar. "Going Up" is set at the time of the Six-Day War in 1967. The narrator tells of his widowed uncle Mendel, who accompanies him across the newly captured Golan Heights. Uncle Mendel sees a dead youth, a Syrian, and is reminded of himself at the age when he first met his wife. The story had begun with the 121st Psalm: "Behold, He who keepeth Israel shall neither slumber nor sleep." Now, upset by the sight of the Syrian corpse, Uncle Mendel responds rebelliously, as did the bereaved hero of "The Blessing": "He never sleeps. One forgets. It wouldn't be so bad if I believed He was asleep." [39] It is the hand of Israel's keeper that struck down Uncle Mendel's other self. With knowledge like this, who can rejoice?

The other story in *A Pile of Stones* that is set in Israel is "The Well." It concerns the troubled relations between man and man rather than the unhappy ones between man and God. The story is told by an Israeli, a member of a *kibbutz*. It opens with a ten-year-old boy who fears that the Bedouins encamped two miles away will kill a newborn camel whose mother wandered into the commune's date grove to bear her colt. The Bedouins' well has gone dry and they need the camel's milk. The colt is shot. Grossman, one of the leaders of the *kibbutz*, persuades the members to share their water with the Arabs. The narrator is European-born, but Grossman grew up with the Arabs, spoke Arabic as a child, and shares the Bedouins' sense of possession of the land that both groups love. The debate is tense because the Jews remember an attack on their commune by the very Arabs whom Grossman wishes to help, but Grossman wins the debate and makes arrangements with the Bedouin friend of his childhood, Ali. The Bedouins come, but Ali's father charges his own people for the water the Jews freely provide. Ali refuses to accept the Israeli notion of equality for all members of his father's tribe. His father's right to tax seems as natural as life and death in a hard country. The Jews refuse to let Sheik Ahmed sell the water they have offered as a gift, and proud Ali leaves. When Grossman goes to their camp, Ali blames the Jews for the Arabs' misery and calls Grossman a "dog of a Jew." Grossman strikes him and drives off.

The story conveys—as paraphrase and comment cannot—a sense of the tragic conflict of two cultures. Two nations, each with a fierce conviction of moral rectitude, lay claim to the same land. The dispute about the water becomes a metaphor, a dramatic enactment of an apparently hopeless situation. It is the breadth of Nissenson's sympathy that enables him to write movingly of Israeli and Arab and, in still another story, to dramatize a young man's troubled acceptance of the burden of the Law.

4   "All Men Are Jews": Bernard Malamud

Although he is not in any important sense a Zionist, Bernard Malamud is almost certain to be mentioned in any discussion of the postwar reaffirmation of Jewishness. He has been acclaimed, in *Judaism,* as "the most Jewish of American Jewish writers." [40] There is, however, a very problematic quality to his fiction. His conception of what it means to be a Jew seems at times to resemble that of Ludwig Lewisohn, at other times that of Philip Roth. His work has been related to that of Sholom Aleichem and the tradition of Yiddish literature; it has also been described as "distinctly in the American grain." [41] Each new publication complicates matters and increases the difficulty of assessing the purport of his career.

Malamud's first book, *The Natural* (1952), had no Jewish characters of any importance. As many critics have noted, the novel combined the myths of the Grail Knight and the Fisher King with the national mystique of professional baseball.[42] The result was a comic hero named Roy Hobbes (the common man as king?), armed with a magic bat named Wonder Boy. The novel is divided into two unequal parts, the first of which is "Pre-Game." In "Pre-Game," the young hero is tested. In an impromptu contest staged by the side of a halted train on which both were travelling, Roy strikes out the "Whammer," the best batter of the day. For his *hubris,* Roy is struck down by a mysterious woman, curiously ornithic Harriet Bird, "a snappy goddess" [43] who tempts him and then shoots him in the stomach (as, in actuality, Eddie Waitkus was shot in 1949 by a temptress in Chicago's Edgewater Beach Hotel). Lucky Roy has a second chance. In "Batter Up!" (much the longer of the two parts), he finds employment with the New York Knights, under Pop Fisher.

Allusions to the medieval myth used by T. S. Eliot are many— Pop Fisher wants rain and gets it when Roy bats. Elements of the psychoanalytic theories of Carl Jung are also part of the composition. Roy lusts for wicked Memo Paris and loses his chance for Iris Lemon, takes a bribe to throw the game and changes his mind when it is too late. Malamud's moral is, therefore, conventional enough— selfishness and dishonesty are deplorable. At the very end, a child asks Roy what a child is alleged to have asked Shoeless Joe Jackson at the time of the Black Sox scandal of 1919: "Say it ain't true, Roy." [44] (p. 237) On the basis of this oddly mythical novel, there was no reason to expect that Malamud was soon to be categorized among "Jewish novelists of the postwar period."

He had, however, already begun to publish the short stories later collected in *The Magic Barrel* (1958). Many of these stories resemble the Yiddish literature of Sholom Aleichem and Mendele Mocher Sforim or tales written in the older conventions of Chassidism. Poor Jews survive by hook, crook, and the grace of God. Two of the stories relate directly to the theme of peoplehood. "The Lady of the Lake" is a parable in the sense that the shorter stories of *Goodbye, Columbus* are parables, but Malamud's moral is very different from Roth's. Henry Levin, "an ambitious, handsome thirty, who walked the floors in Macy's book department wearing a white flower in his lapel," inherits money and heads for Europe.[45] (p. 105) He changes his name to Henry R. Freeman, in an obvious effort to shed his Jewish identity for that of a free man. At Isola del Dongo he meets a girl who rises from the water like Botticelli's Venus, or like Roth's Brenda Patimkin:

> Freeman stared as she sloshed up the shore, her wet skin glistening in bright sunlight. She had seen him and quickly bent for a towel she had left on a blanket, draped it over her shoulders and modestly held the ends together over her high-arched breast. (pp. 111–12)

When the girl asks if he's Jewish, Freeman suppresses a groan and denies the truth. She claims to be Isabella del Dongo, a princess; she takes him on a tour of the palazzo, which has the old-world equivalent of the Patimkins' suburban splendor—works of art. It turns out that the Titians are copies and that Isabella is the daughter of a caretaker. Despite the deception, "Freeman" decides to propose to her, only to be queried again about his identity, only to deny again (like St. Peter) the truth. Then, the irony. She is a Jewess whom the Nazis had placed in Buchenwald:

> Slowly she unbuttoned her bodice. . . . When she revealed her breasts—he could have wept at their beauty (now recalling a former invitation to gaze at them, but he had arrived too late on the raft)—to his horror he discerned tatooed on the soft and tender flesh a bluish line of distorted numbers. (p. 132)

She will not marry him because she treasures the past she suffered for. Before he can explain, she steps among the statues of the palazzo garden. "Freeman" embraces the moonlit stone of a faked masterpiece, which is just what he deserves. The point of the story is almost too plain. Isabella had shown him a tapestry from Dante in which a tormented leper suffers punishment for mendacity; she had asked him if seven mountain peaks did not resemble the Menorah. Still, the story is well told.

"The Last Mohican," another story collected in *The Magic Barrel*, stresses the claim that every Jew has on every other Jew and is, therefore, the counterpart to Roth's "Defender of the Faith" and "Eli, the Fanatic." This story too is set in Italy, where Fidelman, "self-confessed failure as a painter," proves finally to be the man of faith his name proclaims him to be. (p. 155) Greeted in Rome with a cheery "Shalom" from a cicerone-schnorrer named Susskind, Fidelman's heart sinks. But Susskind reveals strange facets. He refuses, for instance, to accept a Jewish organization's offer of a ticket to Israel because he likes the freedom of his hand-to-mouth existence in Rome. He enjoys his precarious autonomy but makes sure that Fidelman feels a sense of responsibility. He demands one of Fidelman's suits. When Fidelman refuses ("I am a single individual and can't take on everybody's personal burden"), Susskind steals his manuscript on the work of Giotto. (p. 166) In pursuit of the bandy-legged thief, Fidelman comes to know the Jews of Rome and even the cemetery where six-pointed stars commemorate those who were murdered at Auschwitz. Eventualy, he finds Susskind (selling rosaries), gives him the suit, and recovers the briefcase. Enraged that Susskind has burned the manuscript, Fidelman pursues him through the streets of the ghetto until he is suddenly transfigured by "a triumphant insight." (p. 182) He recognizes his responsibility to Susskind and cries out that all is forgiven.

Does Fidelman's faith matter? His further adventures, told in *Idiots First* (1963), lead one to wonder. In "Still Life," Fidelman appears again, in love with Annamaria Oliovino, whose name seems to suggest the fruitfulness of olives and grapes (i.e. oil and wine). He paints her as the Virgin Mary and is sexually aroused. His attempts to fornicate with the more than ready *shikse* come to naught when she shouts, "Enough of antipasto," grabs his penis, and brings him to premature ejaculation. She kicks him out, shouting, "Pig, beast, onanist." [46] (p. 48) Eventually, Fidelman dresses as a priest and paints a portrait of himself with a cross. Annamaria Oliovino changes her mind and offers herself once again. "She clasped his buttocks, he cupped hers. Pumping slowly he nailed her to her cross." (p. 56) This is a memorable conclusion but one is puzzled about what to conclude from it. Is metaphoric conversion necessary before Fidelman can enjoy forbidden fruit? Had he donned caftan and yarmulka before coitus, critics would surely have discovered a return to Jewishness. Fidelman's later appearance in "Naked Nude" leaves one equally doubtful. Malamud subsequently wrote three more stories about Fidelman and collected all six in *Pictures of Fidelman: An Exhibition* (1969). In his later treatment of Fidelman's unusual erotic and artistic escapades, the theme of Jewishness is of negligible importance.

A New Life (1961), which appeared while Malamud was working on the various stories of *Idiots First,* is a more conventional work in the pastoral mode.[47] S. Levin goes west to teach at Pacifica College and runs into rather tedious difficulties with foolish colleagues, incompetent administrators, and a coed who questions his masculinity because the unanticipated arrival of her boyfriend cooled instructor Levin's animal ardor. By the end of the novel, Levin accepts the responsibilities incurred by an affair with a colleague's wife, whom he has made pregnant. He drives off with her and her children while her husband gleefully takes pictures. It looks to be one of the most mixed-up of mixed marriages. *A New Life* is not Malamud's "best effort," although some have called it so.[48]

The ambiguities recurrent when Malamud writes of Jews, which he does most of the time, occur even in the two novels that seem at first unambivalently to affirm the responsibility of all Jews to each other. *The Assistant,* published in 1957, represents a turnabout in the fictional treatment of conversion. Now the Gentile gives up the faith of his fathers in order to become a Jew. The significance of the conversion remains somewhat unclear because Malamud's implication is that the Jew can be defined as the man who suffers. The first scene presents the Jew as the much put-upon bearer of burdens:

> The early November street was dark though night had ended, but the wind, to the grocer's surprise, already clawed. It flung his apron into his face as he bent for the two milk cases at the curb. Morris Bober dragged the heavy boxes to the door, panting. A large brown bag of hard rolls stood in the doorway along with the sour-faced, gray-haired Poilisheh huddled there, who wanted one.
> "What's the matter so late?"
> "Ten after six," said the grocer.
> "Is cold," she complained.[49] (p. 3)

Morris Bober's assistant is a petty thief, Frank Alpine, who becomes increasingly involved in Morris Bober's affairs. Frank is fascinated by what one critic has cleverly referred to as the "Cartesian minimum": I suffer, therefore I am.[50] For Morris Bober, the statement seems to have an implied predicate nominative: "I suffer, therefore I am [a Jew]." Frank asks him why Jews suffer "so damn much," and Morris answers that they suffer because they are Jews.

> "If you want to live, you suffer. Some people suffer more, but not because they want. But I think if a Jew don't suffer for the Law, he will suffer for nothing."
> "What do you suffer for, Morris?" Frank said.
> "I suffer for you," Morris said calmly.
> Frank laid his knife down on the table. His mouth ached. "What do you mean?"
> "I mean you suffer for me." (p. 125)

Frank's involvement is in large part motivated by his love of Morris Bober's daughter, who bears the rather classical name Helen.

Like the elders who spied on Susanna, like David who caught sight of bathing Bathsheba (the prototype, perhaps, of Brenda Patimkin and Isabella del Dongo), Frank Alpine hides in a dumbwaiter to catch a sight of Helen Bober: "Her body was young, soft, lovely, the breasts like small birds in flight, her ass like a flower." (p. 75) She returns his love but refuses his sexual advances; eventually, she is saved *from* rape by his intervention, is then raped *by* him, and curses him as an uncircumcized dog. Frank continues his unorthodox courtship, returns to the store despite the fact that Morris had fired him for dishonesty, and—after Morris dies—takes over completely. At the funeral, Frank tumbles awkwardly into the grave and climbs out again, symbolically reborn. Madly in love with Helen, he runs the store.

His religious decision comes when he imagines St. Francis going to the garbage can into which Helen has thrown his gift of a carved rose and presenting it to her. The image of St. Francis has appeared earlier. At a candy store, Frank Alpine thumbed through a magazine and discovered the picture of a monk raising his skinny arms to a flock of birds. Frank identifies with the saint, for whom, after all, he may well have been named. He undergoes circumcision and becomes one of the sufferers whom he had earlier wondered at, a Jew.

But what is this strange identity that Frank Alpine has assumed? In their discussion of the famous dialogue on suffering, critics rarely point to what comes before and after Morris Bober's remark that Frank suffers for him. Earlier Frank asks why Morris keeps his store open on Jewish holidays, why he eats ham. Morris responds as follows:

> "This is not important to me if I taste pig or if I don't. To some Jews is this important but not to me. Nobody will tell me that I am not Jewish because I put in my mouth once in a while, when my tongue is dry, a piece ham. But they will tell me, and I will believe them, if I forget the Law. This means to do what is right, to be honest, to be good. (p. 124)

After Frank's query and Morris Bober's assertion that Frank suffers for him, Morris goes on: "If a Jew forgets the Law, he is not a good Jew, and not a good man." (p. 125) There can be no doubt about the seriousness of this redefinition. At the funeral of Morris Bober, the rabbi preaches on Jewishness:

"When a Jew dies, who asks if he is a Jew? He is a Jew, we don't ask. There are many ways to be a Jew. So if somebody comes to me and says, 'Rabbi, shall we call such a man Jewish who lived and worked among the gentiles and sold them pig meat, trayfe, that we don't eat, and not once in twenty years comes inside a synagogue, is such a man a Jew, rabbi?' To him I will say, 'Yes, Morris Bober was to me a true Jew because he lived in the Jewish experience, which he remembered, and with the Jewish heart.' Maybe not to our formal tradition —for this I don't excuse him—but he was true to the spirit of our life—to want for others that which he wants also for himself. He followed the Law which God gave to Moses on Sinai and told him to bring to the people. He suffered. He endu-red [sic] but with hope." (p. 229)

The rabbi's comments are crucial. Although the rabbi refers to the Law that God gave Moses on Sinai, he has already insisted that Morris Bober is a true Jew despite his numerous infractions of what Orthodox Jews have taken to be the essence of that law.[51] The letter of the Law is less important than the spirit, which turns out to be remarkably like Immanuel Kant's categorical imperative: to want for others what you want for yourself. One critic, disturbed by the implications of the rabbi's speech, has called it "clearly ironic," but this attempt to whisk away the difficulties is too simple.[52] What Malamud has done explicitly throughout his work is widen the definition of "Jew" to the point of meaninglessness. If any good man, measured by Kant's categorical imperative or the Golden Rule or the rabbi's formulation, is doomed to suffer and, therefore, to be a Jew, then the concept has been permanently replaced by its own metaphoric extensions. Frank Alpine's conversion was merely the painful ratification of a prior change of heart. No wonder, then, that Malamud's most famous epigram is the orphic statement: "All men are Jews."[53]

The difficulty, for those anxious to insure the survival of the Jews as a distinct people, is that Malamud's conclusions are too much of a good thing. If all men are Jews, then the divinely drawn line between the Chosen People and the *goyim* has been erased. Robert Alter's comments on Malamud are shrewd and to the point: "Although his protagonists are avowedly Jewish, he has never really written *about* Jews, in the manner of other American Jewish novelists." [54] To Alter, *The Fixer* (1966) is Malamud's finest achievement because the central metaphor of imprisonment is derived from the social facts of Czarist Russia and from the actual details of the career of Mendel Beilis. The novel is certainly Malamud's most intense and sustained dramatization of the responsibilities of peoplehood. The novel tells the story of Yakov Bok, the fictional correlative of the Russian martyr Mendel Beilis. Like "Henry Freeman," Yakov Bok attempts to evade the responsibilities of his identity. He discovers as a child that the life of a Russian Jew is a dangerous one:

> On the third morning when the houses were still smoldering and he was led, with a half dozen other children, out of a cellar where they had been hiding he saw a black-bearded Jew with a white sausage stuffed into his mouth, lying in the road on a pile of bloody feathers, a peasant's pig devouring his arm.[55] (p. 5)

He decides, therefore, to flee, Jonah-like. He drops his bag of prayer articles in the Dnieper River and goes to Kiev and takes the name of Yakov Ivanovitch Dologushev. The name Bok, which signifies scapegoat, was the truer sign. A boy is murdered and Yakov is accused. Under pressure, he admits that he is a Jew. Most of the book is filled with the anguish of his imprisonment and trial, with his terrible disappointments (such as, for instance, the suicide of his sympathetic lawyer), with the dishonest machinations of anti-Semitic officials. Although Yakov Bok is doomed to die because he is a Jew, he rejects the God of his people: "Don't talk to me about God," he answers bitterly when soothed by a friend, "I want no part of God. When you need him most he's farthest away." (p. 256) Advised that "God's justice is for the end of time," he cries out, "I'm not so young any more, I can't wait that long. . . . God counts in astronomy but where men are concerned all I know is one plus one." No more than the Jews of Philip Roth's Woodenton is he impressed by the Biblical myths. How can one respect a God who plays games with men? "To win a lousy bet with the devil he killed off all the servants and innocent children of Job." (p. 258) Although Malamud ends the novel before the execution of the hero-victim, it is clear that Yakov will be sacrificed because the world insists that he is what he has no desire to be.[56]

But Malamud's portrayal of Yakov Bok, whose distinctness was insisted upon by friend and foe alike, suggests that the flamboyant, quotable assertion of the universality of Jewishness is hyperbole. Jews are Jews, in Malamud's fiction as in the popular mind, because their parents or grandparents were believers in the God of Abraham and Isaac and keepers of His Law. Fidelman gives up his suit because he and Susskind share a common fate. Henry Freeman loses Isabella del Dongo because he denies his share in their particular *Schicksalsgemeinschaft*. Malamud sometimes sounds like the contemporary of Philip Roth, but he seems in his heart of hearts to be, like Ludwig Lewisohn, a believer in peoplehood.

5   *The Postwar Revival of Peoplehood*

Of the many postwar novelists who have dramatized the commitment to peoplehood less ambiguously than Bernard Malamud, three definitely deserve discussion—Herman Wouk, Arthur Cohen, and Chaim Potok.* The first of these three men was already a popular novelist when he discovered the appeals of Conservatism in politics and in religion. *Aurora Dawn* (1947) was a gentle satire of the "dear-reader" variety, a commentary on the foibles and wiles of admen. *City Boy,* which came out a year later, was a *Penrod and Sam* for Jewish readers, a genre picture of urban childhood. Despite the sentimentality that pervades Wouk's portrait of Herbert Bookbinder and his playmates, the book demonstrates Wouk's ability to tell a story. Wouk achieved commercial success and caught the eye of numerous literary critics with *The Caine Mutiny* (1951).

The structure of the novel is fairly simple. Throughout most of the

* Among novelists, the most ambitious postwar advocate of Jewishness in all of its facets—from Orthodoxy through an agnostic commitment to peoplehood—has been Charles Angoff, whose multivolume, autobiographical narration of the life of David Polansky has been highly praised in Jewish journals and discussed respectfully in Bernard Sherman's *The Invention of the Jew: Jewish-American Education Novels (1916–1964)*. Miriam Bruce's *Linden Road* (1951), Samuel Astrachan's *An End to Dying* (1956), Sylvia Rothchild's *Sunshine and Salt* (1964), Stephen Longstreet's *Pedlock and Sons* (1966), Judith Papier's *The Past and Present of Solomon Sorge* (1967), and Zelda Popkin's *Herman Had Two Daughters* (1968) are also devoted to the rediscovery of Jewishness. Of these writers, Astrachan and Papier are the most talented.

tale, Wouk demonstrates that Captain Queeg is a paranoid maniac, a petty, willful, tyrannical coward. Incident after incident reveals Queeg's absolute unfitness to command a ship. Nonetheless, when the crew is led into mutiny by a dissident intellectual, Lieutenant Keefer, Wouk suddenly shifts his position and sends the reader's expectations for a tumble. He reverses his emotional vectors and now insists, through the figure of Barney Greenwald, the Jewish defense attorney at the mutineers' court martial, that Captain Queeg was right all the time. Greenwald has demonstrated that Queeg is a mythomaniac and a hysteric. Greenwald has brought him to alienate the court by his mad claims to absolute innocence: "I did not make a single mistake in fifteen months aboard the *Caine* and I can prove it and my record has been spotless until now and I don't want it smirched by a whole lot of lies and distortions by disloyal officers." [57] (p. 436) But at the vulgar celebration of the acquitted mutineers, the lawyer condemns his own clients and tells them that Captain Queeg has kept Greenwald's mother from the soap dish, his inelegant way of referring to the extermination of the Jews in the concentration camps. While other Americans reveled hedonistically through the 1920s and worried over domestic matters in the 1930s, Queeg served with the Navy and was ready to defend them when the time of danger came. The military establishment that fought and defeated Nazi Germany must be affirmed by grateful Jews.

The same novelistic strategy, more skillfully handled, served for *Marjorie Morningstar* (1955). The heroine, whose real name is Morgenstern, is led into temptation by Noel Airman, an assimilationist whose name suggests the ne'er-do-well *Luftmensch* of Yiddish literature, but she returns at length to her institutional commitments to Judaism and its Law.

The novel opens with seventeen-year-old Marjorie about to ride horseback in Central Park with a boy from Columbia University. She is an adolescent victim of "self-hate": "By moving to the El Dorado on Central Park West her parents had done much, Marjorie believed, to make up for their immigrant origin." [58] (p. 4) Her ride is symbolic: she hits the crop-shy horse until he gallops—and she falls. Better to live at one's proper pace. When wicked Vera Cashman urges Marjorie to eat bacon, Sandy Goldstone defends her resolve, but most of her acquaintances encourage her to violate Mosaic prohibitions. Despite her lack of interest in Judaism, Marjorie holds firm to her refusal to eat non-kosher food—until she gets a job in a Catskill resort and meets Noel Airman (born Saul Ehrmann). He seems a veritable Greek god who dances, sings, plays chess, and discusses philosophy more ably than professors can. An older woman acts as a plain-speaking pander: "Margie, you're an infant. The world is all like South Wind, just a lot of eating, maneuvering, guzzling, and fornicating, and everybody is like me and Carlos, loused up, grabbing what fun we can." (p. 125) Marjorie continues to resist.

Section III, "Sodom," contains her spiritual fall. She plays Eliza Doolittle in Shaw's version of the Pygmalion legend and comes to believe that one can be remade, perhaps reborn. Although South Wind "seethes," "crawls," and "ullulates" with "nasty squirming writhing naked bodies," Noel brings Marjorie to the point where she is ready to sleep with him. (p. 180) Providentially, her uncle Samson, planted as a dishwasher in order to keep an eye on her, dies of a heart attack. Only after the funeral does Marjorie realize how close she came to the loss of her virginity.

Time passes, but Noel, now a successful songwriter, continues to pursue Marjorie. He persuades her to eat lobster; the physical mess she makes of it symbolizes the moral horror of the act, but Marjorie promises to order ham the next time they dine out. Under constant pressure from Noel and from other assimilationists, she finally surrenders. The moment of her Fall is the opposite of marvelous. While most modern writers describe coitus in terms once reserved for descriptions of the mystical union of the soul with God, Wouk dramatizes disgust: "There were shocks, ugly uncoverings, pain, incredible humiliation, shock, shock, and it was over." (p. 417) A broken glass, knocked over by Marjorie, is an emblem of her shattered self.

After an affair of a year's duration, Noel goes off to Europe. Eventually, Marjorie follows and meets a psychologist-guru in the guise of a certain Michael Eden. He saves our modern Eve from her high-flying snake in the grass. He tells her that "food disciplines are part of every great religion. Psychologically, they're almost inevitable, and extremely practical." (p. 469) (He does not explain the practical purposes of the rules that restrict women's behavior during and after their "unclean" periods.) Michael reveals later that he knew

Freud but broke with him when he discovered that psychoanalytical theory absolves men from moral responsibility. He also discloses to Marjorie the irony of his family's history—his Jewish forebears had changed their name from Einstein, "the one name that's apt to survive the next twenty centuries." (p. 510) Michael, like Ludwig Lewisohn's Arthur Levy, has recovered his sense of peoplehood.

In Europe, Marjorie finds Noel, who has finally decided that Karl Marx was wrong and that the religion of his ancestors is right. He proposes belated marriage, but she refuses him and sleeps as soundly as a child. Now her future is plain. She marries a politically and religiously conservative suburbanite named Milton Schwartz. Noel Airman weeps for what he has foolishly lost, marries a German, and endures damnation as a TV writer. Marjorie settles in New Rochelle, which was Noel's symbol of witless conformity, and has four children. She is described by an old admirer: "She's a regular synagogue goer, active in the Jewish organization of the town; apparently that takes up a lot of her time." (p. 562) She and Milton keep separate dishes for milk and for meat, as the Law prescribes, and find comfort in faith when their baby dies. Wally Wronken summarizes: "The only remarkable thing about Mrs. Schwartz is that she ever hoped to be remarkable, that she ever dreamed of being Marjorie Morningstar." (p. 564) Nonetheless, Wally writes of her youthful beauty, of the visionary loveliness that she once represented. Wally's memories are the equivalent of a last-minute remark from Barney Greenwald to the effect that Captain Queeg really was a paranoid maniac. The novel's last hundred pages nail down the thesis that religiously observant middle-class domesticity is better than the dream of Romantic love, only to have Wally Wronken pop up with the notion that the dream lingers on. Does Wally want "a warm and happy home" or does he still want "that second kiss from Marjorie under the lilacs"? (p. 565) Perhaps he, like Wouk himself, wants to have it both ways.

The book's popularity is in no way remarkable. It responded to a call that more talented writers refused to answer. It provided a full, if somewhat inept, dramatization of moral death and resurrection, but it called for none of the sacrifices implied by Lewisohn's *The Island Within*.

Wouk's annoyance with the negative critical reaction to his commercially successful work surfaced in his next novel, *Youngblood Hawke* (1962), where one of the characters comments, "I'm getting a little tired of this cult of college professors who keep writing and reviewing novels for each other and about each other, just passing back and forth their own slightly damp gray laundry." [59] (p. 192) The novel, which resembles the massively semi-literate work of Ayn Rand, defends American values—as understood by Wouk—against the menace of alien doctrines. Jewishness is not a theme. Wouk then relaxed from his labors with *Don't Stop the Carnival* (1965), a moderately comic novel about an innocent American who buys a Carribean resort. There is also a minor character named Sheldon Klug, a Jewish atheist who considers himself an existential pagan, writes of the alleged homosexuality of Honoré Balzac, condemns American society, and eats like a pig. Sheldon Klug is not an admirable man.

The fictive world of Arthur Cohen resembles Herman Wouk's literary skeet shoot in that Cohen too is concerned with the responsibilities of peoplehood; other similarities are to be found. Cohen's short novel *The Carpenter Years* (1967) returns to the father-son conflict but with a significant difference. It is now the father who is the apostate and the son who has been disavowed. The title refers to those years in which Jesus of Nazareth lived quietly and plied his mundane profession. The first sentence of the novel raises the relevant issues: "It seemed implausible, ever more implausible as the years passed, that Morris Edelman should have become Edgar Morrison." [60] (p. 3) The suggestion of lost nobility, in the name "Edelman," is appropriate to the tone of the book. Edgar Morrison is morally a coward, a man in flight from his true identity. Ironically, he works for the Young Men's Christian Association and uses his authority to block Jewish boys from the swimming pool (because they won't pledge their belief in Christianity). He refuses to side with Rabbi Kieval on the question of a Nativity scene on the football field.

From the rabbi, Edgar Morrison learns that the son of his abandoned family is about to come to town to work for the local hospital. Edgar Morrison is shattered, gets drunk, walks the streets. Cohen indulges in melodrama:

Edgar began to cry inaudibly, muffling his tears against his coat sleeve, crying not for the wife and child . . . he had deserted, but for the fact that he had remembered and no longer wanted to enact the obligation imposed by memory to light a daylong candle of remembrance for his father. . . . (pp. 38–39)

Minutes later, he passes a synagogue and is transfixed by the Eternal Light burning over the Ark of the Covenant. The light held his eyes "powerless." Cohen then rubs the point in:

Edgar had lost his own Jewish childhood, and his Polish youth, his New York growing up, his whole past, centuries of memory, millennia of history, cut away, burned out as a dead stump is burned out of the earth, roots still clinging. (p. 43)

The climax comes at a party for the new psychologist. The father meets and refuses to acknowledge his son. The son, insulted by one of the prominent citizens of the town, knees him in the groin and returns to New York, proud, independent, amused (despite an automobile accident). The father is left to his gloomy fate, a lesson to us all.

The Carpenter Years received tactful consideration from the reviewers. Chaim Potok's first novel, also published in 1967, was enthusiastically welcomed (and quickly became a best seller). Denying himself simplifications of the sort indulged in by Wouk and Cohen, acknowledging reasons for the rejection of faith, Potok's enactment of the theme of peoplehood deserves to survive the season of its publication. *The Chosen* is an admirable work of art, the most persuasive book of its kind since *The Island Within*.

The narrator, Reuven Malter, tells the story of Danny Saunders, whom he meets in the comically symbolic baseball game that opens the novel:

To the rabbis who taught in the Jewish parochial schools, baseball was an evil waste of time, a spawn of the potentially assimilationist English portion of the yeshiva day. But to the students of most of the parochial schools, an inter-league baseball victory had come to take on only a shade less significance than a top grade in Talmud, for it was the unquestioned mark of one's Americanism . . .[61] (p. 14)

Danny Saunders turns the game into a struggle over the essence of Judaism. His team catcalls that Reuven and his fellow players are *apikorisim,* apostates. Danny bats at the pitcher and injures Reuven. Visiting him in the hospital, he makes the first gestures of friendship.

It happens that Danny, a fanatical reader, has already met Reuven's father, although he was ignorant of the connection. Danny's own father is an almost miraculously learned rabbi who has taught his son a tradition that the son no longer feels. No wonder, then, the displaced hostility against the less Orthodox. The fathers represent two views of Jewish history. Reb Saunders learns of the death of six million Jews in Hitler's *Endlösung* and accepts their death as part of God's will. Reb Malter, however, becomes a Zionist, which enrages Reb Saunders: "God will build the land, not Ben Gurion and his goyim!" (p. 198) The thought that David Ben Gurion can be considered a Gentile may amuse some readers, but Reb Saunders speaks from the same tradition that burned the works of Moses Maimonides and excommunicated Baruch Spinoza. When Reb Malter defends the Zionists, Reb Saunders forbids his son to associate with any of the Malter family. Danny, however, moves further from Orthodoxy than Reuven. While the latter studies to be a rabbi and cautiously introduces modern critical methods into textual analysis, Danny determines to become a psychologist.

The Arab-Israeli war of 1948 brings the Zionists and anti-Zionists together (as did the Arab-Israeli war of 1967). Danny's father finally accepts the fact that his son, without earlocks, will follow Freud rather than Moses. Wisdom accepts the various ways of knowledge and seems, within the world of the novel, the wiser for its acceptance. But the defense of the old has become an elegy.

The sequel, published in 1969, is Reuven's story rather than Danny's. In an effort to repeat the success of his first novel, Potok opens *The Promise* with a symbolically American country fair, where Reuven meets a compulsive, disturbed young Jew named Michael Gordon, son of a modernist scholar. Reuven is interested enough to read Abraham Gordon's books, on the margins of which someone has written, "This is the book of an apostate. Those who fear God are forbidden to read it." [62] (p. 63) Reuven's involvement with the Gordon family is thus a double one: he arranges for

Michael's treatment by Danny Saunders (now a psychologist), and he is persuaded that Abraham's scholarly methods are sound ones.

Tension builds, however, because Reuven is a rabbinical student of a fiercely antimodernist immigrant professor, Jakob Kalman, who denounces the sins of American Jews:

> In America, everything is called Yiddishkeit. . . . A Jew travels to synagogue on Shabbos in his car, that is called Yiddishkeit. A Jew eats ham but gives money to philanthropy, that is called Yiddishkeit. A Jew prays three times a year but is a member of a synagogue, that is called Yiddishkeit. (p. 108)

He asks wrathfully how a school can teach Judaism without the Talmud. He refuses to believe that a modern scholar with knowledge of Greek might be able to explicate a passage better than a medieval sage misled by a botched translation. When he does show an interest in modern methods and asks Reuven for help, it is only to use the information for a vicious assault on Reuven's father's books. And yet, Jakob Kalman has the power to grant or withhold ordination for Reuven Malter. He decides, finally, to grant *smicha* because he doesn't want to drive a gifted student from the *Yeshiva*. The moral victory is paralleled by a psychological breakthrough when Danny Saunders brings Michael Gordon out of his catatonic state.

Although Potok's work can hardly be described as a brief for Orthodoxy or for Chassidism, he has managed to transform the travail of the devout into literature of a fairly high order, which is more than Wouk and Cohen were able to do. Not since Abraham Cahan's *Rise of David Levinsky* had an important writer taken seriously the details of religious observance and the theological controversies among traditional Jews.* Whether Potok's achievement

---

* Sympathetically portrayed rabbis are no longer a rarity. In addition to Myron Kaufmann's *Thy Daughter's Nakedness* (1968), there is Noah Gordon's *The Rabbi* (1965). Gordon's hero has married a convert to Judaism but can still reassure the spirit of his grandmother, who told him not to marry *shikse:* "Don't be afraid, Zaydeh, he said silently into the darkness. Six thousand years is not the wink of an eyelash or the beat of a bird's wing. There is nothing new on the face of the ancient earth, and what could not be erased by bloodbaths and ovens will not be erased by changed names or bobbed noses or the merging of our blood with mysterious bloodstreams." [63] (pp. 388–89)

will win converts from among the *apiḳorisim* is a question that no one can answer.

6 Poems of Jews: Karl Shapiro, Irving Feldman, John Hollander

Poetry may be the only means of touching the heart of the minimally observant or totally secular Jew. But where are the poets? Judaism's denominational magazines do not, of course, suffer from any quantitative scarcity of poets, but where are the Jewish equivalents to T. S. Eliot and the young Robert Lowell? Muriel Rukeyser, Delmore Schwartz, and Howard Nemerov are gifted poets, but their verse is almost without a trace of their Jewish origins (except, perhaps, in such poems as Nemerov's irreverent "Dialogue with a Rabbi"). Other poets (discussed in Chapter 4) have sung of revolution rather than of the traditional "End of Days." Writers who *have* written of Abraham and Isaac offer respect rather than homage. Within the space of a short poem there is room for a *cri de coeur*, for a passionate testament of peoplehood, but the mood passes and the next poem tells of Cassandra or laments a cinema's metamorphosis into the "supermarket's failure of the imagination." [64]

The strange case of Karl Shapiro is not the exception it seems to be. His early poems told of Adam and Eve but also of drugstores, auto wrecks, and—especially—of the life of a soldier: "I smoke and read my Bible and chew gum, /Thinking of Christ and Christmas of last year. . . ." [65] In 1958 he published a selection of his earlier verse with the polemical title *Poems of a Jew*. He wrote of his grandmother "at ragged book bent in Hebrew prayer" and of her final inability to remember the "tongues and tasks of her children's children." [66] (p. 49) He wrote of his own childhood and education, of the creation of the State of Israel, and of the difference between Christianity's cathedrals and Judaism's synagogues, where "Our scrolls are volumes of the thundered law / Sabbath by Sabbath wound by hand to read." (p. 8) In the collection's first poem, he paid tribute to the language of the Law:

> The letters of the Jews are black and clean
> And lie in chain-line over Christian pages.
> The chosen letters bristle like barbed wire
> That hedge the flesh of man. . . . (p. 3)

Shapiro's book was unquestionably the assertion of his identity as a Jew. The question remained: what kind of Jew? "The name," he wrote, is "immortal but only the name." (p. 50) Nietzsche, Flaubert, Edward Lear, and Edgar Allan Poe figure in his poems more than the prophets and sages of Judaism do. "The Murder of Moses" is based, he commented in his notes, on Sigmund Freud's interpretation rather than Talmudic authority. The poem suggests the intractability of the Jews:

> We watched where you overturned the calf on the fire,
> We hid when you broke the tablets on the rock,
> We wept when we drank the mixture of gold and water.
> We had hoped you were lost or had left us.
> This was the day of our greatest defilement. (p. 54)

What kind of Jew? In his introduction, Shapiro asserted that he was not concerned with Judaism, with Jewry, or with Israel. "The religious question is not my concern." For him, the Jew is the "symbol of the primitive ego of the human race," the essential qualities of mankind stripped of nationality and—it seems—religion. "The free modern Jew, celebrated so perfectly in the character of [Joyce's] Leopold Bloom, is neither hero nor victim. He is man left over, after everything that can happen has happened." (p. ix–xi) For a poet who has condemned the excesses of modernist criticism, Shapiro has offered a remarkably metaphoric defense of peoplehood.

Among younger poets who have identified themselves as Jews, two seem especially important—Irving Feldman and John Hollander. Both poets are witty and both—but especially Hollander—are learned. They are, like almost all poets of our time, ironic about themselves. Feldman, "ghetto-born, depression-bred,"

> Learned the cost of life in cents,
> To measure every ring and rag.
> Saw Israel's shining tents
> Fold up like a doctor's bag.[67] (p. 35)

In a poem entitled "The Wandering Jew," Feldman adopted the comic mode: "Why was I born in Brooklyn in the lower middle-classes? / Is that a hero's place? Was Moses freckled! Samson wear glasses!" (p. 96) There are solemn moments in *Works and Days*

(1961), in "A Speech by Abraham" for instance, where the prophet laments the divine necessity that calls upon him to sacrifice his beloved son. "Moses on Pisgah" is also moving:

> Joyless and ashen as one who stalks
> His shadow I go, and do not know
> If I am but His staff Who walks. (p. 16)

There are, however, also poems about Prometheus, Narcissus, Theseus, and other figures from the myths forbidden to Orthodox Jews. Feldman's second book of poems, *The Pripet Marshes* (1965), is more subdued and introspective. In "Poem at Thirty-Five" and in memories of childhood, Feldman seems to brood on what he was and what he has become, on the difference between the little boy fascinated by Yankel the butcher and the man who writes poems inspired by Picasso. Feldman's relation to the exterminated Jews of Eastern Europe becomes the subject of poetic meditation in the title poem and in the penultimate poem, "To the Six Million." In "The Pripet Marshes," the speaker imagines his American friends transported to the *shtetl*. "It is the moment before the Germans will arrive." [68] (p. 44) Can he save them, can he save himself?

> The German motorcycles zoom through the town,
> They break their fists on the hollow doors.
> But I can't hold out any longer. My mind clouds over.
> I sink down as though drunk or beaten. (p. 47)

The poem ends with these mysterious lines, with the suggestion that imaginative re-enactment can have no happier conclusion than reality's piled corpses. This suggestion is supported by the placement of "To the Six Million," which follows "The Pripet Marshes." The poem moves between the massacred Jews and the "I" who survived unscathed and is nonetheless figuratively dead. Like the "death-of-God" theologians who have appeared among rabbis as well as among ministers, the speaker seems to set the old dogmas aside:

> If there is a god,
> He descends from the power.
> But who is the god rising from death? (p. 48)

The gods, it seems, are of many sorts, hostile and competitive. They are not central. The question that is the poem's core concerns the speaker and not the gods:

> Should I have been with them
> On other winter days in the snow
> Of the camps and ghettos? (p. 50)

The answer is that the speaker was one who should have died and who *did* die. He is the resurrected survivor. Or is he? Contraries are asserted. The second section of the poem is an address to the speaker's "dear ones," to whom he offers to speak with the speech of ritual. The ritual is mundane. When they have awakened, he will accompany them in the streets. What these streets are, metaphorically, is left to the reader. The poem seems, finally, in T. S. Eliot's terms, a raid on the inexpressible. Perhaps it is appropriate that the ambiguous identity of the American Jew be the wraithlike theme of a paradoxical poem. Feldman's latest collection, *Magic Papers and Other Poems* (1970), is almost entirely without reference to Jewishness.

The emotional eclecticism of Feldman's first book is to be found in the work of John Hollander, who once looked upon a ruined palace in Poland and described himself as a ruin too, if "a remnant of all the six forgotten / Millions is a true ruin. . . ." [69] Hollander's first book of poems, *A Crackling of Thorns* (1958), bore a title from Ecclesiastes (7:6): "For as the crackling of thorns under a pot so is the laughter of fools; this also is vanity." In the book's epigraph, Hollander quotes a Talmudic interpretation of the verse. The poems themselves are, however, witty invitations to imagine rather than to worship. Consider, for instance, "Susanna's Song":

> There are old men in mastic trees,
> Arms in oaks, and hands in the grass;
> Their shadows will reach above my knees
> And play with the light on me, unless
> The clouds go dark and drift too near
> And sun and shadows disappear.
> But they will stay while I undress
> Not far from where the ground is shady,
> The right place to bathe a lady. [70] (p. 7)

It seems perfectly natural for Hollander, in his third book of poems, *Visions from the Ramble* (1965), to meditate on "The Ninth of

Ab," the fast day that commemorates the destruction of the Second Temple; it seems quite as natural for him to write of Icarus or simply of Central Park. His poem "The Great Bear," which concludes *A Crackling of Thorns,* expresses better than any other I know of the skeptic's regret that things are as they are. Of the Great Bear in the sky, he writes,

> We should not want to train ourselves to see it.
> The world is everything that happens to
> Be true. The stars at night seem to suggest
> The shapes of what might be. If it were best,
> Even, to have it there (such a great bear!
> All hung with stars!), there still would be no bear. (p. 71)

To end a chapter devoted to the conversion of apostates and the recovery of a sense of peoplehood like this—with references to a pair of gifted poets assimilated into the traditions of European civilization—is to indicate the almost hopeless difficulty faced by Ludwig Lewisohn and others transformed by the idea of Zion and anxious to kindle in others a similar sense of the oneness of Israel. In fairness, let the chapter's last quotation be from Lewisohn. Thirty years ago, when Hitler's armies were already on the march in Czechoslovakia and Spain, Lewisohn appealed to American Jews:

> Escape, escape, anything on any irrelevant periphery. Anything but the center, the heart, the blood. Virgin Spain.* The Soviet Fatherland. Anything but the real, the attainable, the given, that for which real work can be done in a world of reality and real sacrifices made and real tears shed and real blood; anything but that to which one is called by nature and unperverted instinct and tradition and where one is wanted and needed and where . . . one can give one's whole heart. Any place but home. Any people except one's own. Any God except the God of one's fathers. . . . Utopia is the opiate of . . . the Jewish people.[71]

* Lewisohn's reference to "Virgin Spain" was aimed at Waldo Frank's book by that title, published in 1926. Frank, a German-American Jew with little or no consciousness of Jewishness, had also written *The Re-Discovery of America* (1929) and many novels, of which *City Block* (1922) is best known. By 1944, Frank came largely to agree with Lewisohn. In *The Jew in Our Day* he attacked the assimilationist tendencies of the "inertial Jew" who did not actively involve himself in the Jewish community.

Utopia is the opiate of the Jewish people—or their truest vocation. Perhaps the only category of conversion to rival in importance that of St. Paul was precisely this conversion to radicalism. Let us investigate.

IV

The Revolutionary Messiah

1 *Jewish Radicals?*

Many observers have noted that the American Jew has, from the 1870s to the present day, played a conspicuous part in the lively drama of radical politics in the United States. The political role of the American Jew as anarchist, socialist, Communist, and "New Left" proponent of romantic revolution has often been explained by references to Judaism and its Messianic tradition. Scholars have maintained that the Old Testament prophets' dream of justice is directly related to the modern Jew's involvement in revolutionary politics. Historians and political scientists have asserted that democratic theory and republican government flourished among the ancient Jews, and Hugo Valentin has claimed that Moses was "the first to proclaim the rights of man." [1] In one of its more sophisticated versions, the argument goes like this:

> The recollection of Egyptian bondage with the concomitant emphasis upon liberty are among the most important facts of Jewish history. In ancient Jewish life these resulted in egalitarian and libertarian emphases in Jewish religious thought and a marked sympathy for the oppressed and enslaved. [2]

It is, moreover, a rare study of Marxism that does not hint that Karl Marx was the reincarnation of the Jewish prophets.

The difficulty with this line of analysis is that it runs counter to

134

the historical evidence, which suggests that the social situation of the Jews, at any moment of history, is a more crucial factor than religious tradition in the explanation of political commitments. Medieval Jews were, for instance, noted for their conservative reliance upon papal and imperial authority and for their antagonism to the nascent institutions of popular authority. Why? Because emperor and pope offered some small protection against persecution. The Holy Roman Emperors, who claimed exclusive jurisdiction over Jews within their realm, found Jews useful as money lenders and as specially reserved victims of their own extortion. Catholic doctrine categorized the Jews as a kind of useful infidel deserving of special toleration. Alexander of Hales and St. Thomas Aquinas agreed that Jews bore witness to the truth of Christianity because of their belief in the Old Testament (which allegedly predicts the events of the New). Salo Wittmayer Baron concludes that

> If one were to attempt any generalization, one might assert that, next to the emperors, the German hierarchy served as the chief and relatively most consistent protector of [medieval] Jewry. Certainly the bishops rarely initiated, even though they did not always strongly enough resist, the popular pressures aimed at the total elimination of Jews from their bishoprics.[3]

Before the Emancipation of the eighteenth and nineteenth centuries, Jews were noted for their conservatism and condemned by many of the advocates of the Enlightenment (who have since been berated for their alleged anti-Semitism).[4] Why? Because Jews of the *ancien régime* had generally been granted some measure of autonomy over their own affairs, which their leaders were quite naturally reluctant to jeopardize by premature trust in democratic forms. In his public statements and in his novels, Benjamin Disraeli maintained that Judaism and conservatism were naturally allied. In their addresses to the Czars, Orthodox Jews made the same assertion. When a contemporary historian tells us that American Jews were not involved in the crusade against slavery until the arrival of the German Jews in the 1840s, he has refuted his own theory of the religious rather than the sociological origin of Jewish radicalism.[5] The truth is that there has been for Jews of the Diaspora a negative correlation between Judaism and political radicalism. Jews who have rejected the political and economic *status quo* have also rejected Torah and Talmud. Their radicalism has meant the abandonment rather than the intensification of their faith in Judaism. "Jewish" radicals have actually been converts to the secular faith in revolution.

It is the twofold alienation of the Jewish radical, from his own traditions and from the society in which he lives, discussed by Thorstein Veblen in 1919, that must be understood by anyone who seeks to understand the Jewish radicalism of the last one hundred years. Veblen's subject was the alleged "intellectual pre-eminence" of Jews in Western culture, but his conclusions apply more strikingly to political radicals than to the others he discussed. Despite the richness of the Jewish heritage, he argued, "the later generations of home-bred Jewish scholars . . . have run into lucubrations that have no significance for contemporary science or scholarship at large." This is, of course, no accident, for Orthodox tradition shuns the secular culture.

> It appears to be only when the gifted Jew escapes from the cultural environment created and fed by the particular genius of his own people, only when he falls into the alien lines of gentile inquiry and becomes a naturalized . . . citizen in the gentile republic of learning, that he comes into his own as a creative leader in the world's intellectual enterprise. It is by loss of allegiance, or at the best by force of a divided allegiance to the people of his origin, that he finds himself in the vanguard of modern inquiry. . . . The young Jew finds his own heritage of usage and outlook untenable . . . The idols of his own tribe have crumbled in decay and no longer cumber the ground, but that release does not induce him to set up a new line of idols borrowed from an alien tribe to do the same disservice.[6]

The middle-class culture of bourgeois Christianity no longer lures the emancipated Jew. "By consequence," Veblen continued, "he is in a peculiar degree exposed to the unmediated facts of the current situation. . . . In short, he is a skeptic by force of circumstances over which he has no control."[7] He is, in the current jargon, doubly alienated. He is Isaac Rosenfeld's "specialist in alienation" who may be led by persecution to "envisage the good society."[8] Every Jew in Christendom knows what many Christians never know—that there is more than one answer to life's ultimate questions. The intellectual of Jewish origin knows still more. He knows that there are at least two answers and that neither one of them will do. He is the wanderer who must imagine the Zion he can return to.

Veblen's brilliant insights were, apparently, ignored by most academic sociologists, but Robert E. Park, drawing upon the work of Georg Simmel, established the theory of marginality in a famous essay published in 1928.

> When . . . the walls of the medieval ghetto were torn down and the Jew was permitted to participate in the cultural life of the peoples among whom he lived, there appeared a new type of personality, namely, a cultural hybrid, a man living and sharing intimately in the cultural life and traditions of two distinct peoples; never quite willing to break . . . with his past and his traditions, and not quite accepted, because of racial prejudice, in the new society in which he now sought to find a place. He was a man on the margin of two cultures and two societies. . . . The emancipated Jew was, and is, historically and typically the marginal man, the first cosmopolite and citizen of the world.[9]

Although Park did not carry the analysis to the next step, it seems reasonable to assume that marginality is an uncomfortable status from which the marginal man seeks to escape. Utopia is the goal of that escape. Political and social revolution is the means.

The validity of this interpretation of the relation between radicalism and Judaism can be seen in the careers of so-called Jewish radicals. Emma Goldman was perhaps the most famous of the turn-of-the-century anarchists. Shortly after her friend Alexander Berkman was imprisoned for an abortive attempt to assassinate the chairman of the strike-bound Carnegie Steel Company in 1892, Emma Goldman was sentenced to a year on New York's Blackwell's Island. "The prison," wrote Emma in her autobiography, was "the crucible that tested my faith."[10] (p. 148) But the faith was anarchism and not the Judaism of her ancestors. It was faith in anarchism that inspired her to denounce the government of the United States until her deportation in 1919. It was that same faith that led her to disillusionment with the Soviet Union and brought her, after more than the Biblical forty years, to the Promised Land of the Spanish Civil War. When, in 1893, the head matron of Blackwell's Island asked Emma what her religion was, Emma answered, "None, I am an atheist." (p. 133) Earlier, in another prison, another matron had offered her a Bible: "Indignantly I flung the volume at the matron's feet. I had no need of religious lies; I wanted some human book." (p. 125) Despite Emma's violence in this particular incident, her relation to Judaism was remarkably calm. She never rebelled; there was no dramatic moment of conversion; she simply came to ignore the traditions and the beliefs that were, supposedly, her heritage. To a man like James Joyce, the Catholicism he rejected meant almost everything. He would have been unthinkable without the Church he hated. Emma Goldman's *Living My Life* (1934), an autobiography of 993 pages, does not even dramatize Emma's renunciation of Yaweh and His commandments.

Alexander Berkman, who made the attempt on Henry Clay Frick's life, shared Emma Goldman's faith in anarchism and her antagonism to religious orthodoxy. He had as a child refused to attend Jewish schools and had been expelled from a Russian *Gymnasium* when he wrote a rather direct essay entitled "There Is No God." While imprisoned in America, he wrote his unrepentant *Prison Memoirs of an Anarchist* (which Emma Goldman published). In his memoirs he denounced "religion" as "the very fountainhead of bigotry and injustice." [11] (p. 122) There is little in the book to indicate that Berkman identified himself as a Jew. The last section of the memoirs is entitled "Resurrection," but the metaphor applies to his release from prison, to his rebirth to the radical movement that was his very life.

Daniel DeLeon, the radical who "Americanized" Marx and led the Socialist Labor Party in its heyday, went beyond Berkman and Goldman. He denied his Jewish background and invented a family tree of Catholic forebears! Few radicals went this far. Nevertheless, as Moses Rischin reminds us in his recent history of Jews in New York, the typical socialist or anarchist was a man who transferred his commitments from Moses to Marx. *Zukunft,* the most distinguished of Yiddish periodicals, adopted a militantly atheistic position. The *Freie Arbeiter Shtimme* did the same and published David Edelstadt's poem, "Anti-Religion":

> Börne, Lasalle, Marx
> Will deliver us from the diaspora

The world wil recognize no distinctions
All will be free, whether Turk, Christian or Jew
Every age has its sacred message
Ours is freedom and justice.[12]

Abraham Cahan, editor of *Forward* and generally recognized as the most important of radical journalists, wrote the parable of Reb Nehemiah: "I had ears but could not hear, because of my ear-locks; I had eyes and could not see because they were closed in prayer. . . . I am Rabbi Nehemiah no longer, they call me Nehemiah the atheist now." [13] And even Samuel Gompers, who can hardly be called a radical at all, turned from Judaism to membership in the Ethical Culture Society.

Despite their quarrel with God, many of the radicals of the 1890s were linguistically restricted to Yiddish and to an audience that spoke Yiddish. The generation that supplied recruits to the Communist Party was not so restricted. Men like Joseph Freeman and Howard Fast were born or reared in America; they spoke and wrote English; their ties to Judaism were even looser than those of the nineteenth-century radicals. Here is Joseph Freeman, the American Communist whose autobiography, *An American Testament* (1936), is one of the few classics of the proletarian movement in American literature: "From my uncle Moishe I heard about the revolution; from grandfather about God and the destiny of the Jewish race. No two ideals could be more sharply at odds. Uncle wanted the whole of humanity to go forward; grandfather wanted his own people, a fragment of humanity, to go backward . . ." [14] (p. 22) Attentive readers predict Freeman's commitment to Uncle Moishe's ideals. As a convinced Marxist, Freeman's loyalties went to the worker, not to the Jew. "In the last analysis, it was obviously not race against race, or nation against nation: it was class against class." (p. 53) The failure of Freeman's faith in Yaweh is treated in one paragraph in a book of 576 pages. Far more dramatic is the account of the journey from the Ukrainian village of Freeman's childhood to the "golden realm" of America. For the seven-year-old boy, as for Mary Antin and for Abraham Cahan's David Levinsky, the migration to America was a spiritual rebirth.

Howard Fast, also a Communist (until the Hungarian Revolution of 1956), indicated his lack of sympathy for the Jewish heritage in a symposium conducted in February 1944 by the *Contemporary Jewish Record*:

> For me, a Jew is a man. He is persecuted; so are other minor-
> ities. He is libeled; so are others. There is discrimination against
> him; is there none against Negroes? He has been murdered,
> tortured, driven across the face of the earth, but isn't that the
> fate of millions who are not Jewish?

The road for Freeman and for Fast and for a thousand others now forgotten led, figuratively, not to Damascus but to the Finland Station. The decisive crossroads came *after* the commitment to Communism. It was neither the abandonment of Orthodoxy nor the disillusionment with *laissez-faire* capitalism; the typical crisis for the Jewish radicals of the 1930s was the conversion experience that transformed them from Stalinists into Trotskyites. In *absolute* terms, the number of Jews in the Communist Party and in the myriad of "splinter groups" formed from the parent organization was never very large; relative to the whole Jewish population, the Jewish radicals were a fairly small percentage. It was the cultural role of the Jewish radicals as editors and propagandists—and writers—that gave them prominence in the history of American radicalism.[15]

2   *Jews and Proletarians*

Although the emergence of proletarian literature in the United States was by no means an exclusively Jewish phenomenon, many of the most important writers of "revolutionary" novels and poems were men converted from Orthodoxy or *Yiddishkeit* to Marxist radicalism. The first important document of proletarian literature was Michael Gold's autobiographical novel, *Jews without Money* (1930). Gold was a writer whom almost any student of literary style can criticize, but *Jews without Money* manages nonetheless to communicate something of the spirit of the ghetto. In itself Gold's book refutes the allegation that "one cannot find an important Jewish poet or novelist who has ever been inspired by the irreligious notions entertained by the proponents of secularist ideology in this country."[16]

Chapter 1, "Fifty Cents a Night," describes the Lower East Side in

terms very different from Henry Roth's *Call It Sleep*. Gold emphasizes the sordid, the pimps, gamblers, "peanut politicians, pugilists in
sweaters," longshoremen, and—especially—prostitutes.[17] (p. 13)

> The Jews had fled from the European pogroms; with prayer,
> thanksgiving and solemn faith from new Egypt into a new
> Promised Land.
> They found awaiting them the sweatshops, the bawdy houses
> and Tammany Hall.
> There were hundreds of prostitutes on my street. They oc-
> cupied vacant stores, they crowded into flats and apartments in
> all the tenements. The pious Jews hated the traffic. But they were
> pauper strangers here; they could do nothing. They shrugged
> their shoulders, and murmured: "This is America." They
> tried to live. (pp. 14–15)

"Fifty cents a night" is the taunt of the small boys when they scream
at the prostitutes, but they discover that even whores are sensitive to
insults. It is all part of their education. Girls became prostitutes not
from choice but from bitter economic necessity.

Jews without Money has no plot in the conventional sense. It is
more like an unstructured memoir than a novel. Characters come
and go: Fyfka the Miser, Mendel the Apostate, a hundred more.
Seasons change. In summer, the East Side women fling their garbage
from their windows until "the East Side heavens rained with potato
peelings, coffee grounds, herring heads and dangerous soup bones."
(p. 57) In winter, the half-frozen East Siders come home to shiver
in flats barely warm enough to sustain life. The narrator's father
curses Columbus and condemns the land where the lice make for-
tunes, and the good men starve. But the narrator accepts America.
It is the only life he knows. He believes in the Messiah (and in
almost no other aspect of Judaism), but he scarcely expects to witness the Messiah's arrival in New York.

The last chapters describe an accumulation of disasters. The narrator's sister is killed in an automobile accident, his mother falls into
a depression from which she never fully emerges, his father fails to
find decent work, and he himself drifts from job to job, his dreams
of college all forgotten.

> At times I seriously thought of cutting my throat. At other
> times I dreamed of running away to the far west. Sex began

to torture me. I developed a crazy religious streak. I prayed on the tenement roof in moonlight to the Jewish Messiah who would redeem the world.

The Messiah comes:

> A man on an East Side soap-box, one night, proclaimed that out of the despair, melancholy and helpless rage of millions, a world movement had been born to abolish poverty.
> I listened to him.
> O workers' Revolution, you brought hope to me, a lonely, suicidal boy. You are the true Messiah. You will destroy the East Side when you come, and build there a garden for the human spirit. (p. 309)

The fictional scene was not far removed from Michael Gold's own discovery of radicalism in 1914, when he came upon a Union Square demonstration and heard a fiery speech from Elizabeth Gurley Flynn.

By the time *Jews without Money* was published in 1930, Gold (whose real name was Irwin Granich) was a veteran of nearly ten years in radical journalism. He had become an editor of Max Eastman's *Liberator* in 1921 and had written his hymn to the masses:

> Masses are never pessimistic. Masses are never sterile. Masses are never far from the earth. Masses are never far from heaven. Masses go on—they are the eternal truth. Masses are simple, strong and sure. They are never lost long; they have always a goal in each age.[18]

In 1928 he had become editor of *The New Masses,* the Communists' most important literary magazine. His book was a commercial success. No wonder then that younger writers took him for their model.

Among the younger writers, Albert Halper and Isidor Schneider wrote novels that can still be read with some pleasure.* Halper, who began with a loosely structured evocation of place in *Union Square*

---

* Among the proletarian poets, Joy Davidman, Sol Funaroff, and Edwin Rolfe were probably the best. All three were nominally Jews (although Miss Davidman later converted to Anglicanism and maried C. S. Lewis). My views on proletarian poetry are contained in "The Brief Embattled Course of Proletarian Poetry," in David Madden's *Proletarian Writers of the Thirties* (Carbondale, Ill., 1968), pp. 252-69.

(1933), found his fictional focus in *The Foundry* (1934) and *The Chute* (1937). The ostensible heroes of the second and third novels are really less important than "the system," symbolized by the electrotype foundry in *The Foundry* and the mail-order house in *The Chute*. Through the dominant metaphors of the machines in the one book and the chute through which packages are hurled in the second, Halper manages to convey a sense of production and consumption in a capitalist society. In both situations, the conditions of labor are very nearly intolerable. Men sicken and die from the strain of the work or run amok in crazed protest against their exploitation by the master class. In *The Foundry*, for instance, when an owner of the plant shouts at a sweat-drenched caster to work more quickly or be fired, the infuriated workman charges at the owner with his knife, forces him to breathe the choking vapors of his wax pot, and is just about to push his obese employer's face into the boiling wax when he is stopped by one of the foremen. *The Foundry* is weakened, however, from a radical point of view, by a good deal of sympathy for the owners of the factory and by extended accounts of the good times of the workers. There is, for example, a thirty-eight-page picnic sequence.

The next novel is a good deal bleaker. The mail-order house has a beach party, but it is marred by the suicide of one of the female employees. At the end of *The Chute*, the corporation devours its employees. One of the managers discovers that he has been tricked by the owner, who now plans to sell the company to a larger competitor, and begins to rip up the merchandise. Attempting in his frenzy to silence a set of ringing bells, he loses his balance: "Then suddenly, swaying, [the boxes] gave way beneath him, pitching him in a wide circle forward, straight forward toward the hole. He uttered one piercing scream as the bells kept ringing, then the chute, as if in triumph, engulfed him. . . ." [19] (p. 550) There is little chance that the reader will miss the significance of Mr. Myerson's demise. Certainly not the reader of Frank Norris's "Corner in Wheat," in which the greedy capitalist is buried by the golden grain. The future, however, belongs to young Paul Sussman and his Italian-American girl friend. They will fight to unionize the industry and, eventually, to bring on the revolution. Ethnic difference is the least of their problems.

Isidor Schneider's novel *From the Kingdom of Necessity* (1935) resembles *Jews without Money* insofar as it is also a *Bildungsroman,* a story of a young man's education. Comparison with *The Rise of David Levinsky* is also appropriate in that both books begin in Europe, in the Jewish Pale. The first scenes of Schneider's novel are far far more subtle than the later sections. Memory is more affecting than ideology. The first chapter shows the effect upon a *shtetl* of a villager who has returned from America and brought with him a Singer sewing machine. The villagers' wonder gives way to imitation and Morris Hyman quickly discovers that his compatriots are more skillful operators than he. Back, therefore, to America he goes, with his wife and children. In America, Judaism ceases to be significant: "They pray 'next year in Jerusalem,' with their mouths, but with their hearts they pray 'next year on Fifth Avenue.' " [20] (p. 42) Like Anzia Yezierska's unfortunate Hannah Breineh, Morris Hyman learns that families can be demoralized by the process of Americanization: "All children go mad in America, and lose their respect. A dollar in their hands makes them kings who rule their parents. It is a lunatic country. May it burn up." (p. 112)

Isaac Hyman, the central character of this obviously autobiographical novel, learns at an early age to question his religious heritage. His father closes a dishonest business deal on Yom Kippur, the Day of Atonement, and the last remnant of Isaac's faith is reduced to ashes. When his father rejoices at God's goodness, Isaac asks if God heard the prayers of the victimized buyer. His father strikes him, as Philip Roth's Rabbi Binder strikes blasphemously inquisitive Ozzie Freedman. Among a people who prize the immediate expression of emotion, slaps and kisses are seldom in short supply.

The main line of the action, however, has more to do with economics than with religion. The great novelistic weakness of *From the Kingdom of Necessity* is the inserted *obiter dictum,* which Schneider seems unable to resist. When the Hyman family seeks a better apartment, Schneider moralizes: "The differences between the rich and poor were known, were realities too great to evade; but as yet, they spurred the poor only to hope for riches—to deny, with hysterical revulsion, their own class, and their class destiny." (p. 25) There is, however, reason for hope, "for among Jewish workers there is an intuitive understanding that their difficult national problem will be solved finally, and only, when a proletarian revolution solves the world's economic problem." (p. 165) Although the reader expects Schneider to display the distortions wrought by capitalism in the world of letters, through which his hero makes his way, there is no Marxist analysis of publishers, advertisers, or audience. There is, instead, a sententious promise:

> He was to learn that no one enters the kingdom of freedom alone. He would return to his class. With it, he would march, taking his place in the advancing lines, in the irresistible movement of the masses of mankind from the kingdom of necessity into the Kingdom of Freedom. (p. 450)

One suspects that Schneider found himself in a technical dilemma; he had carried the story too far for the sudden climactic introduction of the workers' Messiah, but he was apparently unable to demonstrate what *difference* Marxism made in the consciousness of his hero. In Schneider's poems, rhetoric was made to suffice:

> In America the task waits to be done.
> Lead us, Comrade Lenin, we will follow.[21]

But where will Comrade Lenin lead and how will Isaac Hyman follow?

Schneider's difficulty was, of course, widely shared. Much of proletarian fiction ended with a conversion experience or with the determination of defeated strikers to win the final battle of their struggle. Schneider, making use of neither convention, ends with an implied promise that the best of proletarian writers were unable to fulfill.

No Jewish writer of proletarian novels ever equalled the extraordinary literary achievement of Robert Cantwell's *Land of Plenty* (1934), the best of the genre, but Meyer Levin came close with *Citizens* (1940). At first glance *Citizens* seems to be merely a sequel to *The Old Bunch*. Many of the characters are the same. The hero is Mitch Wilner, an important figure in the earlier novel, but there is an entirely different structure. Instead of a large group of characters followed through a long period of time, there is a relatively narrow focus on one man's involvement in a single important action over the course of only twelve months. A series of biographical chapters, in the style of John Dos Passos, widens the range of the book.

There are also frequent references to the Spanish Civil War and other events of 1937–38, but the book is about Mitch Wilner's education, about the radicalization of one man.

There is another way in which *Citizens* differs from Levin's previous novel. *The Old Bunch* was realistic in its treatment of the West Side Jews; *Citizens* is more than "realistic"; it is closely drawn from the tragic events of Memorial Day 1937, when the Chicago police shot and killed ten workers at a struck steel mill, and from the Congressional investigation that followed. (Levin dedicated the book to the ten slain men and discussed in an appendix the parallels between his novel and his sources.)

The book opens with Mitch Wilner and his family on their way home to Chicago after a Fourth of July on the beach in Indiana. The Wilners drive by the struck factory to see if there has been trouble and to set up a first-aid station, which is soon needed. Dr. Wilner witnesses the police firing on the unarmed workers, clubbing the fallen, dragging off a man with a tourniquet, charging into a hospital. He is further educated by Chicago's journalism. The newspaper headlines scream: MOB ATTACKS POLICE, 200 INJURED AS STRIKERS CHARGE, STRIKERS DRUGGED TO ASSAULT POLICE. The mayor of Chicago applauds the brave men in blue. When a Congressional committee investigates, as the LaFollette Committee did in actuality, they are lied to in an outrageous manner.

> . . . as their testimony [the police's] progressed, none admitting firing, none admitting carrying the non-regulation bludgeons they were shown carrying in the photographs, a fright of hopelessness grew in Mitch, for what could be done with men like these? [22] (p. 314)

When the strikers go to court, their lawyer advises them to face reality and plead guilty. Those who insist upon their innocence are ignored by the judge (whose name, Pacelli—that of Pope Pius XII —is probably no accident). Mitch Wilner imagines that the political process might work after all—if not through Congressional action or through the courts, then through the electoral system. Then he learns that even the Communist Party supports the mayor for re-election. After all, they argue, the mayor supports the President and the President deserves the support of all anti-Fascists. By the end of the novel,

Mitch is radicalized but not yet ready to join his sociologist friend Rawley in full-time political activity on behalf of the revolution. The book ends with their discussion of what can be done and with the memorial parade for the slain workers. The line of march passes by a floral wreath and a banner reading, TEN DEAD MEN WILL PICKET HERE FOREVER. The march is a sacrament: "As the people approached the wreath, the column narrowed to a single file, and, passing slowly, one by one they dropped their dark red flowers, like great swollen drops of blood augmenting the spreading dark pool on the ground." (p. 643) The symbolism suggested in 1940 that the blood of the slain was to be augmented until justice is done. In retrospect, the red pool seems also to stand for the twenty-five million doomed to die in the war for which the Spanish Civil War was but a prelude.

3   Paul Goodman's Quest for Community

The tradition of proletarian literature was carried into the 1940s by Howard Fast and, in more attenuated form, by Arthur Miller, whose great success, *Death of a Salesman,* was first produced in 1949, but the most notable literary achievements by secular Jews have been, at least since 1945, inspired more by anarchism than by Marxism.*

There is probably some relationship between the disappearance of Marxism as a mass movement and the decline of revolutionary literature from a Marxist point of view, but the relationship is certainly an indirect and complicated one. It is, however, fairly clear that Marxism was very largely the faith of first- and second-generation Americans. Intellectual disillusionment with Marxist theory was probably a secondary factor. For every radical convinced that the theory of surplus value was conceptually faulty, there were probably a dozen who felt that the Soviet Union and its American supporters had, in their practice, betrayed the promise of a better world. Some writers recoiled from Stalin's purges, which led to the death of an almost incredible twenty million people. Others balked at the Molotov-Von Ribbentrop Pact of 1939. Still others were shocked by the postwar

* Neither Fast nor Miller has written much about Jews or about the process of assimilation. Fast's novel *My Glorious Brothers* (1948) deals with the Maccabean revolt of the second century B.C. The book was clearly related to the creation of the State of Israel, which the Soviet Union helped to sponsor. Miller's first novel, *Focus* (1945), was concerned with anti-Semitism.

extension of Soviet power over Eastern Europe and by the naked use of that power against the Hungarians in 1956 and the Czechs in 1968. Jews have had a special reason to question the success of the Soviet Union: it is now common knowledge that Jewish citizens have suffered from suspicion and from antireligious persecution and that most of the nominally Jewish Bolshevik leaders (of which there were many) were purged by Stalin. There is, moreover, another, more paradoxical reason for the decline of Marxism among Jewish intellectuals. The 1930s were a time of economic and political crisis, which led to the limited reforms of the welfare state. It is common today to condemn the mildly socialistic reforms that have somewhat widened the nineteenth-century definitions of the proper role of the state. It is easy to respond in anger to inequality and to forget that inequalities and injustices were greater in the past than in the present. In short, it has been the resiliency of the system—up to now —which has persuaded onetime Jewish radicals that revolution is unnecessary. Daniel Aaron, whose *Writers on the Left* (1961) is a classic of literary biography, has argued that the improved status of Jews—if not of all Americans—was a fundamental factor in the disenchantment with Communism: "With few exceptions, the Jewish Left-Wing writer's break with Communism became irreparable at that moment in American history when the barriers that had hemmed him in and kept him a 'hyphenate' began to crumble." [23] The prestigious professor who publishes reminiscences about his days in the Young Communist League is almost a commonplace.

New Deal and post-New Deal reforms have, however, taken the form of a pragmatic, more or less piecemeal institutionalization of social democracy. These reforms have vastly increased the number and the importance of governmental functions in our society. Even without racism and the tragic folly of the Vietnamese War, the inadequacies of an immensely complex bureaucratic government are precisely the sort to bring forth a romantic reaction in the name of spontaneity, immediacy, and the intuitive. In the words of Paul Goodman, ". . . the programs of Populism, the labor movement, and Debs socialism have, for the most part, become the law of the land; but in their effect they have been entirely transformed by becoming bureaucratized and administered from above." [24] The young radical of the 1970s calls for love and/or sensual gratification. Committed to the "greening" of America, he has no patience with "planning." It is, therefore, at least plausible to assert that Marxism made a great deal more sense in 1933, at a time of almost completely unregulated private economic power, than it does now, when many of us feel that too much of our lives has already been nationalized. It is at least plausible to assert that the romantic anarchism of Paul Goodman and of the later Norman Mailer makes more sense in the 1960s and 1970s than the faithfully dogmatic Marxism of Herbert Aptheker and Morris Schappes.

Paul Goodman is probably better known today as an essayist and public speaker than as a writer of fiction and poetry. After working for years in relative obscurity, Goodman attained prominence in 1960 with *Growing Up Absurd*, his appeal for decent treatment of the contemporary adolescent. Goodman's early work, however, deserves more sympathetic consideration than it has yet received.

In *The Facts of Life* (1945) and *The Break-Up of Our Camp* (1949), two collections each containing stories from the 1930s and the 1940s, Goodman dealt with the question of Jewish identity. In the second book, the brief allegory "A Prayer for Dew" (1935) concerns the traditional auction of the right to read from the Torah and the ironic result of the prayer: in the midst of a thunderstorm, the Jews pray for water. The implied moral is that American Jews do not know when they are well off. There is more ambiguity in other stories. The title story of *The Facts of Life*, for instance, deals with a progressive family whose daughter is denigrated at school as an "old-time Jew." She asks what that means. Her father maintains that religion is central to the definition of "Jew" and she is, therefore, not a Jew: ". . . you *can't* be a Jew if you're *not* a Jew!" His wife, born Martha de Havilland, insists that a "person's a Jew if his grandparents were Jews," but she also needles her husband when he boasts of Jewish achievements: "If it weren't for the Jews," she says, "there wouldn't be any anti-Semitism." [25] (pp. 28, 32, 44) The inconclusiveness of the story indicates that its young author wasn't entirely sure of his own thought on these matters. There is a similarly tentative quality to the last piece collected in *The Facts of Life*, "Jonah: A Biblical Comedy with Jewish Jokes Called Far and Wide." The humor is quite conventional, the purposeful incongruity of modern speech within Biblical myth. Requested to set forth on his mission to

Nineveh, Jonah answers the Angel in Brooklynese: "To *Ninevah!* I should go to Ninevah? *There* I'll be popular! A prophet they need, you should pardon the expression, like a pain in the arm." (p. 208) The tone of the play, which ends with a joke, suggests that Jewishness is a theme with no permanent appeal for Goodman.

Goodman has, however, devoted himself like a modern Jonah to the Nineveh that is contemporary American society. In more than a score of books he has castigated us for our hardness of heart and lured us with a sparkling cascade of utopian proposals and practical suggestions. His vision is that of the philosophical anarchism of the great Russian prophet of peaceful cooperation, Pyotr Kropotkin; his technique is to offer pragmatic expedients that *seem* utopian because they "do not follow the usual procedures." [26] He has very little patience with "our moronic system of morals and property," [27] with the mistaken notion that men "socialized to an unsatisfactory situation" are representatives of uncorrupted human nature.[28]

In the face of centrally administrated bureaucracies, Goodman preaches the gospel of decentralization. He recognizes that *some* centralized administration is necessary but argues persuasively that "the centralizing style of organization has been pushed so far as to become ineffectual, economically wasteful, humanly stultifying, and ruinous to democracy." [29] Bureaucratic organizations have an innate tendency to reduce people to personnel, to adopt a manipulative orientation, to involve themselves in the *how* and to forget the *why*.

Although Goodman discusses General Motors, the Federal government, and an enormous number of other institutions, he is mainly interested in the dysfunctions of urban life and in the failures of schools and colleges. The fullest exposition of his views on the city is to be found in the book he wrote with his brother Percival, an architect: *Communitas: Means of Livelihood and Ways of Life* (1960). The first part of the book is a critical history of planned cities. The second is a series of paradigms: the city of efficient consumption (today's model improved and rationalized), the city of "planned security with minimum regulation" (in which the whole society seems to emulate the spare economy of Henry Thoreau), and the "new community" (in which the difference between work and play is eliminated, in which labor becomes once again meaningful). The details of the schemes are less important—within the present context—than the insistently offered choice between centralization and a city made up of neighborhood-sized communities.

Goodman's most persistent criticism has been of the educational system and its effects upon the young. *Growing Up Absurd* is about the dishonesty of automobile repairmen and the humiliation of grown men paid to compose jingly advertisements and the frustrations of the adolescent imprisoned in "educational" institutions that do not educate. Colleges and universities have, in Goodman's analysis, betrayed their function. The administrative apparatus has grown disproportionately large, while professors have sought advancement through publication and coerced students through the grading system. The medieval "community of scholars" has become another giant bureaucracy soullessly committed to the production of standardized units. Although most professors are allegedly "servants of the public and friends of the cops," [30] there is also the idealistic remnant, the "veterans" of experience who love knowledge and seek to impart it. What should they do? "The simplest remedy is the historical one, for bands of scholars to secede and set up where they can teach and learn on their own simple conditions." [31] Black Mountain College was, during its brief lifetime, an example of successful secession.

One of Goodman's complaints against American society in general and against the educational system in particular is that they "dampen . . . animal ardor." [32] High-school students are in an especially unfortunate situation. "Is it an eccentric opinion," asks Goodman, "that an important part of the kids' restiveness in school from the onset of puberty has to do with puberty?" [33] In "youth culture," which is in part the flamboyant assertion of sexual liberation, Goodman finds reason for hope. "The most portentous libertarian and populist counter-force," he writes, "is the youth movement." [34] Goodman finds too little joy and too little spontaneity in the sexual antics of the young, but he sees them as allies in his own efforts to loosen the system and to end its unnecessary repression of instincts. Although Goodman is not unambivalent about the new radicalism in America, he is moderately hopeful that adolescent rebellion may be the harbinger of a general rejection of bureaucratic giantism.

Except for *Empire City* (1959), Goodman's novels and poems tend to concentrate thematically on the need for sensual freedom.

That Jews and Gentiles should be free to love each other (sexually as well as liturgically) is taken for granted; Goodman urges freedom for miscegenation and for homosexuality as well. These views are poignantly embodied in a short novel that ought to be more widely known than it is. *Parents Day,* published by a small press in 1951, is narrated by a recently divorced homosexual who finds employment in a private school. He puts his own situation as a homosexual matter-of-factly: "I chose during my adolescence to avoid guiltiness by means of what eventually, when I was an adult, roused much greater guiltiness." [35] (pp. 8–9) The narrator encourages the students to masturbate and continually surprises them with his advice. When one of them says he'd like to suck Deborah Lowenstein's breasts, the narrator replies, "Why don't you do it?" (p. 85) He himself falls in love with young Davy Drood and, despite his conviction that teachers should not have affairs with their students, indulges in an awkward sexual act. He is betrayed by one of the children (no utopian child-worship here) and told by the school's director that he must go elsewhere. When Davy Drood's mother arrives, the narrator lectures her on her evasions, shows her a poem written for her son, and wins her over. He weeps when he departs, "I had made many stupid errors," and then the bus comes. (p. 223)

Despite the tin-eared awkwardness of Goodman's prose (what other important writer refers to "an university"?), *Parents Day* is a successful book in the confessional mode. It is a pity that it did not secure the critical attention given *Empire City,* an enormously convoluted, torturedly allusive attempt to write of "a kind of real persons living in an illusory system." [36] Of the book, one despairing reviewer remarked, ". . . difficult as it is to read at first sight, at second sight it is impossible." [37] This is an exaggeration, but any reader not embarked upon an obligatory excursion through Goodman's entire literary *corpus* is well advised to move on to *Making Do* (1963). The book places the narrator, named Paul Goodman, within a community of anarchists and pacifists. The sexual relations transcend every conceivable barrier between people—race, class, religion, and gender are of little moment if two partners want each other. The language too is intentionally "honest." The narrator, for instance, is worried about the emotional instability of the group: "I was too old for these strenuous games. I had too much real work to do in America to be exhausted by the inevitable fuck-ups of my young friends and these hang-ups of my older friends who should have known better than to marry crazy persons." [38] (p. 3) (Goodman's poetry is equally direct: "His cock is big and red when I am there / and his persistent lips are like sweet wine." [39]) At a conference, the narrator meets and soon falls in love with a youth who continually underestimates the narrator's moral character. He assumes, for instance, that homosexuality has destroyed his integrity so that he can now be blackmailed. Eventually, Terry (the youth) responds to the narrator's affection and is taken into the commune. His leadership of a group of boys gives Goodman opportunity for another sermon. A game of handball is stopped by "authority," and he writes: "What appalled me, as a city planner, was the thought of that bleak tan useless wall and the boring empty stretch of pavement, which Terry had made for an hour bound with ordered life." (p. 150) The plot thickens when a befriended Puerto Rican, Ramón, turns against the community and smashes the apartment of two of the members. All is, however, forgiven. Conflicts with the town are worked out, difficulties with the police are resolved. The narrator's wife is pregnant and the struggle for a humane society goes on: "No. 'The Lord has yet more light and truth to break forth,' as John Robinson said to the Pilgrims embarking toward America." (p. 276) It seems appropriate that the seventeenth-century New England historian who compared his contemporaries to the Israelites of old should be quoted by a twentieth-century secular Jew transfixed by the transcendent vision of what America might yet become.

It is easier to admire Paul Goodman's literary intentions than to praise his novels. It is difficult, for me at least, to read with pleasure the "Ballad of the Pentagon" and other poems collected in *Hawkweed* (1967). No such doubts need qualify esthetic judgments of the work of Norman Mailer.

4 *The Apocalyptic Vision of Norman Mailer*

Within the literary generation that followed Ernest Hemingway and William Faulkner, of the writers come to prominence since 1945, Norman Mailer is unquestionably among the most gifted. He is also among the most radical: "The sour truth," he wrote in 1959, "is that I am imprisoned with a perception which will settle for nothing less than making a revolution in the consciousness of our time." [40] Mailer has shown no patience whatsoever with the passive, timid, pathetic underdogs of Yiddish literature; he likes least to be thought of as a Jewish writer. If the traditional Jew of the *shtetl* is meek in his encounters with authority, then Mailer's characters (and Mailer too) will be defiant and bellicose. He will have none of the ancestral determinism of Horace Kallen's theory of cultural pluralism. He described himself, in the December 1962 issue of *Commentary,* as a non-Jewish Jew, that is, as a secular Jew for whom the customs of conventional Jews are of little importance. In the explosive and protean variety of his literary and political postures, he can be taken to represent the extraordinary energy of the gifted Jew described in Veblen's essay. He is the Jew released from his ethnic identity and invited to act out whatever roles are now within reach of his imagination.

His first and most successful novel was initially taken to be a defense of Marxist values against the threat of an American brand of Fascism. The book betrayed, however, a fascination for Fascism and a romanticism that became increasingly apparent as Mailer moved further and further from the literary tradition of Realism. In the twenty years following *The Naked and the Dead* (1948), Mailer has dramatized the appeals of Trotskyism, the decadence of contemporary society, the attractions of charismatic power (as symbolized in part by John F. Kennedy), the obsession with apocalypticism, and—most recently—a new kind of irony that questions radicalism as well as the *status quo.* It is a career full of twists and turns, instructive rather than representative, awesome and perhaps even frightening.

The Naked and the Dead is a "modern" book in the sense that it puts together the literary techniques of Realism (or Naturalism) and symbolism. The surface is realistic, the tragicomic outcome seems preordained, the symbolism is pervasive. Mailer himself offered the literary antecedents for his first novel in a collection of essays, *Advertisements for Myself* (1959), which document his indebtedness to Hemingway and Faulkner, whose influence in the novel is clear enough. The structure of the book, however, is derived from John Dos Passos. There is an attempt to catch the whole of American

THE REVOLUTIONARY MESSIAH 155

society through a variety of characters and through a technical trick, the "Time Machine," which takes us back into the past of each major character. The language is plain and usually understated, Hemingwayesque rather than Faulknerian.

Mailer begins with nameless American soldiers about to wade ashore on the Japanese-held island of Anopopei. He then focuses on a small group of men with whom he stays, or to whom he returns, for the length of the novel. The leader of these enlisted men is Sgt. Croft, ruthless and competent. The third chapter shifts to the ostensible hero, Lt. Robert Hearn, an officer whose sympathies are with the enlisted men. The vulgarity and stupidity of his fellow officers disgusts him. When he objects to their reactionary politics and to their obscene racism, they turn on him and he is rescued by General Cummings, the ostensible villain of the novel.

Cummings is a Nietzschean figure, reminiscent of Wolf Larson, the powerful hero of Jack London's *The Sea Wolf*. Hearn becomes Cummings' protégé in a literal sense. There is also a strong suggestion that Cummings is homosexually drawn to Hearn. But when Hearn refuses to accept Cummings' domination, he is sent on a hopeless mission with the men of Sgt. Croft's squad.

By the time this has happened, Mailer has characterized every member of the squad, explored the tiny social system ruled by Croft, and prepared for a climax in which Croft betrays Hearn and sends him into an ambush that Croft knows awaits him. Most of the squad manages to return safely to the beach, but not before Croft attempts to lead them to the top of Mount Anaka, brooding symbol of inaccessible mystery.

While the squad is gone, Cummings plots his offensive, goes off to secure an "indispensable" destroyer from the Navy, and returns to discover that his blundering assistant, Major Dalleson, has accidentally overrun Japanese headquarters and thus concluded the campaign. The *Übermensch* has been surpassed by a boob too stupid to realize that he has actually defeated the enemy. Mailer's irony here is like Tolstoi's: warfare, and perhaps life itself, is indeed a chaos where ignorant armies clash by night, where arrogant leaders delude themselves with dreams of dominance.

The irony is complicated by the fact that the author has lost control over his own characters. Although Hearn is drawn in large part from Mailer himself, who also went to Harvard and absorbed radical ideas, Hearn's Marxism seems flimsy and ridiculous when set against the *Machtpolitik* of Cummings. In their debates, Cummings triumphs. Compared with Cummings, Hearn is simply ineffectual. Cummings has a grandness of design, a vision, and the determination to carry his ideas through and to realize them. He controls an entire army—to the degree that control is possible. His conception of world politics is simply an extrapolation from the military relationship of a general to his troops. He imagines a postwar empire:

> There are countries which have latent powers, latent resources, they are full of potential energy, so to speak. And there are great concepts which can unlock that, express it. As kinetic energy a country is organization, co-ordinated effort, your epithet, fascism. . . . Historically the purpose of this war is to translate America's potential into kinetic energy. The concept of fascism, far sounder than communism if you consider it, for it's grounded firmly in men's actual natures, merely started in the wrong country, in a country which did not have enough intrinsic potential power to develop completely.[41]
> (p. 321)

Hearn attempts to dispute these assertions and denies that he too feels the urge to omnipotence, but when he finds himself in command of a squad of men and exercises his authority, he experiences a surge of pleasure that seems to validate Cumming's authoritarian *Weltanschauung*.

Cummings remains an unattractive person, despite the effect of his personality on Hearn, but Croft emerges as the covert hero of the book. He is sadistic, but he is also a natural leader. He tries, like Herman Melville's Captain Ahab, to mold the divergent personalities of his men into the forged instrument of his purpose. And it is *his* purpose. Just as the pursuit of sperm oil is the overt end of Ahab's voyage, the reconnaissance is Croft's official function, but in actuality he wants to experience some mysterious Ultimate, for which Mount Anaka becomes the symbol. He *will* scale the mountain. But he fails, like Captain Ahab. His quest ends comically, absurdly, when the men blunder into a hornet's nest and flee. Defeated by nature, they return to the beach, unable to complete a mission that was pointless when conceived. Croft "found a limit to his hunger." (p. 701)

This interpretation of Croft as the real hero has found support from Mailer himself. In an interview reprinted in *The Presidential Papers* (1965), he said, "Beneath the ideology in *The Naked and the Dead* was an obsession with violence. The characters for whom I had the most secret admiration, like Croft, were violent people." [42] (p. 136)

Mailer's infatuation with power was to become painfully evident in the collections of essays published between 1959 and 1968, but his second and third novels are variations on the overt radicalism of *The Naked and the Dead*. Although *Barbary Shore* (1951) was stylistically experimental, almost surrealistic, it is thematically the most conventional of Mailer's novels.

The action takes place almost entirely within the various rooms of an apartment house, a microcosm of American society, a twisted mirror in which the tensions of the 1950s are weirdly reflected. Mailer's own assessment of *Barbary Shore* is vivid and authoritative:

> . . . it could be that if my work is alive one hundred years from now, *Barbary Shore* will be considered the richest of my first three novels for it has in its high fevers a kind of insane insight into the psychic mysteries of Stalinists, secret policemen, narcissists, children, Lesbians, hysterics, revolutionaries— it has an air which for me is the air of our time, authority and nihilism stalking one another in the orgiastic hollow of this century.[43]

The term "orgiastic" reveals Mailer's mid-fifties interest in the orgone psychology of Wilhelm Reich; the conflict is between authoritarianism and nihilism rather than between legitimate authority and nihilism, but Mailer's comment does suggest the claustrophobic atmosphere of the novel.

The major characters include an old radical, McLeod, who is a veteran of the Spanish Civil War, a Trotskyite. He is repeatedly interrogated by a counterintelligence agent named Hollingsworth, who resembles him in his furtive hole-and-corner existence. Since Hollingsworth is having an affair with the proprietress of the house, who turns out to be McLeod's wife, the complications of plot are manifold. Among the characters is Monina, the proprietress's enigmatic daughter, one of the most unnatural children since Hawthorne's Pearl Prynne.

Into this situation come Lovett, the young narrator, and Lannie, a girl who is as lost and alienated as he. Lovett, whose loss of identity is symbolized by his amnesia, is gradually drawn into Lannie's troubles and also into the mysterious struggle between McLeod and Hollingsworth. Despite the nightmarish atmosphere and the entanglements of both prose and plot, Mailer's narrator's passionate response to the vision of radical change is clear. Where else in American literature, or in American political rhetoric, has the appeal of Trotsky been more vividly remembered?

> There was a great man who led us, and I read almost every word he had written, and listened with the passion of the novitiate to each message he sent from the magical center in Mexico . . . For a winter and a spring, I lived more intensely in the past than I could ever in the present, until the sight of a policeman on his mount became the Petrograd proletariat crawling to fame between the legs of a Cossack's horse. . . . There was never a revolution to equal it, and never a city more glorious than Petrograd, and for all that period of my life I lived another and braved the ice of winter and the summer flies in Vyborg while across my adopted country of the past, winds of the revolution blew their flame, and all of us suffered hunger while we drank at the wine of equality. . . .[44] (pp. 125–26)

It is as if John Reed's *Ten Days That Shook the World* were distilled to a single set of images.

The revolution for which Trotsky fought, which he described in his own *History of the Russian Revolution,* eventually became the *ancien régime* of Josef Stalin. Mailer's McLeod describes Stalin's repressions in Spain during the civil war in which he fought. He laments the Soviet Union's support of bourgeois democracy and its betrayal of revolutionary radicalism. Lannie, meanwhile, tortures him with the memory of what the Stalinists have done to Trotsky:

> He was the man I loved, the only man I ever truly loved with heart and not with body, the man with the beard because he was a fool—a brilliant man and I loved his beard, and there was the mountain ax in his brain, and all the blood poured out, and he could not see the Mexican sun. Your people raised the ax. . . . (p. 188)

Although Lovett's response to McLeod's radicalism is hesitant and ambivalent, he finally accepts the trust that is bestowed upon him. McLeod commits suicide and leaves to Lovett a mysterious heritage, "the remnants of my socialist culture." (p. 311) The dream of radical social reconstruction is passed on, but Mailer's description of the novel suggests that this hint of optimism was forced. In his next novel, authority continues to be repressive, but revolutionary fervor turns to the nihilism referred to in his description of *Barbary Shore*.

The Deer Park (1955) was savagely and foolishly reviewed upon its appearance, but it is now generally recognized as a remarkable novel as well as an indispensable document. As in *Barbary Shore,* a youngish narrator becomes involved in the affairs of an older radical. Sergius O'Shaugnessy comes home from the Korean War and enters the hostile world of Desert D'Or, Hollywood's equivalent of the "deer park" of Louis XV. He is befriended by Charles Francis Eitel, the fictional counterpart of the Hollywood directors who lost their positions when they refused, in the early 1950s, to answer questions put to them by Congressional committees hunting for Communist infiltration in the movie industry.

Sergius becomes a part of the scene, has an affair with Lulu Meyers (one of Eitel's ex-wives), and is questioned by the F.B.I. Sergius is frightened; Eitel—unlike McLeod—breaks down and confesses to the committee. His artistic work shows similar inability to resist pressure. He is, however, the mentor who helps Sergius discover the liberating possibilities of sexuality (in the theoretical framework of Wilhelm Reich).

Sexuality is the metaphor for sickness as well as health. Hollywood, and by implication all of America, is sexually as well as politically perverted. One symbol of the sickened system is Teddy Pope, a homosexual star who is engaged to Lulu Meyers because their fans will, presumably, be excited by the vicarious marriage. Another symbol of perversion and decay is Marion Faye, in whom one prescient critic saw, as early as 1964, a prediction of Mailer's subsequent career: "Marion Faye seems . . . to have led Mailer into areas which are structurally and theoretically tangential to his novel but which bring him closer to his future interests. Marion deliberately tests his own will . . . by violating the codes of his society and by exposing himself to his worst terrors." [45] It is now possible to see that Marion's drive to the edge of the desert contains in embryo form much that was to preoccupy Mailer during the 1960s. Looking toward the nuclear laboratories at Los Alamos, he thinks,

> Let this explosion come, and then another, and all the others, until the Sun God burned the earth. Let it come, he thought, looking into the east at Mecca where the bombs ticked while he stood on a tiny rise of ground trying to see one hundred, two hundred, three hundred miles across the desert. Let it come, Faye begged, like a man praying for rain, let it come and clear the rot, and the stench and the stink, let it come for all of everywhere, just so it comes and the world stands clear in the white dead dawn.[46] (p. 161)

Although Faye is not the central figure in the book, it is he who is subsequently revealed to have been, like Sgt. Croft, the clue to Mailer's development. The theme of the Apocalypse became increasingly important throughout Mailer's next four books.

Advertisements for Myself (1959) is quite frankly a book about Norman Mailer, about his ambitions, his frustrations, his achievements, the dark nights of his ego. He reprinted his early stories, some written while an undergraduate at Harvard, and a selection from his essays. To them he added intercalated commentaries, his "advertisements" for and explanations of these earlier pieces. Simply as materials for a study of Mailer's development as a writer, these exercises after the manner of Hemingway and of Faulkner are invaluable. As evidence of Mailer's state of mind at the end of the Eisenhower years, the commentaries are indispensable.

Mailer began politically: "like many another vain, empty, and bullying body of our time, I have been running for President these last ten years in the privacy of my mind, and it occurs to me that I am less close now than when I began." [47] (p. 17) He turns continually to the world of letters and politicizes it. His acid comments on rival writers indicate his sense of literature as a political arena in which writers compete for whatever power and influence can be won with words. Analogies to the political realm are frequent. Jack Kerouac, for instance, is defeated with a phrase when Mailer refers to him as "an Eisenhower gypsy." (p. 21) At the same time, the extraliterary world is seen novelistically, through metaphor, irony, and the manipulation of syntax, but it is not fictive. In other words, Mailer glories in a mix of modes. It is highly unlikely that he has made or ever can make a "revolution in the consciousness of our time," but he has created a new kind of journalism in which the who, what, when, and where are subordinated by the novelistic journalist's insistent question, Why?

The stated ideology of *Advertisements for Myself* is socialism, in one form or another. At one point, Mailer describes himself as "libertarian socialist." But the thrust of this book, and of Mailer's next three books, is in another direction. Mailer espoused at this time the romantic irrationality that Georg Lukacs, Ernst Nolte, and Karl Dietrich Bracher have identified as a basic component of contemporary Fascism. He praised Freud as well as Marx but seemed—as has been indicated in my comments on *The Deer Park*—much more a disciple of Wilhelm Reich. In his condemnation of American society, Mailer can also sound like a new Nietzsche striking out against the bourgeoisie. He condemned cowardice rather than injustice, asserted that "pleasure comes best to those who are brave," and praised James Jones because he was "the only one of us who had the beer-guts of a broken-glass brawl," which is hardly a conventional literary judgment. (p. 463)

The most memorable and significant essay in the book is undoubtedly the widely admired (and condemned) piece entitled "The White Negro" (1957). The counters of the essay are the terms "hip" and "square," labels for the rebel and the conformist. The romantic language is a symphony of nineteenth-century themes, variations on Edgar Allan Poe and Charles Baudelaire. The only response to contemporary society, writes Mailer, is to divorce oneself from it. Since "society" means the institutions of white men, the Negro is by definition the outsider, characterized (in this essay) by his music, by jazz. Insofar as they refer to the intellectual subculture and not to the "man in the street," Leslie Fiedler's spirited remarks are apropos:

> At the moment that young Europeans everywhere . . . are becoming imaginary Americans, the American is becoming an imaginary Jew. But this is only half of the total irony we confront; for, at the same moment, the Jew whom his Gentile fellow-citizen emulates may himself be in the process of becoming an imaginary Negro.[48]

Mailer's "white Negro" is the Caucasian who emulates the black man's "existential" authenticity, who surrenders himself to an "incandescent consciousness which the possibilities within death has opened." (p. 342) In his rage against the dullness of rationalized process, Mailer praises a group of boys who murdered a shopkeeper. Like the characters of Simone de Beauvoir or Jean-Paul Sartre, or like Bigger Thomas in Richard Wright's *Native Son,* they have struck out for freedom and significance. Mailer's description of the "American existentialist—the hipster" is a paean:

> If the fate of twentieth-century man is to live with death from adolescence to premature senescence, then the only life-giving answer is to accept the terms of death, to live with death as immediate danger, to divorce oneself from society, to exist without roots, to set out on that uncharted journey into the rebellious imperatives of the self. In short, whether the life is criminal or not, the decision is to encourage the psychopath in oneself, to explore that domain of experience where security is boredom and therefore sickness, and one exists in the present, in that enormous present which is without past or future, memory or planned intention, the life where a man must go until he is beat, where he must gamble with his energies through all those small or large crises of courage and unforeseen situations which beset his day, where he must be with it or doomed not to swing. (p. 339)

The sentences are almost a catalogue of Romanticism—the immediate, the spontaneous, the dangerous, the unknown, the uniquely personal, the active.

The romantic dream quickly became apocalyptic and thus fulfilled the prayer of Marion Faye—in words. By 1966, Mailer was able to suggest that the followers of Adolf Hitler embodied at least one important virtue when they acted on the belief that "the weak are happiest when death is quick." [49] In the interim between *Advertisements for Myself* and *Cannibals and Christians* (1966), there was the phenomenon of John F. Kennedy, the existentialist as good guy.

The essays that comprise *The Presidential Papers* (1963) touch frequently on American literature, on sexuality in general and on the orgasm in particular, and on whatever Mailer or his interviewers happen upon, but the central fascination is with the possibility of a hero who is both romantic and constructive. Kennedy becomes the

Faust of Goethe's last act, the socially purposeful adventurer, the man bold enough to jar Americans loose from conventional politics.

Mailer became, in his own mind, Kennedy's aide-de-camp. His essays were "papers written *to* the President, *for* him, they are his private sources of information." (p. 1) Mailer suggests, apparently in earnest, that his praise for Kennedy swung enough votes to secure victory in that closely contested election. Once Kennedy was in office, Mailer continued his calls for duels between condemned prisoners and their putative executioners and for other forms of "existential legislation," but Kennedy's support for the invasion of Cuba by Cuban exiles thoroughly alienated Mailer, who wrote, "Tin soldier, you are depriving us of the Muse." (p. 79) In bitter disappointment, Mailer began to sound repeatedly the note that characterizes his next collection—modern American society is already totalitarian. The F.B.I., the American Medical Association, the pacifists as well as the Pentagon—all are collectivities that destroy differences and turn the social system into a kind of paste. His favorite recurrent metaphor for the process is cancer, the undifferentiated orgy of the cells. The political opinions of these years were—to speak mildly—novel. They have since been described by Mailer as a "private mixture of Marxism, conservatism, nihilism, and large parts of existentialism." [50] The conservative elements are not conspicuous. Mailer's political opinions prior to 1964 have also been anatomized, somewhat less generously, by Christopher Lasch, one of the most acute analysts of American radicalism:

> With Norman Mailer, the body of ideas and assumptions which I have called the new radicalism achieved some kind of final and definitive statement. The confusion of power and art, the effort to liberate the social and psychological "underground" by means of political action, the fevered pursuit of experience, the conception of life as an experiment, the intellectual's identification of himself with the outcasts of society—these things could be carried no further without carrying them to absurdity. Perhaps Mailer had carried them past that point already. [51]

But for the Mailer of that time, to be called "absurd" was to be flattered.

The year before the appearance of *Cannibals and Christians,* Mailer published his fourth and most controversial novel, *An Ameri-*

can Dream (1965). The hero, "half-Jewish" Stephen Rojack, is the existentialist man praised in "The White Negro" and *The Presidential Papers*. That he murders his wife is less significant than the fact that the murder is described in terms of a visionary and religious experience. Rojack—veteran of World War II, friend of John Kennedy, former member of Congress, husband of wealthy Deborah Caughlin Mangaravidi Kelly, and mystic lover of the moon—quarrels with his wife and struggles with her as if with a ritual animal. She is described as strong, as bull-like. He chokes her to death in what has already become one of the most notorious scenes in American literature:

> I struck her a blow on the back of the neck, a dead cold chop which dropped her to a knee, and then hooked an arm about her head and put a pressure on her throat. . . . My eyes were closed. I had the mental image I was pushing with my shoulder against an enormous door which would give inch by inch to the effort.
>
> One of her hands fluttered up to my shoulder and tapped it gently. Like a gladiator admitting defeat. I released the pressure on her throat, and the door I had been opening began to close. But I had had a view of what was on the other side of the door, and heaven was there, some quiver of jeweled cities shining in the glow of a tropical dusk, and I thrust against the door once more. . . .
>
> [Rojack continues his pressure until] the wire tore in her throat and I was through the door, hatred passing from me in wave after wave, illness as well, rot and pestilence, nausea, a bleak string of salts. I was floating. I was as far into myself as I had ever been and universes wheeled in a dream.[52] (pp. 30–31)

Like Emerson, Thoreau, and Whitman, Mailer's hero has had a transcendental experience. He comments upon it, "I was weary with a most honorable fatigue, and my flesh seemed new. I had not felt so nice since I was twelve." (p. 32) In only one other place in this novel is there a similar moment, and that comes one hundred pages further, as part of orgasmic experience: "I was passing through a grotto of curious lights, dark lights, like colored lanterns beneath the sea, a glimpse of that quiver of jeweled arrows, that heavenly city which had appeared as Deborah was expiring in the lock of my arm." (p. 128)

Minutes later, while Deborah's body lies upon the floor, Rojack looks into the maid's room and finds Fräulein Ruta "lying on top of the covers with her pajama pants down, a copy of a magazine in one hand . . . and her other hand fingering . . ." (p. 41) Without a word, Rojack takes advantage of his unusual opportunity. Alternating between anal and vaginal intercourse, which he describes as raids on the Devil and trips back to the Lord, he finally chooses the Devil: ". . . I jammed up her ass and came as if I'd been flung across the room." (p. 46) The imagery justifies Tony Tanner's assertion that the intercourse with Fräulein Ruta is "an analogue to a more metaphysical ambiguity," [53] but Rojack's sexual choice—the Devil—suggests not indecision in the face of ambiguity but rather a satanic choice that takes one back, in literary terms, to Byron's *Cain* and the diabolism of the Marquis de Sade.

Within the context of the novel, the sadistic association of love and death is in some measure ironic. The novel is written almost as if it were a parody of comic strips or of pop art. The characters are flat, vividly colored, and stereotyped. Deborah's father, for instance, is a kind of Daddy Warbucks (from the famous cartoon strip "Little Orphan Annie"). An affair with Cherry, the night-club singer, is reminiscent of scenes in films. One can, for example, easily imagine the role played by the late Marilyn Monroe. The simplified form of the novel makes the very lack of ambiguity seem ambiguous. What *does* Mailer mean by these murders, orgasms, interviews with the police, hints of astrology and espionage, by Rojack's terminal trip to Yucatán?

The critical response to *An American Dream* was remarkable for the range of its diversity; readers tended either to loathe the book or to admire it with an electric intensity. Elizabeth Hardwick, writing in *Partisan Review*, condemned the novel on aesthetic, moral, and intellectual grounds. She called it "a fantasy of vengeful murder, callous copulations and an assortment of dull cruelties." [54] The contrary view is that the fantasy is really a fable of redemption and regeneration. Emphasizing Rojack's test of wills with both Deborah and her father (whom Rojack bests in a mysterious penthouse combat), comparing *An American Dream* to Milton's *Samson Agonistes*, Shelley's *Prometheus Unbound*, and Bunyan's *Pilgrim's Progress*, Barry H. Leeds maintained that "Rojack's movement through the world of this novel represents a pilgrimage in the strictest religious sense of the word. He is a man who moves from imminent damnation to a state of grace by intimately encountering evil in many forms." [55] Still another defense is possible. Leo Bersani, replying to Hardwick's verbal barrage, argued that Mailer's novel expressed "private obsessions and dreams of power ideally demonic." The fabulous "playfulness" of the language, asserted Bersani, is more important than the action of the fable. It is inventive exuberance and linguistic virtuosity that matter, not the plot, which is the occasion of the verbal art.

> This means, of course, that the *playfulness* of the novel is by no means a frivolous attitude toward "dirty" or "ugly" events, but rather the natural tone of a man for whom events have become strictly literary-novelistic situations to be freely exploited for the sake of a certain style and the self-enjoyment it perhaps unexpectedly provides. [56]

This line of argument was carried further by William H. Pritchard; agreeing with Bersani, he went on with characteristic sublety to discuss the "narrative voice" heard in Mailer's "extravagances." [57] The difficulty with this position is that Norman Mailer has always stressed the moral purpose of his art. The themes of his essays are also the themes of his novels. Diana Trilling, who knows Mailer the man as well as his work, observed in 1962 that Mailer's "moral imagination is the imagination not of art but of theology, theology in action. . . . His writer's role . . . is much more messianic than creative." [58] The connection between the moralistic essayist and the prophetic artist is clear and direct. In the last essay of *Advertisements for Myself,* Mailer had attempted to clarify his argument about the morality of violence. To restrain from murder is comparable to a refusal to confess under torture. Restraint is *physically destructive:*

> . . . if one is going to confess eventually it is wiser to do it soon, do it now, before the damage is irrevocable. So with the desire to murder. Each day we contain it a little of that murder is visited upon our own bodies, the ulcers seat themselves more firmly, the liver sickens, the lungs wither, the brain bursts the most artful of our mental circuits, the heart is sapped of stamina and the testicles of juice . . . Yes, to hold murder too long is to lose the body, hasten that irreversible instant when

the first cell leaps upon the habit of stale intelligence and gives itself as volunteer to the unformed cadres in the future legions of barbarian and bohemian. (p. 517)

In plainer words, to refuse to murder is to risk cancer.

If any doubts of Mailer's views remained, they ought to have been dissipated by an interview in *Mademoiselle* magazine in February 1961: "If you're going to grind your heel into the face of a dying man, I still insist on the authority of my existential logic: let the act finally be authentic. If you're going to do it, *do it*." [59] On the twenty-first of November, 1960—less than three months before publication of this interview—Mailer was arrested in New York and charged with an attempt to murder his wife, who had been admitted to University Hospital thirty-six hours earlier for wounds in her upper abdomen and back. The alleged victim claimed to have hurt herself accidentally, and the charge was dropped. When one ponders "the relation between an ideology of violence set forth in an essay and a charge of felonious assault set forth in a police affidavit," [60] when one meditates further on the relation between these two documents and *An American Dream,* one simply cannot believe that events "have become strictly literary-novelistic situations to be freely exploited for the sake of a certain style and the self-enjoyment it perhaps unexpectedly provides." I, at least, am unable to accept the Bersani-Pritchard thesis, preferable as it is to the outrageous attempt to pass Mailer's vision of violence off as a pilgrimage of regeneration. To look with Mailer into the heart of darkness is one thing; to look upon it and call it good is quite another.

Mailer's most recent novel, *Why Are We in Vietnam?* (1968), is another linguistic revel, another romp through the realms of pop art, another challenge to conventional morality. The language is comic, imaginative, and almost uninterruptedly obscene. His own satisfaction with the stylistic experiment is evidenced in a comment; he writes that he had "kicked goodbye . . . to the old literary corset of good taste, letting [my] sense of language play on obscenity as freely as it wished, so discovering that everything [I] knew about the American language (with its incommensurable resources) went flying in and out of the line of [my] prose with the happiest beating of wings." Whatever others may think, Mailer felt the language to be "very literary in the best way." [61]

The narrator is apparently (the matter is obscure) a disk jockey from Texas who refers to himself as D.J. His scatological account of his mother's neuroses and his father's crass ambitions is clearly designed (by the narrator and of course by the author) to *épater le bourgeois*. The humor is gross and finally tiresome, but the action gains in interest and significance when the narrator, his father, his best friend Tex, and numerous minor characters set forth on an Alaskan hunt. D.J. and Tex break away from the group (after a symbolic Faulknerian bear is slain by D.J. and claimed by his father) and journey into the unknown territory to the north. In the night, the narrator achieves a sense of communion that is almost accompanied by a homosexual rape. He and Tex return from the hunt in order to depart for Vietnam. The final words are reminiscent of those that end *The Naked and the Dead*: Major Dalleson thinks of teaching map-reading by laying a grid over a pin-up girl, and cries out, "Hot dog!" (p. 721) Now D.J. announces that he is turning off and cries out, "Vietnam, hot damn." [62] (p. 208) Although Norman Mailer's public statements and political activities are those of an *opponent* to the war in Vietnam, this novel—and the works that preceded it—tempted more than one reader to wonder if Mailer didn't secretly condone the violence committed in Asia. It is, after all, a kind of adventure, an arena for the demonstration of what is taken to be virility, and an opportunity for "existential" actions. When Mailer commented in a speech that Lyndon Johnson felt apropos of the war "like the only stud in a whorehouse on a houseboat," [63] it was hard not to think of Sergius O'Shaugnessy in *The Deer Park* and of an orgiastic story entitled "The Time of Her Time."

The grounds for Mailer's opposition to the war appear in *The Armies of the Night* (1968). Given the development of romantic and frequently apocalyptic and even nihilistic themes in the works prior to 1968, this book represents a new turn. The tone is far more rational and the ironies are gentler. Mailer appears, rather suddenly, as someone newly attracted to certain bourgeois virtues.

Although the book is pretentiously subtitled "History as a Novel: The Novel as History," it is essentially an autobiographical account of Mailer's participation in the October 1967 march on the Pentagon by protesters of the war in Vietnam. The techniques are novelistic, as often in autobiography, but the assumption is that we deal with the "real" and not with a fictive world. This assumption is supported by Mailer's quotation from *Time* magazine. The magazine's version, published October 17, 1967, falsifies. "Now," remarks Mailer, "we may leave *Time* in order to find out what happened." (p. 4)

Appropriately, Mailer describes himself, his commitment to drugs, his dislike of telephones, recent events in his own life, and, especially, his highly ambivalent agreement to participate in the planned demonstration. "Mailer," he writes in the third person, "wished as the Washington weekend approached that the Washington weekend were done." (p. 10) A party given by "Liberals" enables Mailer to characterize his friends and rivals. Paul Goodman, Robert Lowell, and Dwight Macdonald are brilliantly characterized. Speaking, for instance, of the last's fascination for *The New Yorker,* Mailer imagines "Disraeli on his knees before Victoria." (p. 26) The occasion also permits a denunciation of the "liberal technologues":

> His deepest detestation was often reserved for the nicest of liberal academics, as if their lives were his own life but a step escaped. Like the scent of the void which comes off the pages of a Xerox copy, so was he always depressed in such homes by their hint of oversecurity. If the republic was now managing to convert the citizenry to a plastic mass, ready to be attached to any manipulative gung ho, the author was ready to cast much of the blame for such success into the undernourished lap, the overpsychologized loins, of the liberal academic intelligentsia. (p. 15)

They are servants of the social machine.

The next important scene is a speech, or series of speeches, in which Mailer drunkenly harangues his audience, the "troops" that will on the morrow challenge the government. His opinion of the demonstrators is not without ambiguity:

> These mad middle-class children with their lobotomies from sin, their nihilistic embezzlement of all middle-class moral funds, their innocence, their lust for apocalypse, their unbelievable indifference to waste . . . Yes, these were the troops: middle-class cancer-pushers and drug-gutted flower children. (pp. 34–35)

In the various exchanges and speeches, Lowell is clearly the most impressive person—cool, diffidently patrician, a gentleman forced by occasion to revolutionary acts, quite in the tradition of his Bostonian ancestors.

In the march itself, Mailer's excitement is clearly related to the excitement of military combat: "Going to battle! He realized that he had not taken in precisely this thin high sensuous breath of pleasure in close to twenty-four years, not since the first time he had gone into combat." (p. 90) Although the horrors of modern war are mentioned, the struggle here in Washington is characterized as the struggle between romanticism and rationalism, between the spontaneously intuitive individual and the relentlessly manipulated mass. The Pentagon is diabolical less for what it does than for the way it does it. It is the symbol of what Mailer calls "technology land." And now, "In the capital of technology land beat a primitive drum. New drum of the Left!" (pp. 93–94) The devotees of magic try their arts. Mailer is arrested.

But he is no longer unambivalently among the romantics. Chapter 7, "Why Are We in Vietnam?," proves that Mailer's radicalism has taken a turn toward the rational. He is not among those who polarize modern conflicts into a choice between love and war. The language is highly charged, but the analysis is cogent, with summaries of arguments pro and con. Mailer suggests that the expansion of Communism leads to its own "containment," in that no centralized monolith can possibly rule half of Europe and most of Asia. But political analysis of this sort is not Mailer's strength. After an account of his hours in confinement and his release, Mailer ends Part I and opens Part II, an attempt to provide a more or less objective account of the march. It is anticlimactic except for the last section, which is a meditation on the meaning of America, "once a beauty of magnificence unparalleled, now a beauty with a leprous skin." (p. 288)

No one who has followed Mailer's zigzag career is likely to be surprised by his reports on the political conventions of 1968. *Miami and the Siege of Chicago* (1968) is novelistic journalism of the sort Mailer had perfected with his article on the middle-class mob that nominated Barry Goldwater to be President of the United States. Characterizations continue to be imaginative in a manner that

Mailer tolerates only in his own work: Nelson Rockefeller is "Spencer Tracy's younger brother gone into politics"; Richard Nixon's posture on stage "gave him the attentive guarded look of an old ball player—like Rabbit Maranville, let us say, or even an old con up before Parole Board." [64] (pp. 21, 44) Miami itself is described as a hideous whiteness constructed upon the mangrove swamps. There is perhaps a deliberate analogy between the all-white city and the lily-white convention. Mailer, however, confesses that the rhetoric of Black Power bores him. The claims for Black superiority have no appeal for the no-longer-very-young writer who measures himself against all comers at any hour.

In Chicago, Mailer has his chance to prove himself once more. In that memorable combat between Mayor Daley's police and all those who taunted them, thwarted them, annoyed them, or got in their way, Mailer went through the dark night of the soul. He found himself tired of revolutionary activity, he found himself worried about his comforts: Mailer

> looked into his reluctance to lose even the America he had had, that insane warmongering technology land with its smog, its super-highways, its experts and its profound dishonesty. Yet it had allowed him to write—it had even not deprived him entirely of honors, certainly not of an income. He had lived well enough to have six children, a house on the water, a good apartment, good meals, good booze, he had even come to enjoy wine. (pp. 186–87)

For a man with these doubts, physical confrontation with evil is a necessity. Like Stephen Rojack walking along the terrace wall of his father-in-law's penthouse high above the streets of Manhattan, Mailer ventures out to risk his manhood against the cops. He gets into a dispute over the radical kids and is menaced by the officers of the law, who are ready to manhandle him. When he realizes that he is not afraid of them, he is happy—as he hasn't been since the assassination of Robert Kennedy. Triumph.

The trouble for me is that *Miami and the Siege of Chicago* is not a work of fiction and the Mailer of the book is not the invention simply of his own fantasy. I am pleased that his courage has not been eroded by comforts, but his personal *hombria* seems less important than the heads broken in the streets by the defenders of law and

order. If Norman Mailer had single-handedly outfought six policemen, the nation would still have had to choose between Richard M.
Nixon and a man who had supported the intervention in Vietnam
and refused to intervene in the streets of Chicago. The confusion of
virility with morality is, after all, one of the difficulties of American
foreign and domestic policy.

Where Mailer will go next is unknown. What is unmistakable is
that he has already explored most of the phases of American radicalism. He is too various, too eccentric, too individualistic to be taken
as the representative of any single ideology. He is certainly the
spokesman for no institutionalized dogma. If he is the secular Jew
as revolutionary, he is also the reincarnation of Friedrich Nietzsche
and the personification of a mood shared by many intellectuals in
this present crisis of our civilization. His incandescent articulation of
the anguish of marginality and alienation make him a central figure
in the consciousness of the very people he denounces. Sometimes
comic, sometimes nihilistic, once violent, now meditative, he is a
modern prophet who demands attention even when he cannot command fealty.

5   *Allen Ginsberg and the Angelheaded Hipsters*

Paul Goodman and Norman Mailer are, of course, only two of the
many nominally Jewish writers who dream of a new Zion here in
the American wasteland. Herbert Gold's novel *The Prospect Before
Us* (1954) is the epitaph of a stubborn hotelkeeper who defies the
prejudices of white America and rents a room to a Negro girl—and
dies for love of her. In novels and in essays, Harvey Swados has
documented the degradation of factory life and debunked the myth
of the happy worker. Clancy Sigal's *Going Away* (1961), perhaps
the most minutely thorough novelistic criticism of American society
since Dos Passos's *USA*, sends its hero driving from Los Angeles to
New York in search of that lost world of the 1930s where "unions"
meant sit-down strikes rather than racial discrimination and support
for war, where "Spain" meant the defense of Madrid from Fascism
rather than another come-on in *Holiday* magazine: "I really wanted,
while I was on the road, to look at America and try to figure out
why it wasn't my country anymore." [65] (p. 244) The 1950s were not

the age of political apathy that journalistic myth presently holds them to have been.

In October of 1956, one month before the re-election of President Eisenhower, a young poet offered his radically different vision of the state of the nation:

> I saw the best minds of my generation destroyed by madness,
>   starving hysterical naked,
> dragging themselves through the negro streets at dawn looking
>   for an angry fix. . . .[66] (p. 9)

Allen Ginsberg's *Howl* seemed then a manifesto of the "Beats," a hallucinatory accompaniment to Jack Kerouac's novel *On the Road* (1957), but it appears now to have a much more general significance. Ginsberg's manner was as revolutionary as his matter. The poems demonstrated as well as proclaimed a new life-style. The New Left is many Lefts, including Black Panthers and Weathermen whose nominally Jewish members pride themselves on opposition to the "Nazism" of the State of Israel, but one important type of young radical is certainly the long-haired, drug-inspired dropout who is dead set against the "middle-class hang-ups" of an older generation. Allen Ginsberg is his bard. It was, therefore, appropriate and comic when the author of "Howl" was introduced into the trial of the Chicago Seven to tell Judge Julius Hoffman about the "angelheaded hipsters" that roam the poet's mind.

If the autobiographical elements of the title poem of Ginsberg's second volume, *Kaddish and Other Poems* (1961), are distantly related to the facts of the poet's life, his childhood and youth were a time of domestic horror. His mother had come to America as a girl, married, borne children, and gone mad. The poem "Kaddish" takes its title from the Hebrew prayer for the dead and tells in thirty pages the story of Naomi Ginsberg's decline and death.

> "I am a great woman—am truly a beautiful soul—and because of that they (Hitler, Grandma, Hearst, the Capitalists, Franco, Daily News, the 20's, Mussolini, the living dead) want to shut me up—Buba's the head of a spider network—" [67] (p. 26)

There seems to be no detail too horrid for description:

> One time I thought she was trying to make me come lay
> her—flirting to herself at sink—lay back on huge bed that
> filled most of the room, dress up round her hips, big slash
> of hair, scars of operations, pancreas, belly wounds, abortions,
> appendix, stitching, of incisions pulling down in the fat like
> hideous thick zippers—ragged long lips between her legs—
> . . . (p. 24)

And yet, even when his mother has become a lobotomized crone,
Ginsberg remembers her as a young Communist beauty with long
black flower-crowned hair. Her final letter seemed a revelation. She
wrote of the key in the window, of the key in the sunlight, and
asked her son to marry. His grief does not seem insincere.

In his earlier poem "America," published in *Howl*, he revealed
ironically, humorously, what it was like to be the child of radical
parents:

> . . . when I was seven momma took me to Communist Cell
> meetings   they sold us garbanzos a handful per ticket
> a ticket costs a nickel and the speeches were free
> everybody was angelic and sentimental about the workers. . . .
> (p. 33)

The stanza concludes with the observation that "everybody" must
have been a spy. In "Kaddish," Ginsberg tells more of his ambitions,
of inspiration from Sacco and Vanzetti, Norman Thomas, Eugene
Victor Debs and—unlikely influence!—Edgar Allan Poe. He introduces Hebrew phrases into his poems, but his education is hardly
reminiscent of David Levinsky's. His adult heroes are more likely
to be literary than political in the conventional sense. His frequently
allusive poems contain references to Blake and Keats, Rimbaud and
Apollinaire, Mayakovsky and García Lorca, W. C. Fields and Harpo
Marx—among others. Whether Communist agitators or Romantic
poets or American clowns, his mentors had in common a rejection
of middle-class culture. In the 1960s he became increasingly fascinated by the Oriental mysticism that was present in his first book.
By the time of his above-mentioned entry into the trial of the Chicago Seven, he was as much guru as poet, as much the utterer of the
mystic "OM" as explicator of the conditions that had, allegedly,
destroyed the best minds of his generation.

Even for readers long accustomed to the idea that the evening might be stretched out like a patient etherized upon a table, Ginsberg's poems are likely to be a strange experience. The "angelheaded hipsters" who "coughed on the sixth floor of Harlem crowned with flame under the tubercular sky surrounded by orange crates of theology" [68] are described by fifty-nine other clauses that begin with "who" in a sentence that runs for eight pages. The imagery is sometimes associative to the point where it seems comparable to an inkblot test. What, for instance, is meant by "orange crates of theology" or "the drunken taxicabs of Absolute Reality"? [69]

The second section of "Howl" consists largely of the cry "Moloch!" For example, "Moloch! Moloch! Nightmare of Moloch! Moloch the loveless! / Mental Moloch! Moloch the heavy judger of men!" The anaphoric judgment is plain enough to understand here, but the form is unusual. The third and last section of "Howl" consists of nineteen variations on an assertion beginning, "I'm with you in Rockland. . . ." There is then a "Footnote to Howl," which starts off with the word "holy" repeated fifteen times. (pp. 17–22) Again, the sense is clear enough but the form resembles the oral pattern of a religious revival—which may be appropriate.

The influence of Walt Whitman is strongly evident. In the words of one perceptive critic, "The notorious *Howl* of Allen Ginsberg turns to its account the semi-affirmative line of Walt Whitman to protest the decline of the American promise Whitman had once celebrated." [70] Ginsberg's howl is probably a conscious variant on Whitman's "barbaric yawp." His cry "The tongue and cock and hand and asshole holy!" is analogous to Whitman's claim that he was "the poet of the Body" as well as the poet of the Soul: "If I worship one thing more than another," sang the Brooklyn carpenter in "The Song of Myself," "it shall be the spread of my own body, or any part of it . . ." Similarly, Ginsberg's ecstatic assertion that the wretched of the earth are as holy as the seraphim is a correlative of Whitman's famous invitation to the table set for one and all, for prostitutes and spongers and slaves as well as for the more respected citizens of the day. Any doubts about the pervasive influence of Whitman ought to have been settled by "Love Poem on Theme by Whitman," published in *Reality Sandwiches* (1963). Whitman had written:

I am a free companion, I bivouac by invading watchfires,
I turn the bridegroom out of bed and stay with the bride myself,
I tighten her all night to my thighs and lips.

Those lines are presumably the inspiration for Ginsberg's poem:

I'll go into the bedroom silently and lie down between the
    bridegroom and the bride,
those bodies fallen from heaven stretched out waiting naked and
    restless. . . .[71] (p. 41)

Numerous other rather obvious comparisons await their destined
cataloguer.

Nearly as important an influence is the poetry of William Carlos
Williams. In *Paterson* (1948–58), the older poet's panegyric to the
mundane, several admiring letters from Allen Ginsberg appear over
the initials "A.G." Ginsberg's affection is also expressed in "Death
News," an elegy for Williams that was published in Ginsberg's most
recent collection, *Planet News* (1968). The famous triadic line that
became the mentor's trademark appears also in Ginsberg's "Sakyamuni Coming Out from the Mountain":

He drags his bare feet
            out of a cave
                    under a tree. . . .[72]

Other influences can easily be noted, but Ginsberg's poems are original events.

They are also, as already suggested, contributions to a conscious
rebellion against American society and against the more structured
formal poetry of academically admired poets. Any writer influenced
by Walt Whitman and ready to associate God with the Lone Ranger
is obviously formed in part by the society he rejects, but this is no
cause for wonder. It has always been possible to appeal from the
everyday America we live in to the democratic vistas imagined by
those for whom America has been an unfinished dream. It is the
Jewishness rather than the Americanness of Allen Ginsberg (and
Abbie Hoffman and Jerry Rubin and a great many others associated with the New Left) that seems problematical. Child of a family that had already converted from Judaism to Communism, he has

become a guru whose benevolent visage beams from uncounted dormitory walls. In "Kral Majales," he proclaimed himself a "Buddhist Jew." [73] He has far more in common with citizens of Woodstock Nation than with the Reform Jews of suburbia (not to speak of the Chassidic enclave of Williamsburg). His comic failure to communicate with Judge Julius Hoffman, who evidently decided that his testimony was a sign of madness, represents a gap that is more religious than generational. It is inevitable that Allen Ginsberg and Julius Hoffman have been and will continue to be identified as Jews, but anyone who attempts to discuss them as if they shared the same faith deserves a citation for contempt of common sense.

V

Mr. Bellow's America

1 *Dangling Man*

It was Saul Bellow's friend Isaac Rosenfeld who popularized the thesis that the modern Jew is the marginal man, the doubly alienated figure caught—sometimes uncomfortably, sometimes exhilaratingly —between his own inadequate but inalienable heritage and the miragelike promise of modern civilization. Born in Lachine, Quebec, reared in Chicago, at home with Yiddish literature and with the classics of Western culture, Bellow himself is *par excellence* the explorer of marginality, concerned with men situated somewhere between old and new, with comic and tragic characters in quest of their uncertain identities.

What, after all, is *Dangling Man* (1944), Bellow's first novel, if not a study in marginality? To dangle is, metaphorically, more extreme than to be rootless. The narrator's desperate plight is comparable to that of the characters of Franz Kafka and Jean-Paul Sartre. Joseph is linked by name to Kafka's Josef K. and by situation to Sartre's Antoine Roquentin. Behind these exemplars of alienation stands their shadowy prototype, Dostoevsky's underground man. The literary influences manifested in *Dangling Man* have not gone undiscussed, but there is a realistic quality to Bellow's first novel that is not to be found in *Der Prozess* or in *La Nausée*. The action of the novel seems almost a case study in the sociology of Emile Durkheim, whose seminal analysis of suicide Bellow almost certainly encountered in his undergraduate study of anthropology and sociology.

Durkheim's analysis of suicide rates in France led him to the concept of *anomie*—goallessness, rootlessness. Many suicides, he argued, have motives plausible enough to satisfy the researcher: incurable illness, bankruptcy, social disgrace, disappointment in love. But others occur with no apparent motive. Durkheim, therefore, introduced an argument to explain various hitherto unrelated phenomena. Suicide is more likely in the summer than in the winter, for instance, because warm weather abets visible group activities and thus intensifies the sense of isolation in those who are excluded. Protestants are more likely to commit suicide than Catholics because they have fewer social bonds and are thrown more on their inner resources; they have fewer institutional supports in time of crisis. Orthodox Jews have very low rates, while secular Jews have very high ones.

Bellow's first published work was an exploration of the theme of *anomie*. "Two Morning Monologues," which appeared in the *Partisan Review* in 1941, begins with the thoughts of a young man who cannot find employment. His life is boredom. "Here we are," he thinks. "What'll it be today, the library? museum? the courthouse? a convention?" [1] Young Mandelbaum is Joseph's precursor. Joseph's diary is an extension of Mandelbaum's monologue.

Bellow's diary-keeper suffers from *anomie* when he resigns his job in order to wait for induction into the army. He creates for himself the equivalent of what Erik Erikson terms a "psychosocial moratorium." He enters a period of suspension between his now abandoned ordinary life and the new roles of his future "profession." With his freedom, Joseph imagines that he can become the earnest huntsman of himself, the introspective discoverer of identity. Describing himself in the third person (i.e. "objectively"), he writes: "He wants to avoid the small conflicts of non-conformity so that he can give all his attention to defending his inner differences, the ones that really matter." [2] (pp. 27–28) He learns that the self is an intersection of sets, the fabric woven by the crisscross of social roles. To withdraw from society and to look within is to discover the abyss.

The diary's first entry records defensiveness:

> There was a time when people were in the habit of addressing themselves frequently and felt no shame at making a record of their inward transactions. But to keep a journal nowadays

is considered a kind of self-indulgence, a weakness, and in poor taste. For this is an era of hardboiled-dom. (p. 9)

There is little doubt that Joseph sees Ernest Hemingway as the man behind the tough-guy code: "The hard-boiled are compensated for their silence; they fly planes or fight bulls or catch tarpon, whereas I rarely leave my room." (p. 10) Nonetheless, he proclaims his right to keep a journal rather than shoot big game. At the time of the story, Joseph has already been jobless for almost seven months and has accepted financial support from his wife, with whom his role-reversed relations have become increasingly strained.

The world's belligerent frenzy accelerates while Joseph's lassitude grows daily greater. Although Joseph had intended to resume the role of essayist, which he had tentatively begun and then dropped, he is unable to do more than jot down random thoughts in his journal. He begins, figuratively, to fade away as a person. Complaining to a friend, he tells how he approached a man with whom, in the Communist Party he had once been close: "I said hello to him, and he acted as if I simply wasn't there." (p. 32) When Joseph attempts to cash a check at the bank, the vice-president riffles through his identification cards and queries him, "How do I know you're this person?" (p. 174) How, indeed, when Joseph himself has reason to doubt?

Without the support of a fixed habitation and a place in the world's work, Joseph grows increasingly irritable. Annoyances soon become grievances. Mr. Vanaker, for instance, fellow denizen of the rooming house, drinks, coughs, throws empty bottles into the yard, steals small articles, and leaves the bathroom door open when he relieves himself. To celebrate the New Year, Mr. Vanaker ends his revels with a fire. Joseph's impatience intensifies until he rushes into the lavatory, traps Vanaker, shouts at him, brings the other tenants to the scene, and quarrels with them too. Eventually, he is threatened with eviction.

The deterioration of his relations with others in the house is paralleled by strains in his various friendships and by quarrels within his family. Visiting his father-in-law, sick in bed, he asks him, "How did you ever manage to stick it out so long, Mr. Almstadt?" Stick what out? "With her." (p. 21) That is, with Mrs. Almstadt. Although the old man has frequently criticized his wife, he naturally grows angry when others usurp his socially accepted role. Relations with Joseph's wealthy brother Amos and his family are even worse. Listening to a Haydn divertimento on his niece's record player, Joseph is interrupted. "I want to play these Cugat records Mamma gave me." (p. 69) Joseph refuses to remove his record and is informed by his niece, "Beggars can't be choosers!" (p. 70) In response, Joseph seizes the girl and spanks her, to the expected outrage of her parents. She then accuses Joseph of theft (because he tried secretly to return money thrust at him by Amos). Joseph's wife Iva is estranged by the shrillness of the petty contretemps:

> She did not speak to me on the streetcar and, when we got off, she huried home ahead of me. I reached the door of our room in time to see her drop to the edge of the bed and burst into tears.
> "Dearest," I shouted. "It's so nice to know that you at least have faith in me!" (p. 74)

It is plain that Joseph's own faith has waned.

The marriage weathers away in flurries of picayune disagreements that seem, in the unnatural arena of Joseph's voluntary isolation, catastrophic. A book clandestinely loaned to Joseph's mistress becomes a bone of contention when Iva suddenly desires to read it. Joseph's attempts to reclaim the book turn into a break with his mistress (who is in bed with another man when he bangs on her door). Simple matters—who will cash Iva's check?—become struggles of will against will. Joseph and Iva's sixth anniversary celebration is ruined by the accidental sight of a man collapsed on the street, an occasion for morbidity in a man who no longer needs an external *memento mori*. Joseph can all too easily identify with the fallen.

The incidents chronicle the disintegration of Joseph's personality, while the imagery and the random thoughts jotted down in his journal extend and complicate the theme. He writes, for instance:

> I feel I am a sort of human grenade whose pin has been withdrawn. I know I am going to explode and I am continually anticipating the time, with a prayerful despair crying "Boom!" but always prematurely. (pp. 147–48)

The "Boom!" comes with the change of seasons, so that April is the cruelest month for Joseph as well as for the speaker of T. S. Eliot's poem. The disgraceful fight with Mr. Vanaker is the nadir of Joseph's troubles. He decides that his situation cannot be borne: "I believe I had known for some time that the moment I had been waiting for had come, and that it was impossible to resist any longer. I must give myself up." (p. 183) The language associates Joseph with some outlaw, some fugitive from the authorities, which is appropriate to this moment in the narration. His dream of absolute freedom was a moral misdemeanor.

Joseph notifies his draft board that he is ready for immediate induction. Goethe was right to argue that "All comfort in life is based upon a regular occurrence of external phenomena." (p. 18) (Joseph quotes him in his journal.) Joseph's family draws together to wish him goodbye and the book ends with a paean to routine:

> I am no longer to be held accountable for myself; I am grateful for that. I am in other hands, relieved of self-determination, freedom cancelled.
>   Hurray for regular hours!
>   And for the supervision of the spirit!
>   Long live regimentation! (p. 191)

The much-debated acceptance of things as they are by Moses Herzog, the hero of Bellow's sixth novel, is prefigured here in Joseph's flight from the intolerable strain of an order derived from inner necessity. He turns in relief and even in joy to external, institutionalized authority. He is unable to take advantage of the dreadful freedom offered by marginality. It has been maintained that

> In *Dangling Man* the burden of what Bellow says is that freedom is the necessary condition for man if he is to pursue his chief end as a man—the knowledge of himself; successful in his quest, man's energies may then be released in love.[3]

But this assertion seems based on the critic's own commitment to libertarian and Socratic views rather than on the text of the novel. The reader must not credit Joseph with a strength of character shown in later novels by Augie March and Henderson the Rain King. Richard Lehan's comment is astute: "Joseph is the completely autonomous hero who is unable to direct his energy outside of himself and almost burns himself out in fits of insignificant restlessness."[4] Self-knowledge is, for Joseph, bad news.

It has also been maintained, by widely respected critics, that there is a Chassidic quality to the joy expressed in Bellow's work. If one looks ahead to Bellow's third and fifth novels, the assertion is plausible. Equally plausible (or implausible) is the argument that Bellow's characters are essentially Jewish because they suffer, that "their distinctive dimension arises from the fact that they wear the heart on the sleeve as if it were the Star of David." [5] If one looks carefully at *Dangling Man,* however, one sees the secular Jew as marginal man.* Joseph is, moreover, the marginal man for whom the tensions of marginality are too much. Joseph turns—within the time of the novel—from a position that is markedly Protestant and Romantic to one that is shared by Judaism and Catholicism. He gives up the quest for freedom and accepts the strictures of institutional commitment. It is certainly arguable that Joseph has returned metaphorically from the empty wilderness within in order to surrender himself to a secular equivalent of *Chalakah,* the Law. Within the emotional economy of the novel, it is nonetheless a defeat.

2   The Victim

Asa Leventhal, the protagonist of *The Victim* (1947), is also a secular Jew, and the question of Jewish identity is one of the main themes of the novel, which was not the case in *Dangling Man*. Circumstance rather than choice puts Leventhal in a position where he seems a "displaced personality." The situation is carefully prepared. The seasons play a part in *The Victim,* as they do in *Dangling Man*. The book opens with the weather:

> On some nights New York is as hot as Bangkok. The whole continent seems to have moved from its place and slid nearer the equator, the bitter grey Atlantic to have become green and tropical, and the people, thronging the streets, barbaric fellahin among the stupendous monuments of their mystery. . . . [6] (p. 3)

The muggy, windless air, especially oppressive in the technological jungle of New York, remains a factor, a pressure upon Asa Leven-

---

* A single reference to Gehenna (Hell) is one basis for the assumption that Joseph is nominally a Jew; the names of the characters are another. A reference to the Hindu deity Shiva should, however, caution one against hasty inferences.

thal, a metaphoric reminder of conditions beyond our control. Social ties are temporarily severed, as they are in *Dangling Man*. In this case, the absence of Asa's wife Mary deprives him of one source of support just when he is called upon to support his absent brother's family.

The first crisis of the novel occurs when Elena, his Italian-American sister-in-law, calls him to leave work and rush over to Staten Island, where her younger son Mickey is seriously ill. The illness grows increasingly severe, and Asa become progressively more involved in his brother's family, but the story of this involvement is not continuously narrated. The hospitalization, death, and burial of Mickey Leventhal form a sequence that is repeatedly (and realistically) interrupted by other obligations and by the entirely unexpected demands made by Kirby Allbee, a forgotten acquaintance who blames Leventhal for his hardships. Down-and-out Allbee blames Leventhal for his degradation and demands what he, Allbee, imagines to be justice. During these crises, the matter of identity comes to the fore, so that the drama of the novel includes the moral transformation of Leventhal and his eventual acceptance of his fate.

Allbee's anti-Semitism is foreshadowed by a remark made by one of Leventhal's colleagues on the afternoon of Elena's emergency telephone call: " 'Takes unfair advantage,' Mr. Beard continued. 'Like the rest of his brethren. I've never known one who wouldn't.' " (p. 5) Allbee leads Leventhal into an increasingly complicated analysis of guilt and responsibility. His incessant demands and allegations activate the relatively latent question of identity. He also forces Leventhal to rethink his status in the social system and his personal self-evaluation.

Although the discussions of responsibility and the problems of identity are woven together in the novel, analysis here calls for a certain amount of unravelling. The first problem—who victimizes whom? what is the nature of complicity?—has received extensive attention from the critics. It is undeniable that Bellow sees complicity in evil as a central truth of the relationship between Allbee and Leventhal. The two are *Doppelgänger,* twinned by fate. The present situation, in the time scheme of the novel, has origins that are gradually unfolded as the situation grows more complicated in development. Allbee, at a party given by a mutual friend named Williston, had insulted Daniel Harkavy, Leventhal's best friend. Nonetheless, Leventhal had gone to Allbee for an introduction to Allbee's boss. The interview was a disaster in which Leventhal insulted the notoriously tyrannical and ill-tempered Mr. Rudiger. Subsequently, Allbee lost his job and, gradually, sank to his present level. Was Leventhal responsible?

He insists that Allbee had jeopardized his position through drunkeness and was, therefore, wholly responsible, while Allbee pictures himself simply as the victim. He haunts Leventhal, sleeps on a cot in his apartment, intrudes into his thoughts. Leventhal goes to Harkavy for moral support and is disappointed. Harkavy puts him off with generalizations: "The truth is hard to get at." He tells him, when pressed, that Williston thought Leventhal *was* partly responsible: "Williston thought you made trouble for this fellow when you went to Dill's and you acted up. He kind of hinted that it was intentional." (pp. 87–88) Eventually, Leventhal learns the same from Williston. Whether or not he had intended evil, the consequences were dismal for Allbee.

> You take it for granted that I think you got Allbee in trouble purposely. I didn't say that. Maybe you aimed to hurt him and maybe you didn't. My opinion is that you didn't. But the effect was the same. You lost him his job. (p. 116)

This point is also made in the novel's epigraphs, one of which is a quotation from the *Thousand and One Nights,* which tells of a boy accidentally killed by a carelessly hurled date stone.

Confused and upset, Leventhal begins to accept the fact of complicity. In his own actions, he comes to resemble Allbee—he drinks too much, he spends the night at Harkavy's house. There is even a moment when his relationship to Allbee resembles that of a pair of lovers or of a man and wife. He is "drawn with a kind of affection" and allows Allbee to play with the tangles of his hair, to admire its thickness.[7] (p. 224) They seem more like brothers than Asa and Max Leventhal (who returns to bury his son).

As Allbee's version of the past becomes somewhat more acceptable, his behavior in the present becomes increasingly abominable. He continues to drink. He turns the apartment into a pigpen. In a moment of farce, Leventhal enters the apartment to find Allbee in bed with a prostitute. Leventhal throws him out, but Allbee returns in the night, closes the windows, and turns on the gas. Leventhal awakens in time to prevent what he later refers to as a "kind of suicide pact without getting my permission first." (p. 286) Allbee flees. Leventhal's "spiritual shock-treatment" [8] is finished.

After the attempted suicide and the departure of Allbee, the time of the novel suddenly accelerates. After an almost hourly report of Leventhal's moods and thoughts, Bellow begins Chapter XXIV with a jump ahead to autumn and then, in the next paragraph, to a time several years after the action of the previous chapters. There is a final encounter in a theater foyer between Leventhal and Allbee, both of whom have prospered since their strange summer together. Allbee says, "I've made my peace with things as they are." (p. 294) Leventhal too has a new sense of himself and a new kind of ease in his social position (which a change of jobs has improved). This new sense is not dramatically presented. The attempted suicide may have represented a symbolic death and rebirth, but regeneration seems commonplace. "Having denied Leventhal and Allbee any perception of their fault as a result of their experience," complains one analyst of Bellow's fiction, "he uses an unjustified change in character to insure our perception of it." [9] The truth of the change must be tested by the reader's own experience of the novel. My own sense is that Bellow's omission of the evidence for a dramatic change in character is appropriate to the kind of change at issue here. Leventhal accepts himself as an ordinary man. A subtle image ends the novel: "The bell [announcing the end of the theater's intermission] continued its dinning, and Leventhal and Mary were still in the aisle when the house lights went off. An usher showed them to their seats." (p. 294) Here is acceptance of one's place as a spectator, offstage. Leventhal is not Prince Hamlet and was not meant to be, but he takes his seat nonetheless.

A small achievement, no doubt, but Bellow's novels repeatedly insist upon the validity and the worth of the ordinary as well as the heroic. This insistence is made explicit in the eloquent arguments of a character named Schlossberg. (His name, "castle mountain," suggests his authority.) Schlossberg, a theatrical journalist who holds sway in a Fourteenth Street cafeteria, is an impressive man to whom Leventhal is enormously drawn. Schlossberg urges an almost Aristotelian view of man: "I'll tell you. It's bad to be less than human and it's bad to be more than human." (p. 133) What this means—to be human—is, of course, determined by standards other than statistical ones. To be human means to forgo the Faustian desire to be divine and, simultaneously, to avoid the temptation to be bestial. It means to accept man as he is. Schlossberg comes to a peroration:

> I am as sure about greatness and beauty as you are about black and white. If a human life is a great thing to me, it *is* a great thing. Do you know better? I'm entitled as much as you. And why be measly? Do you have to be? Is somebody holding you by the neck? Have dignity, you understand me? Choose dignity. Nobody knows enough to turn it down. (p. 134)

When Schlossberg is done, Shifcart, an agent for actors, laughingly tosses him his card. "The card fell near Leventhal, who seemed to be the only one to disapprove of the joke." (p. 135) Leventhal is not amused because he feels the truth of Schlossberg's words. This is a serious matter. By the end of the novel, he has in his small way chosen dignity.

To the degree that Allbee challenges Leventhal's status as a secular Jew assimilated into American society, the book's repudiation of Allbee is an affirmation of an identity conditioned by but not limited to origins. Allbee's narrow view is actually the precipitant of the sequence of events that leads to his claims against Leventhal. At Williston's party, Harkavy "and a girl he had brought to the party were singing spirituals and old ballads." Allbee interrupts:

> "Why do you sing such songs?" he said. "*You* can't sing them."
> "Why not, I'd like to know?" said the girl.
> "Oh, you, too," said Allbee with a one-cornered smile. "It isn't right for you to sing them. You have to be born to them."

Allbee then tries to bully Harkavy into singing a psalm or "any Jewish song. Something you've really got feeling for." (pp. 39–40) Allbee's view resembles Horace Kallen's theory of cultural pluralism. Ancestry determines.

His view is related to his own sullen sense of dispossession. He tells Leventhal, much later, of his ancestors. "Do you know, one of my ancestors was Governor Winthrop. Governor Winthrop!" He goes on to bewail fiercely his sense that he is an outsider in his own country: "The old breeds are out. The streets are named for them. But what are they themselves? Just remnants." (pp. 144–45) The assertion that the old breeds die out is almost certainly an echo of Longfellow's poem on the Jewish cemetery at Newport, a bit of subtle irony. In this same conversation, Allbee complains, ". . . last week I saw a book about Thoreau and Emerson by a man named Lipschitz." (p. 145) His confusion is manifested by his reference a moment later to the Book of Job, to which he attributes the argument that suffering is the consequence of sin. His allusion characterizes him in that he feels no awkwardness in citing what is, after all, a Jewish book. The irony is compounded by the fact that he misinterprets the Book of Job and cannot possibly have read Thoreau and Emerson, who actually *did* hold views like those he attributes to the Biblical author.

Leventhal rather angrily rejects Allbee's comments about the impropriety of Mr. Lipschitz, but he himself is uneasy about the position of Jews within European and American society. In the cafeteria discussion referred to a moment ago, Leventhal had expressed doubts about the status of the assimilated Jew. Several of the men debate the identity of Benjamin Disraeli—Jew or Englishman? Despite the fact that Disraeli's father was born in England and Disraeli himself was raised as a Christian, one of the group refers to him as "an Italian Jew." The argument grows involved and Leventhal remarks, "I understand they never took him in." Although at first Leventhal is reluctant to speak, he discovers "he was unable to hold back his opinions." It is probable that Allbee's challenge has awakened doubts hitherto repressed. He becomes agitated and even eloquent:

> "Why do you have it in for Disraeli?" demanded Harkavy.
> "I don't have it in for him. But he wanted to lead England. In spite of the fact that he was a Jew, not because he cared about empires so much. People laughed at his nose, so he took up boxing; they laughed at his poetic silk clothes, so he put on black; and they laughed at his books, so he showed them. He got into politics and became the prime minister. He did it all on nerve." (pp. 128–30)

It was all, Leventhal insists, to prove something. It was a weakness rather than a strength of character.

Debating Allbee in the next chapter, Leventhal has shifted positions. Although Bellow does not leave the point without a large portion of ambiguity, Leventhal seems finally to have accepted the fact that he is both Jew and American. Like all Americans, his identity is a combination of inheritance and acquisition. In their last encounter, Allbee notices Mary's pregnancy and remarks, "Congratulations. I see you're following orders. 'Increase and multiply.'" (p. 292) The intimation is, of course, that Leventhal is under orders and follows the God of the Old Testament, as Allbee presumably does not. But Leventhal is now able to accept the remark as a pleasantry rather than a malicious insinuation. Without the dramatic moment of perception of the tragic hero and without the momentous moment of a conversion, without any *conscious* attempt to sort out and to reorder his experience, Leventhal has come to terms with himself. What part of this new sense of self can be attributed to Allbee's assault on Leventhal's sensibility? What part can be traced to traumatic experiences accompanying the death of his nephew (for which Elena seems to blame him)? Bellow never specifies. This is typical of him. If there is one constant in the negative criticism directed against his work, it is that he does not show why his heroes end as they do. In this, his books are as mysterious as life itself. It is enough for us to know that Leventhal has been ushered to his seat.

3   The Adventures of Augie March

Both *Dangling Man* and *The Victim* are well-written novels in the tradition of Gustave Flaubert and Henry James, serious almost to the point of morbidity. In the five years that separated *The Victim* from *The Adventures of Augie March,* Bellow began to publish pieces of a comic nature, like "Sermon by Doctor Pep" and "Address by Gooley MacDowell to the Hasbeens Club of Chicago." [10] Secure now in his sense of himself as a writer, he was ready to indulge himself as an unsurpassed comedian. The themes of *Augie March* are variants of the familiar ones, but the style is transformed. Augie

March is the picaresque hero who tells his own story with a gusty eloquence beyond that of Bellow's previous characters. The language is so appropriate to the theme that one is tempted to say the language *is* the theme. One young critic found "a willed and empty affirmation which showed itself in the forced spontaneity of the prose," [11] but the book was Bellow's first great critical and commercial success.

The first paragraph is characteristic of Bellow's new style:

> I am an American, Chicago born—Chicago, that sombre city— and go at things as I have taught myself, free-style, and will make the record in my own way: first to knock, first admitted; sometimes an innocent knock, sometimes a not so innocent. But a man's character is his fate, says Heraclitus, and in the end there isn't any way to disguise the nature of the knocks by acoustical work on the door or gloving the knuckles.[12] (p. 3)

The language is loose, colloquial, with parenthetical inserted remarks rather than clauses of subordination and superordination. The metaphors are drawn "free-style" from the many realms traversed, vicariously or actually, by the much-traveled and much-read narrator. The allusion to Greek philosophy is tossed into the paragraph amidst a scatter of images from sports, business, and engineering. The variety of the language and the range of the allusions are very like the variety and range of Melville's *Moby-Dick*, directly alluded to later in the text. Emerson wrote that "America is a poem in our eyes" and encouraged poets to explore the commonplace. Bellow follows in the line of those who have taken Emerson at his word. He fills his book with minutely particularized descriptions of Chicago in the 1920s and 1930s:

> In the [elevator] cage we rose and dropped, rubbing elbows with bigshots and operators, commissioners, grabbers, heelers, tipsters, hoodlums, wolves, fixers, plaintiffs, flatfeet, men in Western hats and women in lizard shoes and fur coats, hot-house and arctic drafts mixed up, brute things and airs of sex, evidence of heavy feeding and systematic shaving, of calculations in concrete to be poured or whole Mississippis of bootleg whisky and beer. (p. 39)

He fills his book with a thousand references to the tragic, the comic, the villainous and noble through the span of history. Augie March knows how to use the freedom that Joseph, in *Dangling Man,* did not.

Curiously, Augie March and Henderson the Rain King derive, like poor Joseph, from concerns first articulated in 1941 in "Two Morning Monologues." The second monologue was a gambler's. He told of the excitement of winning and losing, of taking life as a game. Augie's own view is that there is a share for him in all that has happened. He too wants to be cut in on life's deal. He can *see* greatness, can *understand* the extremes of heroism and humiliation, can respond to the gestures and speeches fixed forever in history and in literature. His realism is never the renunciation of romance; he names Caesar, Ulysses, Machiavelli, and goes on:

> . . . if we don't have any special wish to abdicate into some different, lower form of existence out of shame for our defects before the golden faces of these and other old-time men, then I have the right to praise Einhorn and not care about smiles or derogation from those who think the race no longer has in any important degree the traits we honor in these fabulous names. (p. 60)

He likens crippled Einhorn to Socrates and himself to Alcibiades and insists that he is free to model himself on whom he will:

> We had title just as good as the chain-mail English kings had to Brutus. If you want to pick your own ideal creature in the mirror coastal air and sharp leaves of ancient perfections and be at home where a great mankind was at home, I've never seen any reason why not. (p. 76)

Despite his enthusiasms, Augie has no foolish notions about his own ability to fall, like Cato, on his sword, or to stand as Roland stood at Roncesvalles. Unlike his brother Simon, who was taken in by Tom Brown's schooldays and a number of other influences "we were not in a position to afford" (p. 4), Augie lacks the illusions that are prerequisite to disillusionment. He writes with an eye to perfection but also with a sense of the abyss that separates the actual from the imagined. Like the speaker of John Hollander's "The Great Bear," he knows that desire alone does not establish fact.

> Everyone tries to create a world he can live in, and what he can't use he often can't see. But the real world is already created,

and if your fabrication doesn't correspond, then even if you feel
noble and insist on there being something better than what
people call reality, that better something needn't try to exceed
what, in its actuality, since we know it so little, may be very
surprising. (p. 378)

Like Asa Leventhal, Augie March accepts the conditions within
which we live. But Augie makes a good deal more of them.

One symbol of Augie's ironic and disorganized passion for greatness (in others) is the fire-damaged set of classics that he inherits
from Einhorn. He drags with him President Eliot's unwieldy dis-
tillation of the world's wisdom (so that he is deep in Schiller's *History of the Thirty Years' War* when Mimi Villars comes to involve
him in an up-to-date disaster). Augie is the comic hero who looks
at his own misadventures and grins, "That's the *animal ridens* in
me . . ." (p. 536) He ends his story with the thought of a new
beginning, with one last allusion to greatness:

> Why, I am a sort of Columbus of those near-at-hand and be-
> lieve you can come to them in this immediate *terra incognita*
> that spreads out in every gaze. I may well be a flop at this line
> of endeavor. Columbus too thought he was a flop, probably,
> when they sent him back in chains. Which didn't prove there
> was no America. (p. 536)

Augie is the Columbus of the commonplace, another Whitman, in
open shirt and panama hat. Although persistent efforts have been
made to connect Augie with the archetype of the *schlemiel* (who
never gets anything right), his breezy confidence, his appetite for
experience, his extraordinary self-awareness, and his obvious delight
in the gamut of the American language relates him to the speaker
of "Song of Myself" rather than to the plaintive protagonist of Isaac
Bashevis Singer's "Gimpel the Fool." [13] For Augie, marginality is
possibility. If his story is, as has been asserted, a confession, he is a
remarkably cocky penitent.[14]

Although Augie is not literally an orphan, "People have been
adoptive towards me, as if I were really an orphan." (p. 103) Metaphorically he *is* an orphan or, in his words, "an adoptee." The irony
is that he is more at home in the world than those who wish to
adopt and thus to define and limit him. It is, moreover, possible to

see the entire novel as a series of episodes in which families and individuals attempt to adopt Augie while he, always tempted by the attractions of *stasis*, manages nonetheless to evade them.

The family into which he is literally born is no family at all. His father has deserted his mother long before the narration commences. Mrs. March is a kind but nearly helpless creature under the domination of "Grandma" Lausch, who is actually no relative of the Marches. Grandma is the first of many who attempt to wrest Augie to their will. The old woman, with her pretensions and passions, dominates the first chapter. Remembering her outburst when he came back from the library with a book on religion ("because it says Tolstoi on the cover" [p. 11]), Augie is reminded of her irreverence and of his own minimal Jewishness.

Although Grandma Lausch never attends the synagogue, eats bread on Passover, and loves canned lobster, she still burns a candle on the anniversary of her husband's death. She is not quite an atheist. She practices a "kitchen religion" that "had nothing to do with the giant God of the Creation who turned back the waters and exploded Gomorrah but it was on the side of religion at that." Augie's relationship to the Law is even more peripheral:

> . . . sometimes we were chased, stoned, bitten, and beat up for Christ-killers, all of us, even Georgie, articled, whether we liked it or not, to this mysterious trade. But I never had any special grief from it, or brooded, being by and large too larky and boisterous to take it to heart. . . . (p. 12)

The metaphor from the era of apprenticeship is significant. There is a strangely contractual quality to the relationship. It is a contract that Augie breaks effortlessly and almost without thought: "It wasn't my nature to fatigue myself with worry over being born to this occult work." (p. 12) He dismisses his status as a Jew as one might dismiss theosophy or the heresies of the Hindus. Augie is, as he says, an American, Chicago born. Nonetheless, critics have gone on at length about his Jewishness:

> Augie is a *talmid* (permanent student) and this is a prime characteristic of a Jew. . . . To sit at the feet of a sage is very much the act of a Jew. The succession of men who counsel Augie, generally at the metaphysical level, are rabbis, if we take the word in its true meaning—teacher.[15]

In his happy application of the philosopher's stone, the uncritical critic has missed the point. Augie March is not one who has been chosen. Among the myriad factors that condition choice, he will pick and choose for himself.

Much of the time, his choice is simply the refusal to let others choose for him. Chapter 2 sets Augie in the midst of the Coblin family, his relatives. Bellow describes the Coblins and their milieu in great detail. He creates a whole new context that momentarily displaces the world dominated by Grandma Lausch. Detailed characterization of the Coblins—for example, of Anna Coblin's boastful brother, "Five Properties"—makes Augie's adoption into this household eminently plausible. Anna Coblin sees him as an inadequate replacement for her son, who has run off to the Marines, and as an appropriate husband for her daughter. She *greets* him with the announcement of her plans: "Hear, Owgie, you'll be my son, my daughter's husband, *mein kind!*" But Augie fails her. "Even at that time I couldn't imagine that I would marry into the Coblin family." (p. 17) And he fails his brother Simon, who has moved from childish dreams of chivalry to the humdrum, mundane, and mildly dishonest vending of newspapers, magazines, and cigars. Augie proves to be a poor clerk and, in the next chapter, a totally inadequate thief.

In Chapter 5, Augie moves into the orbit of William Einhorn, a crippled manipulator of men and money, "the first superior man I knew." (p. 60) Again, Bellow creates a whole new world of Einhornism to displace the environments from which Augie has come. A plethora of Einhorns crowd the stage and push the Marches and the Coblins into the wings. Einhorn's father, half-brother, son—they all play important parts. Each is amply characterized. Einhorn wants Augie not as son and heir but as retainer, servant, and disciple. He is the Sun King of South Chicago and Augie is his Chamberlain. There is no doubt that crippled Einhorn's compensatory energy attracts Augie. His rhetoric is so similar to Augie's that certain speeches might have been made by either man. He too broods on Socrates and Alcibiades. He begins to quote Shakespeare and ends in Yiddish: "What a piece of work is a man, and the firmament frotted with gold—but the whole *gescheft* bores him." (p. 75) He too is an assimilator, a lover of images and episodes, an almost insane collector of commercial samples, come-ons, offers, odds and ends. Einhorn becomes almost a parody of Augie's own *Weltan-schauung*, a pathetic figure carried to a brothel on Augie's back in complicated reversal of the mythical prostitute whom legend placed on the back of love-stricken Aristotle.

From Einhorn's sphere of influence, Augie moves on to that of the Renlings. Mr. Renling, a haberdasher, outfits Augie in a version of English style, arranges for riding lessons, sends Augie on excursions. Mrs. Renling takes him as a companion to the resort at Benton Harbor, plans for his education, and formally proposes adoption. Augie refuses, partly because he is now in love with beautiful Esther Fenchel, whose sister Thea loves him (and will return to carry him off to Mexico).

Between Benton Harbor and Mexico, however, Augie passes through a maze of adventures and avoids each *cul de sac*. Falling foolishly under the influence of Joe Gorman, a gangster, he goes off to smuggle immigrants in from Canada and must himself flee the police, hitchhike, ride the rails, spend a night in jail, and feel him-self lucky to return safely to Chicago. Much more important is the influence of Augie's brother Simon, who wants him to marry as Simon has into the Magnus family. Simon is now the disillusioned and cynical young man on the make. Ruthless and talented, he is clearly bound to be rich. He employs Augie and arranges his en-gagement to Lucy Magnus, but Augie—although he thinks himself ready to settle for ordinary existence—becomes involved with Mimi Villars, a girl sought by several of his friends, a large-busted, tight-skirted young lady with "high heels that gave a tight arch of impa-tience to the muscles of her calves. . . ." (p. 204) When her boy friend gets her pregnant, she seeks an abortion, which is bungled. It is Augie who sticks by her through a wild night in which he and a friend find a hospital that will take her in. Spotted by a hostile member of the Magnus clan, Augie is reported and the engagement is off. Simon is enraged and Augie is bemused. It was inevitable.

He becomes the organizer of a union and begins an affair with a chambermaid, Sophie Geratis, but Thea Fenchel reappears to prove that his political commitments are superficial. When she knocks at his door, Sophie rises from his bed and departs in as good a humor as can be expected in such circumstances. The union is forgotten. Thea is consumed by a purpose: "She was one of those

people who are so certain of their convictions that they can fight
for them in the body." (p. 316) Augie turns to her as Ishmael turned
to crazy Captain Ahab. Thea's plan is to train an eagle to hunt
iguanas. The "fiery hunt" is now *with* rather than *for* a symbolic
animal.

Augie bewails his foolishness:

> Oh, you chump and weak fool, you are one of a humanity that
> can't be numbered and not more than the dust of metals scat-
> tered in a magnetic field and clinging to the lines of force,
> determined by laws, eating, sleeping, employed, conveyed, obedi-
> ent, and subject. So why hunt for still more ways to lose
> liberty? (p. 316)

He protests weakly, "Do we have to go to Mexico?" (p. 323) But
against her he is as ineffectual as Starbuck against Ahab. Off they
go.

The Valley of Mexico blazes with blue as it did for D. H. Lawrence, and Augie is soon excited by Thea's impetuous prospect. The
situation is richly comic. Augie is not a hero:

> Seeing that fierce animal in his cage, I felt darkness, and then
> a streaming on my legs as if I had wet myself: it wasn't so, it
> was only something to do with my veins. But I really felt dazed
> in all my nerves when I saw with what we would have to deal,
> and dark before the eyes. The bird looked to be close kin to the
> one that lit on Prometheus once a day. (p. 331)

The bird perches in the bathroom on the waterbox and seems to
menace Augie in his least heroic moments: an image of the visionary within the mundane. The eagle is appropriately named Caligula,
for the mad emperor (who attracted Albert Camus as well as Bellow), when the Spanish boys shout *"El águila, el águila!"* The
ironies are intensified when it turns out that Caligula is a coward.
Bitten by a lizard, he flees; in the face of opposition, he gives up.
Thea is furious; Augie is sympathetic.

After suitable further adventures, Augie is "adopted" by a certain
Stella, who asks him to help her evade her lover. The flight is comic.
It begins with Thea's attempt to halt them, leads to the brink of
disaster (when the car nearly goes over a cliff), and ends with the
"one appropriate thing." (p. 390) They make love. Augie returns

for the moment to Thea, but it is Stella whom he will eventually marry, for reasons which she sees clearly at this time: ". . . one of the things I thought is that you and I are the kind of people other people are always trying to fit into their schemes. So suppose we didn't play along, then what?" (p. 384) Before Augie realizes that Stella is the perfect match for his restless adventuresomeness, he pursues Thea, returns to Chicago, makes the rounds and visits the personages of his life, and works briefly as research assistant for a fanatical millionaire who wants to write a pre-Galbraithean book on the miseries of abundance Finally, he returns to Stella. To her Armenian friend, Mintouchian, on the fifty-eighth story of a building in mid-town Manhattan, Augie articulates the truth he has discovered: "I will never force the hand of fate to create a better Augie March, nor change the time to an age of gold." (p. 485) With the mysterious blessings of Mr. Mintouchian, Augie marries Stella, ships out with the merchant marine, survives a torpedo and the insanity of a man with whom he shares an open boat, moves to France for the postwar high life, and writes his autobiography.

Stella makes movies. Augie makes money, in more or less legal deals sponsored by Mintouchian. They live in Paris, which Augie refers to as the City of Man. He wants to open a school for orphans, for poor fellows as disadvantaged as his brother Georgie (a half-wit who plays his small part in the novel),* but Augie knows that he never will. His dream is the perennial dream of Arcadia, of the pastoral landscape:

> What I had in my mind was this private green place like one of those Walden or Innisfree wattle jobs under the kind sun, surrounded by velvet woods and bright gardens and Elysium lawns sown with Lincoln Park grass seed. However, we are meant to be carried away by the complex and hear the simple like the far horn of Roland when he and Oliver are being wiped out by the Saracens. (p. 515)

The dream of a foster home was "not a preoccupation but one of those featherhead millenarian notions or summer butterflies. You should never try to cook such butterflies in lard." (p. 516)

---

* It is possible that Bellow shows the reader the March family, with its simple-minded mother and half-wit son, to suggest the impossibility of Augie March's finding any sanctuary in domestic institutions.

Augie's acceptance is not despair. He insists on the word uttered despite the silence, on the act committed despite its apparent futility: "When finally you're done speaking you're dumb forever after, and when you're through stirring you go still, but this is no reason to decline to speak and stir or to be what you are." (p. 519) Acceptance for him is alignment with the "axial lines" of fate, but his fate is to be ordinary in an extraordinary way. He is indeed fated to be the Columbus of the commonplace, and he will accept that fate. He will endow the diurnal with a wonder comparable to that of the Conquistadores.

4 *Seize the Day*

Augie March succeeds. Tommy Wilhelm, hero of *Seize the Day* (1956), fails. The differences between them are more remarkable than the similarity of their circumstances, but their circumstances *are* similar in that both are figuratively orphans, both are men without a fixed place in the social system. In Tommy Wilhelm's case, his father—aged, rich, successful Dr. Adler—is physically present but emotionally distant. (One can also conjecture that the doctor, whose name means "eagle," is somehow related to Augie's Caligula: the intractable other.) Tommy's adolescent rebellion failed in a fizzle of infantile aspirations that he himself recognized were doomed. Now a grown man with an estranged wife, he continues to seek his father's love. He remains unable to accept his fate as an ordinary man among others of no special significance. Unable to follow Schlossberg's advice and to "choose dignity," he becomes a buffoon. *Seize the Day* is, therefore, a cautionary tale.

Augie knows that greatness is a rare and risky thing, but Tommy doesn't. He and his father, a retired professor of medicine, live in the aptly, ironically named Hotel Gloriana on or near Upper Broadway. "Among these old people at the Gloriana, Wilhelm felt out of place," because he is "comparatively young" but also because their identities are set, their lives lived, their fates known or calculated.[16] (p. 4) In an image, Bellow characterizes him:

> He saw his reflection in the glass cupboard full of cigar boxes, among the grand seals and paper damask and the gold-embossed portraits of famous men, Garcia, Edward the Seventh, Cyrus the

Great. You had to allow for the darkness and deformations of the glass, but he thought he didn't look too good. (p. 6)

He has set his goals too high and has failed to reach them. Augie March, knowing that greatness was a complex fate, settled for less, but Tommy continues to rush, more and more frantically, up and down the closed corridor of his life. There is no magic door through which one steps to glory.

Tommy's first great mistake, now recognized by him as foolishness, was his desire to become an actor: "He was to be freed from the anxious and narrow life of the average." (p. 23) On the basis of a screen test that turned out badly, against the advice of an agent, and against his parents' will, Tommy rushed out to Hollywood, changed his name, and barely survived as an extra. The screen test revealed the truth, as the glass of the cupboard did: there is a weakness in him, a lesion in the sense of selfhood.

Tommy has also, some months before the action of the novella begins, given up his job as a salesman and walked out on his wife and children. He has, immediately before the story's single day of action, given the last of his money to a certain Dr. Tamkin, an enigmatic figure who represents both a father and a tempter. He promises riches (through investments in lard and other commodities), and he offers the concern and advice that Dr. Adler refuses. Tamkin's advice is by no means eccentric: "The past is no good to us. The future is full of anxiety. Only the present is real—the here-and-now. Seize the day." (p. 66) Unfortunately, Tamkin encourages Tommy in his worst fault, in his tendency to see within the here-and-now some sudden opportunity that, if seized, will bring to realization his dreamy wish for success. Tamkin claims to have lived among the great and to have shared their life, to have been accepted, for example, among the princes and princesses of pre-Nasser Cairo. Tommy distrusts him but falls into temptation, gives him his last seven hundred dollars, loses all, and collapses.

Between the handing over of the money and the final collapse, Tommy tries vainly to penetrate the defenses that surround his father. His father, like some hidden god, wants filial worship but no requests, no entreaties. He suggests that Tommy give up drugs and take up exercise. When Tommy leaves a note asking that he "carry him" with the hotel's cashier, he refuses to play Aeneas for the youthful Anchises. Tommy begs his father for love, but Dr. Adler, sprawled upon the hotel masseur's table, raises himself up and rejects his son:

> You want to make yourself into my cross. But I am not going to pick up a cross. I'll see you dead, Wilky, by Christ, before I let you do that to me. . . . Go away from me now. It's a torture for me to look at you, you slob! (p. 110)

The reference to the cross suggests a host of analogies. Dr. Adler is certainly similar to the distant God who allowed Job to suffer while his rival tempted and afflicted him.

Although Tommy is the secular son of a secular Jew, he turns frantically to prayer. His prayer is not traditional:

> Oh, God. . . . Let me out of my trouble. Let me out of my thoughts, and let me do something better with myself. For all the time I have wasted I am very sorry. Let me out of this clutch and into a different life. For I am all balled up. Have mercy. (p. 26)

The language and the intent are both pathetic. By the end of the book, Tommy is capable only of sobs. His wife and he have fought over the telephone. His money is gone, and Tamkin has disappeared. His father has denied him. He wanders desperately into a Jewish chapel and encounters what he least needs, a corpse. Dead hopes? Dead dreams? The symbolic significance is uncertain, but it is the occasion for the final outburst of tears. The last words of the tale are among the most quoted in all of Bellow's work:

> The flowers and lights fused ecstatically in Wilhelm's blind, wet eyes; the heavy sea-like music came up to his ears. It poured into him where he had hidden himself in the center of the crowd by the great and happy oblivion of tears. He heard it and sank deeper than sorrow, through torn sobs and cries toward the consummation of his heart's ultimate need. (p. 118)

Almost every commentator on *Seize the Day* has seen the conclusion as a rebirth. *"Seize the Day,"* writes one of the more acute critics, "does not end in Tommy's masochistic acceptance of his role as victim; it ends in hope for a new life." [17] The final scene is one in which he drowns metaphorically, but it "is also a symbolic rebirth out of water." [18] In Tommy's capacity for grief, there is "the possibility of his freedom." Another critic agrees and extends the argument:

> If Wilhelm "dies" because he has sought to deny the human condition, he also accepts the pain of his human identity at the same time that he transcends it. . . . In the Jewish funeral home he accepts his racial heritage; before the corpse of a stranger he accepts his human heritage.[19]

The difficulty with such interpretations is that marine imagery and Tommy's prior quotations from "Lycidas" and from Shakespeare do not enable the reader to conclude that Tommy has been reborn.[20] The reference to the racial heritage seems quite gratuitous. Bellow never indicates the nature of Tommy's heart's ultimate need. To accept his own failure? It is impossible to say. At this moment, Tommy seems pitiable but hardly tragic. He lacks Augie March's "larky" acceptance of fate and Asa Leventhal's ability unconsciously to assume his place in life's theater. Able neither to struggle greatly nor to adjust to mediocrity, he is the victim of his own weakness and confusion. He is the rebel unable to carry through his rebellion, the emigrant who changes his name and his environment and is then stranded in a romantically imagined noplace. Weeping pathetically before the image of his own death, he is cautionary rather than exemplary.

5   Henderson the Rain King

Reviewing *Henderson the Rain King* in April of 1959, Richard Chase rightly considered *Henderson* a romance and Henderson himself a "brutal, loony, yet finally ennobled" character who is "the momentary equal . . . of the greatest heroes of comic fiction." [21] Chase was in the minority then and still is. *Henderson* was and is a great novelist's only undervalued novel. Some have niggled at what they called "pseudo-portentous mumbo jumbo" and complained that Bellow's Africa is not the Africa of the morning newspaper;[22] other critics have lamented the novel's lack of political reference and found Henderson's "emotional abundance . . . Slavic or Hebraic perhaps but not entirely American. . . ." [23] From the Queen's University in Belfast, Ireland, we are told that Henderson's language is not authentically American.[24] Most often, the conclusion is condemned as inconclusive: Has Henderson really learned anything and, if he has, can he tell us what it is? "How much of what he learned in Africa can be exported?"[25] Why, asks Daniel J. Hughes, does Bellow not bring his hero, at the end, all the way back to the United States? "The flight to a symbolic Africa is inevitable, but so, according to the rhythmic expectation, is Henderson's return [to society]."[26]

What can one answer? Fabulous Henderson's comic quest is ended when he learns to replace one verb (*want*) with two others (*imagine, love*). He cannot tell us what to imagine or whom to love any more than he was able to tell us what it was he wanted. Saul Bellow can tell us how it was that Henderson moved from one verb to another. The movement *is* the book. To want more is to be as Henderson was before he learned to love and to imagine.

Henderson begins where Jay Gatsby would have ended if he could have had all that the green light across the water symbolized —wealth and status, money and love. Of Henderson the envious say, "His great-grandfather was Secretary of State, his great-uncles were ambassadors to England and France, and his father was the famous scholar Willard Henderson who wrote that book on the Albigentsians, a friend of William James and Henry Adams."[27] (p. 7) From his famous father, Henderson inherited three million dollars and a country house designed to flush the countenance of a Jamesian observer. But the money is useless. The first great image of the book is Henderson in the library, literally in pursuit of wisdom in words read and forgotten: "The forgiveness of sins is perpetual and righteousness first is not required."

> I searched through dozens of volumes but all that turned up was money, for my father had used currency for bookmarks— whatever he happened to have in his pockets—fives, tens or twenties. Some of the discontinued bills of thirty years ago turned up, the big yellowbacks. For old times' sake I was glad to see them and locking the library door to keep out the children I spent the afternoon on a ladder shaking out books and the money spun to the floor. But I never found that statement about forgiveness. (pp. 3–4)

Seeking wisdom and finding only money, Henderson is the ironic hero of an age of affluence. Heir to all that Henry James's Kate Croy schemed for and Millie Theale lost and Maggie Verver finally won, Henderson suffers from the inner voice that says incessantly, "I *want!*"

Henderson marries a girl of his own social class: "A remarkable person, handsome, tall, elegant, sinewy, with long arms and golden hair, private, fertile, and quiet." (p. 4) Unsatisfied Henderson moves from bourgeois to Romantic love, from Frances to Lily. The courtship takes place amid a dozen digressions (like all the actions in a novel replete with anticipations and remembrances). Important among the digressions is the confrontation of Henderson and an ominous octopus who swims in relation to Henderson very much as Theodore Dreiser's lobster and squid swim in relation to young Frank Cowperwood in *The Financier*. As Henderson tells it,

> The eyes spoke to me coldly. But even more speaking, even more cold, was the soft head with its speckles, and the Brownian motion in those speckles, a cosmic coldness in which I felt I was dying. The tentacles throbbed and motioned through the glass, the bubbles sped upward, and I thought, "This is my last day. Death is giving me notice." (p. 19)

Through the novel, Henderson is haunted by this vision of death. Inauspiciously begun, the marriage fails to satisfy Henderson, and the "terrible repetition within" ("I want! I want!") continues.

Drunkenness and fights are diversions only. Henderson labors with a Protestant's seriousness and turns for his vocation, like Henry Thoreau before him, to the pastoral mode. With a difference. Thoreau was determined, he tells us in *Walden*, to know beans. Henderson attempts to know pigs; he makes of his estate, in defiance of his outraged neighbors, "a pig kingdom, with pig houses on the lawn and in the flower garden." (p. 20) He empathizes with pigs and thinks of the prophecy of Daniel to Nebuchadnezzar: "They shall drive thee from among men, and thy dwelling shall be with the beasts of the fields." But pigs are not enough.

And art is as useless as money, love, and labor. With Lily at Chartres Cathedral, "in the very face of . . . holy beauty," Henderson threatens suicide. (p. 17) Alone in the basement of his house, he plays the violin and seeks thereby to reach his father: "I played in the basement to my father and my mother, and when I learned a few pieces I would whisper, 'Ma, this is "Humoresque" for you,' Or, 'Pa listen—"Meditation" from *Thais*.' " (p. 30) Most important, Henderson plays from Handel's *The Messiah*: "He was despised and rejected, a man of sorrows and acquainted with grief." The voice of his griefs ("I want!") is louder than the music.

The Messiah introduces, in a book where all things make known other things, still another mode. Henderson's daughter Ricey comes home from Danbury, on the morning of the winter solstice, with a colored baby she has found, she says, in a parked car. Although a virgin has come home with a newborn child, the much put-upon father is, if anything, worse off. "I had to withdraw my daughter from . . . school." (p. 37) Two pages later, the references are pagan rather than Mosaic and Christian:

> In her yard [Mrs. Lenox] had an old catalpa tree of which the trunk and lower limbs were painted light blue. She had fixed little mirrors up there, and old bicycle lights which shone in the dark, and in summer she liked to climb up there and sit with her cats, drinking a can of beer. (p. 39)

Mrs. Lenox, unlike Virgil's sibyl, is mortal. One morning she starts Henderson's breakfast, and dies. He finds breakfast on the stove and Mrs. Lenox on the floor. "Not knowing what else to do, I wrote a note DO NOT DISTURB and pinned it to the old lady's skirt. . . ." (p. 39) Death, however, means as little as birth. Except that Henderson, appalled by the wasted life visible in the old woman's testamentáry half-century of accumulated rubbish, decides to go to Africa.

Henderson moves on from the pastoral to the primitive. The heroes of Henry James and the villains of T. S. Eliot follow Irving's Geoffrey Crayon eastward, to the castles and cathedrals and country houses of a civilization parent to our own; Henderson set off, like Cooper's Natty Bumppo, like Melville's Tommo and Ishmael, like Hemingway's African hunters, to "the real past, no history or junk like that. The prehuman past." [28] (p. 46)

The book, fantastic from the start, becomes an increasingly fabulous series of adventures richly imagined in themselves and doubly effective as ironic parallels to Old Testament stories and anthropological data lifted from *The Golden Bough*.[29] Reaching the

Arnewi in company with a guide (whom Elizabeth Hardwick hit off as a "Travelogue Queequeg"),[30] Henderson performs his first Old Testament miracle: "Without waiting for Romilayu's advice I took out the Austrian lighter with the drooping wick, spun the tiny wheel with my thumb, and immediately a bush went flaming, almost invisible in the strong sunlight." The cows gallop off and the children run away. Henderson is clearly no Moses. "The embers of the bush had fallen by my boots." (p. 48)

Although reluctant to fight ("Your Highness, I am really on a kind of quest"), Henderson wrestles ceremonially with Prince Itelo of the Arnewi, and, like an inverted version of the angel who vanquished Jacob, digs his thumbs into Itelo's thigh and throws him down. "I felt almost as bad as he did." (p. 68) Itelo's aunt, to whom Henderson is introduced by the beaten prince, has no answers. She asks instead, who are you?

> Who—who was I? A millionaire wanderer and wayfarer. A brutal and violent man driven into the world. A man who fled his own country, settled by his forefathers. A fellow whose heart said, *I want, I want*. Who played the violin in despair, seeking the voice of angels. Who had to burst the spirit's sleep, or else. (p. 76)

For Queen Willatale and her sister Mtalba, Henderson sings the thematic aria from *The Messiah*; from them, he receives a bit of wisdom which Bellow clearly recognizes as a cliché from the days of E. M. Forster and D. H. Lawrence: "Grun-tu-molani. Man want to live." (p. 85) In gratitude for this perception, Henderson sets off on another misadventure. The land is stricken by a drought and the cistern is clogged with frogs. With a do-it-yourself bomb constructed of flashlight case, shoelace, and Band-Aid, Henderson is a Connecticut Yankee in the Court of the Fisher King, Rube Goldberg's Grail Quester, a utilitarian Moses fanatically turned against the frogs. The bomb destroys the cistern and leaves the stricken Arnewi worse off than before. It is, remarks J. C. Levenson in one of the best essays on Bellow, "a fable against salvation by good works which puts Graham Greene's *Quiet American* in the shade." [31] Mtalba's comment is, in Romilayu's translation, "Goo' by. Fo'evah." (p. 111)

Henderson and Romilayu move, with echoes of Joseph's voyage to Egypt, to the land of the Wariri. They spend their first night moving and removing a corpse left in the hut. (They later learn that the corpse is the recently deceased Rain King, whom Henderson will succeed.) The next day Henderson watches ceremonies that owe more in their sources to genius than to Rider Haggard. Amazons dance. One plays a game with King Dahfu. The two of them toss through the air the ribboned skulls of Dahfu's predecessors:

> The woman threw her skull. The thick purple and blue ribbons made it look like a flower in the air. I swear before God, it appeared just like a gentian. In midair it passed the skull coming from the hand of the king. Both came streaming down with the blue satin ribbons following, as if they were a couple of ocean polyps. . . . She behaved like a priestess, seeing to it that he came up to the mark. Because of the gold paint and Braille marks on her face she looked somewhat inhuman. As she sprang, dancing, her breasts were fixed, as if really made of gold, and because of her length and thinness, when she leaped it was something supernatural, like a giant locust. (pp. 174–75)

After the game and the dances that follow, Henderson attempts to move the gigantic idol Mummah, which no native has been strong enough to move. Henderson succeeds and becomes the Rain King. Whereupon the Amazons chase him through a cloudburst and pound him, throw him into the mud, and leave him, finally, "in my coat of earth, like a giant turnip." (p. 202)

Henderson is now ready for his descent into the Underworld. Dahfu guides him downward, to the cage of the lion Atti. Comparisons with Melville's emblematic whale and Faulkner's mythic bear (and Augie March's eagle) are inescapable and probably intentional. The contrasts are greater than the points of likeness. Ahab hunts in order to destroy the visible symbol of an invisible and intolerable malignity, in order to "burst his hot heart's shell upon it." Ike McCaslin hunts in order to be initiated into the realm of primeval nature existing before man and after him. Henderson seeks only to quiet the voice "repeating, *I want,* raving and demanding, making a chaos, desiring, desiring, and disappointed continually, which drove me forth as beaters drive game." (p. 210) In

fear and trembling, Henderson fulfills the thrice-quoted prophecy
of Daniel:

> And so I was the beast. I gave myself to it, and all my sorrow
> came out in the roaring. My lungs supplied the air but the
> note came from my soul. The roaring scalded my throat and
> hurt the corners of my mouth and presently filled the den like
> a bass organ pipe. This was where my heart had sent me, with
> its clamor. This is where I ended up. Oh, Nebuchadnezzar!
> How well I understand that prophecy of Daniel. For I had
> claws, and hair, and some teeth, and I was bursting with hot
> noise, but when all this had come forth, there was still a re-
> mainder. That last thing of all was my human longing.

The voice is unstilled. "When I could do no more I fell flat on my
face." (pp. 267–68) Henderson (recovered) is ready for Dahfu's
praise of the creative imagination.

> Birds flew, harpies flew, angels flew, Daedalus and son flew.
> . . . You flew here, into Africa. All human accomplishment
> has this same origin, identically. Imagination is a force of na-
> ture. Is this not enough to make a person full of ecstasy?
> Imagination, imagination, imagination! It converts to actual.
> It sustains, it alters, it redeems! (p. 271)

Imagination is, of course, the "shaping spirit" of Romantic poets
from Coleridge to Wallace Stevens, of philosophers from Nietzsche
to Sartre. The ecstasy Bellow shares with Camus (in *his* African
essays); the comic qualifications are Bellow's own acknowledgment
of the triteness of truth and his chastisement of those whom possibility makes solemn.

One step more leads Henderson to the most common discovery
of all: we must love one another or die. He writes a long letter to
Lily and asks her to enroll him in medical school (as Leo E. Henderson) so that he can follow the course of Albert Schweitzer. As
he writes of Franklinian desires, Whitmanesque imagery blossoms:

> It is very early in life, and I am out in the grass. The sun flames
> and swells; the heat it emits is its love, too. I have this self-
> same vividness in my heart. There are dandelions. I try to
> gather up this green. I put my love-swollen cheek to the yellow
> of the dandelions. I try to enter into the green. (p. 283)

Henderson might almost go on from Whitman's "Song of Myself":

> I depart as air, I shake my white locks at the runaway sun,
> I effuse my flesh in eddies, and drift it in lacy jags.
> I bequeath myself to the dirt to grow from the grass I love,
> If you want me again look for me under your boot-soles.

To Lily, Henderson writes (or thinks—he himself is unclear): "I had a voice that said, I want! *I* want? I? It should have told me *she* wants, *he* wants, *they* want. And moreover, it's love that makes reality reality." (p. 286) The movement is from verb to verb, from *want* to *imagine* and to *love;* the movement is also one of pronouns, from *I* to *they*. And Henderson is as good as his grammar. He joins Dahfu in the hunt for the lion Gmilo, Dahfu's father reincarnated. The terrible hunt ends as Dahfu falls from his frail platform into the reach of the lion (who turns out not to have been Gmilo after all).

Henderson weeps not for himself but for his friend, until he discovers that the Rain King is the king's successor.

> Then I said, "Your Majesty, move over and I'll die beside you. Or else be me and live; I never knew what to do with life anyway, and I'll die instead." I began to rub and beat my face with my knuckles, crouching in the dust between the dead lion and the dying king. (p. 312)

In the conventional philosophical terms that Henderson himself used in an early colloquy with Dahful, Henderson embraces the world as Becoming and rejects the world as Being. Henderson *had* longed for Being; "Being people have all the breaks. Becoming people are very unlucky, always in a tizzy. The Becoming people are always having to make explanations or offer justifications to the Being people." (p. 160) He has learned now to accept himself as one of the Becoming people. He can play the roles of Rain King and leonine roarer *de profundis* and aide-de-camp in Dahfu's campaign to trap his father's transposed spirit; but he will not *be* a lion or a king. He grabs up a lion cub (whom he names Dahfu) and flees.

The book ends with two magnificent scenes, one remembered,

one enacted. Henderson remembers Smolak the bear, with whom he had, as an adolescent, ridden a roller-coaster in an amusement park: "By a common bond of despair we embraced, cheek to cheek, as all support seemed to leave us and we started down the perpendicular drop. I was pressed into his long-suffering, age-worn, tragic, and discolored coat as he grunted and cried to me." Henderson then describes himself in the Biblical metaphor that was one of Melville's favorites (and Hawthorne's): "Smolak was cast off and I am an Ishmael too." (p. 338) Now Henderson follows the reference to Ishmael with a Transcendentalist's interpretation. "Nature," wrote Emerson, "is the symbol of spirit. . . . Particular natural facts are symbols of particular spiritual facts." This perception maddened Ahab, for whom "all visible objects" were but "pasteboard masks" to be struck through in an effort to destroy the malign something they surely symbolized. But Emerson's perception is turned by Henderson to happier uses:

> If corporeal things are an image of the spiritual and visible objects are renderings of invisible ones, and if Smolak and I were outcasts together, two humorists before the crowd, but brothers in our souls—I enbeared by him, and he probably humanized by me—I didn't come to the pigs as a tabula rasa. (pp. 338-39)

Who but Bellow could mix references to Melville, Emerson, pigs, and John Locke?

In the final scene, Bellow dramatizes love and imagination. While the plane bringing Henderson home refuels in Newfoundland, he grabs up another outcast, an American boy born in Persia and bereft of father, mother, and mother tongue. With the orphan in his arms and the cub in the plane, Henderson runs in the cold morning air, round and round the plane:

> Laps and laps I galloped around the shining and riveted body of the plane, behind the fuel trucks. Dark faces were looking from within. The great beautiful propellers were still, all four of them. I guess I felt it was my turn now to move, and so went running—leaping, leaping, pounding, and tingling over the pure white lining of the gray Arctic silence. (pp. 340-41)

Kindred spirit now to Walt Whitman, who contained multitudes and rejoiced to imagine himself "stucco'd with quadrupeds and birds all over," Henderson leaps with joy that men can love airplanes and orphans and lion cubs. The world is, as again and again in American literature, newly found (i.e. Newfoundland) in the renaissance of dawn. ("There is more day to dawn," wrote Thoreau characteristically; "The sun is but a morning star.") The world lies white and silent all about, not with the terror of ambiguity (as in Poe's *Narrative of Arthur Gordon Pym* or Melville's "The Whiteness of the Whale"), but with the joy of possibility. Marcus Klein, in an excellent essay, wrote that Henderson achieves the "consummation of his heart's desire" (the phrase is from *Seize the Day*) through a "Nietzschean notion of heroic self-transcendence based on freedom . . ." [32] but Americans too have been Transcendentalists. Emerson, Whitman, and William James, in their very different ways, wrote of human freedom in lovely imagined worlds ever various and new. We find it hard today, if not impossible, to sustain their enthusiasm. Bellow's achievement counters the current. He acknowledges, through the ironic hyperboles of the comic mode, the qualifications dramatized in the darker tradition of Hawthorne and Melville; nonetheless, he masters art's paradox and reproduces in written language the excited, disorderly buzz and bloom of life itself. Should we not, even in an age of anxiety, leap with joy as best we can?

6   Herzog

Moses Herzog embodies a much less strenuous version of Bellow's acceptance of the human condition. His professional milieu is quite unlike that of Bellow's previous protagonists, but *Herzog* (1964) is clearly a continuation of the themes and tricks of style of its author's earlier books. The milieu *is*, of course, important, as Moses Herzog might say, with a quotation from Hippolyte Taine. American literature now includes numerous novels set within colleges and universities, but few of them have characters as authentically intellectual as Moses E. Herzog. Small wonder then that academic critics, with very few exceptions, embraced Bellow's hero as one of them. Here is the secular Jew in one of his most familiar social roles, the professor.

Moses Herzog, despite his name, is no lawgiver to his people. From the German possibilities of his surname, he may be seen as a man of noble heart, a feel-er rather than a do-er. He remembers his childhood in Montreal, his mother and father, the life of Canadian Jews, but his energies are divided between his academic efforts to write the definitive book on Romanticism and his personal struggle to survive domestic shipwreck. Since the domestic crisis is intimately related to the Romanticism of the scholarship, there is no real division between the professional and the private man. The symbol of this unity, and the literary device most notable in the book, is the series of letters, mostly unmailed, which Herzog writes to everyone under the sun. The ideas of his intellectual life enter into personal letters, into communiqués, appeals, ruminations. Finally, his attainment of a provisional peace with himself is integrally related to his rejection of the Romantic fascination with sickness, alienation, the apocalypse. Here is Bellow's provisional farewell to marginality, his adoption of the pastoral motif.

The book opens and closes in the country, in Western Massachusetts, in a rambly house in the Berkshires. Herzog is a new Thoreau who has signed a truce with American culture. "Normally particular about food, he now ate Silvercup bread from the paper package, beans from the can, and American cheese." [33] (p. 1) The first two pages characterize Herzog as a man transcendentally tranquil. His first unspoken words suggest madness, "If I am out of my mind, it's all right with me, thought Moses Herzog," (p. 1) but it is sanity that has seized him, not madness. The rest of the book concerns the devious ways that have brought him to live at peace with field mice and the stars.

The book's structure is enough to overtax the casual reader. After approximately a page and a half of the present, in the Berkshires, the action shifts to several different pasts—the distant past of Herzog's childhood, the previous fall, winter, and spring, and the week immediately prior to Herzog's arrival in the Berkshires. Since the time often shifts within a sentence, the reader is forced to become an active participant in the reconstruction of Herzog's life.

"Late in spring," begins the explanation, "Herzog had been overcome by the need to explain, to have it out, to justify, to put in perspective, to clarify, to make amends." (p. 2) His classes had disintegrated into thoughtful rambles. He saw himself then as narcissistic, masochistic, anachronistic. He saw himself a failure in the network of social relations—a bad son, citizen, father, husband, scholar.

Among a thousand moments, one stands out with special clarity, the moment when Herzog realized that his second wife, Madeleine, wanted to leave him. The moment is remembered with peculiar detachment:

> In the window on glass shelves there stood an ornamental collection of small glass bottles, Venetian and Swedish. They came with the house. The sun now caught them. They were pierced with the light. Herzog saw the waves, the threads of color, the spectral intersecting bars, and especially a great blot of flaming white on the center of the wall above Madeleine. She was saying, "We can't live together any more." (p. 9)

Even as she spoke, he realized that it was a rehearsed performance to which it was the duty of the sophisticated man to pay respect. The villain in the piece is one Valentine Gersbach, who has been described as "a paper imitation of the real man of heart, an *ersatz* Herzog." [34] Surrendering his wife to the gimpy, ungainly, disloyal friend of his first residence in the Berkshires, Herzog sought recompense in the traditional Romantic way. "Herzog had Ramona." She is almost a parody of the heroine of Romantic opera:

> She walked with quick efficiency, rapping her heels in energetic Castilian style. Herzog was intoxicated by this clatter. She entered a room provocatively, swaggering slightly, one hand touching her thigh, as though she carried a knife in her garter belt. It seemed to be the fashion in Madrid. . . . (pp. 14, 16)

From her, Herzog rushes to Libbie Vane and her third husband, on Martha's Vineyard, and from the Vineyard back to New York, without staying a night on the island.

Memories are more important than sexual distractions, but the memories are often of other women—a Polish beauty, a voluptuously soapy Oriental. Other memories concern Dr. Edvig, Herzog's "calm Protestant Nordic Anglo-Celtic" psychiatrist, prophet of a fashionable Romanticism that Herzog rejects: "I've read your stuff about the psychological realism of Calvin. I hope you don't mind my saying that it reveals a lousy, cringing, grudging conception of human nature. This is how I see your Protestant Freudianism." (pp. 53, 57–58) Herzog berates Dr. Edvig because Madeleine, whom the doctor had called a saint, took his daughter and called the police to make sure Herzog wasn't able to see the child.

In his denunciation of Valentine Gersbach, Herzog takes out after the philosophy of Martin Buber, the most widely read Jewish theologian of the twentieth century. Gersbach, a celebrator of modernized Judaism, admired Buber's books and presented them to Herzog, who disparages them to Edvig:

> I'm sure you know the views of Buber. It is wrong to turn a man (a subject) into a thing (an object). By means of spiritual dialogue, the I-It relationship becomes an I-Thou relationship. God comes and goes in man's soul. And men come and go in each other's souls. Sometimes they come and go in each other's beds, too. You have dialogue with a man. You have intercourse with his wife. (p. 64)

The preacher of the I-Thou relationship turns to carnal relationships and then, complains Herzog, claims to be the greater sinner and therefore the greater sufferer—and, therefore, the most worthy of sympathy. But Herzog feels excessively, at this moment, that *he* deserves the sympathy.

The sixth (unnumbered) section concludes with what Herzog refers to as Reality Instruction. After a night with Ramona, Herzog goes to consult with a lawyer and wanders in to observe a series of courtroom scenes. Some are comic, but one chills Herzog to the bone. A crippled woman with an I.Q. of 94 stands trial for the murder of her illegitimate son. The boy, a malnourished three-year-old whose body showed signs of frequent beatings, was hurled against the wall until he died. How can anyone believe in "Progress" or in the "Fatherhood of God and the Brotherhood of Man" when the death of innocents takes place every day?

> The child screamed, clung, but with both arms the girl hurled it against the wall. On her legs was ruddy hair. And her lover, too, with long jaws and zooty sideburns, watching on the bed. Lying down to copulate, and standing up to kill. Some kill, then cry. Others, not even that. (p. 240)

No wonder then that Herzog's sentimental desire for "potato love," for universal undifferentiated affection, withers away.

Herzog flies from New York to Chicago, goes to his stepmother's house, takes his father's pistol and some Czarist money (emblems of his father and of Europe), and sets out to kill Valentine Gersbach. Finding him bathing his daughter June, Herzog has not the heart for murder. Unseen, he departs.

> To shoot him!—an absurd thought. As soon as Herzog saw the actual person giving an actual bath, the reality of it, the tenderness of such a buffoon to a little child, his intended violence turned into *theater,* into something ludicrous. (p. 258)

He arranges, instead, to spend a day with June. He turns out to be the hapless *schlemiel* of Yiddish literature. Wrecking his rented car, he is found with pistol and Russian rubles, taken to the police station, and denounced by vindictive Madeleine—more instruction in Reality. Giving up the pistol and the rubles, Herzog symbolically surrenders the past. He is now on his own.

Herzog borrows money from his brother and returns to the Berkshires and to the novel's present time. The last thirty pages represent an end to alienation and acceptance of reality despite its manifest imperfections, despite the omnipresent spectre of the horrors visited upon man by man. While working out the complications of his second divorce, Herzog has come to some useful conclusions about the Romanticism that was his academic interest. He sets himself squarely against the mainstream of modern intellectual revolt. He rejects the fashionable apocalypticism of our own time as forcedly as Norman Mailer's Stephen Rojack affirms it. Herzog's credo appears in a long letter to Professor Mermelstein, whose book he was supposed to review:

> I venture to say Kierkegaard meant that truth has lost its force with us and horrible pain and evil must teach it to us again, the eternal punishments of Hell will have to regain their reality before mankind turns serious once more. I do not see this. Let us set aside the fact that such convictions in the mouths of safe, comfortable people playing at crisis, alienation, apocalypse and desperation, make me sick. We must get it out of our heads that this is a doomed time, that we are waiting for the end, and the rest of it, mere junk, from fashionable

magazines. Things are grim enough without these shivery games.* (p. 316–17)

Herzog's moral stance is not unlike old Schlossberg's:

> We love apocalypses too much, and crisis ethics and florid extremism with its thrilling language. Excuse me, no. I've had all the monstrosity I want. We've reached an age in the history of mankind when we can ask about certain persons, "What is this Thing?" No more of that for me—no, no! I am simply a human being, more or less. (p. 317)

Bellow's well-read protagonist may well have taken for his motto the words of Melville's Ishmael in the moment of *his* rejection of Romantic passion: "There is a wisdom that is woe; but there is a woe that is madness." In the millennia of human history, there has never been a single second in which some men have not been in pain, but to dwell *exclusively* upon this awful fact is to go mad. Herzog's conclusion is similar to Augie March's, but with a difference. Augie decides that greatness is not for him. Herzog, who once dreamed that he might become a "marvelous Herzog," now sees that the "greatness" of many men is empty strut, a display of courage (or self-pity) in the face of horrors that they themselves have imagined. No, the world itself is bad enough without our efforts to make it worse. Things are grim enough without these shivery games.

Herzog's final philosophic epistles are part and parcel of his acceptance of himself as an American. Attempts have been made to link the pastoral conclusion of the novel with the ritual use of Eden in the poetry of John Milton, but Walden Pond is much closer to the Berkshires than Milton's garden is.[35] Returning to the house in the Berkshires, he thinks of Robert Frost at the inauguration of John F. Kennedy:

---

* Much earlier in the novel, Herzog, writing to Professor Shapiro, held the elitism of T. S. Eliot, Wyndham Lewis, and their followers partly responsible for the totalitarianism of the 1930s and 1940s: "Reaching at last the point of denying the humanity of the industrialized 'banalized' masses. It was easy for the Wastelanders to be assimilated to totalitarianism. Here the responsibility of artists remains to be assessed. To have assumed . . . that the deterioration of language and its debasement was tantamount to dehumanization led straight to cultural fascism." (p. 76)

> . . . the house rose out of weeds, vines, trees, and blossoms. Herzog's folly! Monument to his sincere and loving idiocy, to the unrecognized evils of his character, symbol of his Jewish struggle for a solid footing in White Anglo-Saxon Protestant America ("The land was ours before we were the land's," as that sententious old man declared at the Inauguration). (p. 309)

The garden is hopelessly overrun and the house is dilapidated, and he no longer has the will to work to repair it. Why bother? What is there to prove? He spends two or three days sending off his mental messages to all and sundry.

His peace is disrupted by a call from Ramona. She is, of course, lovely. Bellow describes the traditional attractions of woman and the traditional responses of man:

> The perfume of her shoulders reached his nostrils. And, as almost always, he heard the deep, the cosmic, the idiotic masculine response—*quack*. The progenitive, the lustful quacking in the depths. *Quack. Quack.* (p. 337)

Inviting Ramona to dinner, Herzog asks Mrs. Tuttle, the helpful Yankee, to tidy up the house, in which Herzog is now satisfied simply to be, "to be just as it is willed, and for as long as I may remain in occupancy." (p. 340) His surrender to pastoral domesticity has brought forth enraged protests from critics, who speak of "a fatty sigh of middle-class intellectual contentment" [36] and, more elegantly, of "entropic stasis." [37] To deem Herzog's presumably temporary withdrawal "paralytic" rather than "regenerative" is to insist on the apocalyptic activism that Herzog has, within the world of the novel, definitively abnegated. The final scene asserts the momentary primacy of rest:

> He wanted to tell [Mrs. Tuttle] to sprinkle the floor. She was raising too much dust. In a few minutes he would call down to her, "Damp it down, Mrs. Tuttle. There's water in the sink." But not just yet. At this time he had no messages for anyone. Nothing. Not a single word. (p. 341)

Given our knowledge of Herzog, we need not be scornful of his pastoral impulse. It is as much in character as Henderson's frenzied joy.

The most indefatigable researcher into the Jewishness of American literature has maintained that Jewishness plays an important part in *Herzog*. The argument is that Jewishness can be "vaguely defined as family feeling or heartfelt truth." [38] Since Gentiles have also been known on occasion to acknowledge kinship's claims and to respond emotionally to verity, it seems more reasonable to see in *Herzog*'s conclusion the rewards of marginality understood and overcome. The professor deserves a moment's peace.

7 Mr. Sammler's Planet

Between the appearance of *Herzog* in 1964 and *Mr. Sammler's Planet* in 1970, Bellow published a collection, *Mosby's Memoirs and Other Stories* (1968), which included three stories originally collected along with *Seize the Day* and three stories gathered from those written since 1956. The difference in mood between the earlier and the later stories predicted the more somber tones of Bellow's most recent novel. "Looking for Mr. Green" (1951) may be taken as representative of an optimistic view of the human condition. Although George Grebe finds it maddeningly difficult to deliver Tulliver Green's relief check in the Negro district of Chicago, he persists in the stubborn belief that Mr. Green *can* be found, *must* be found. (Interestingly, the epigraph of the story is a line from Ecclesiastes that Paul Goodman quoted in his early, optimistic story, "A Cross-Country Runner at Sixty-Five": "Whatsoever thy hand findeth to do, do it with thy might. . . .") "Mosby's Memoirs," first published in 1968, concerns an American diplomat, with some of the lineaments of George Kennan, whose *Autobiography* is an obvious source. Having disposed of all things human in his foreign-service career, he is curious to encounter God. He descends into a Zapotec temple near Mitla, Mexico. The descent is the equivalent of the chaotic experience in the Marabar Caves in E. M. Forster's *Passage to India*. Forster's Mrs. Moore discovers that the tidy religions and philosophies of the West are pathetically inadequate to the universal mystery symbolized by the "BOUM" that echoes through the caves. Mosby, too, has his revelation:

> There was a heavy grille, the gate. The stones were huge. The vault was close. He was oppressed. He was afraid. It was very

damp. On the elaborately zigzag-carved walls were thin, thin pipings of fluorescent light. Flat boxes of ground lime were here to absorb moisture. His heart was paralyzed. His lungs would not draw.[39] (p. 184)

The confident master of the fate of nations has become the Underground Man.

Mr. Sammler's blue-green swirling planet is a home rather than a prison, but a home under siege. The larky, jaunty quality of the major works of Bellow's middle phase, the free style of Augie March and the zany antics of Eugene Henderson—these are replaced by the somber thought of an elderly man who has seen the world go to pieces once and would rather that it didn't happen a second time. Bellow's choice of Cracow-born, Bloomsbury-mannered Artur Sammler is, in itself, extremely suggestive. The protagonists of his other novels are all Americans. All but Henderson are Jews, but Jewishness means little to them, except for Moses Herzog, who reflects on the ethnic origins of modern scholars (including one Moses Herzog, of Napoleon Street, Montreal). Like the others, Sammler is nominally rather than religiously Jewish, but he, unlike them, has been shaped rather than influenced by European culture. It seems appropriate, for those who like ends to resemble beginnings, that the latest masterpiece of Jewish writing in America returns to the experiences of an immigrant. Mr. Sammler is not about to lay a curse on the head of errant Columbus, but he wonders what will become of not just the Jews but all of us—Americans, Europeans, all of us who are travellers in spaceship earth.

Mr. Sammler's familial situation is complicated enough to occupy the talents of two or three crafty novelists. He is a widower dependent upon his nephew Elya Gruner, who brought him and his daughter Shula to the United States after the war. He lives with his late wife's niece, Margotte Arkin, on New York's West Side. The illness and death of Elya Gruner help bring about an intellectual and emotional crisis from which Mr. Sammler emerges with what little wisdom it is man's lot to attain. The domestic crisis is aggravated by the almost nymphomaniacal behavior of Elya's daughter Angela and by the screw-loose money-making schemes of her brother Wallace. The latter buzzes the family's house in New Rochelle, to experiment with aerial photography of mansions, while his father dies in the hospital. Sammler's daughter Shula, who habitually turns Catholic at Easter and once kept an Easter chick until it turned "into a hen that squawked on the edge of the tub," [40] (p. 27) complicates her father's life by stealing a Hindu scholar's manuscript on the moon, for her father's memoir of H. G. Wells.

Sammler's thoughts are partly of his rather wacky family, partly of the war, in which he was left for dead by a German death squad, only to escape, to kill a German soldier caught alone in the forest, and to be threatened by the Poles with whom the Jews had cooperated. "In Zamosht Forest the Polish partisans turned on the Jewish fighters. The war was ending, the Russians advancing, and the decision seems to have been taken to reconstruct a Jewless Poland. There was therefore a massacre." (p. 140) But Sammler had, once again, survived. Hidden by a Polish gravedigger in a mausoleum, Sammler had endured hunger and cold and the pain of an eye blinded by the Germans and had come through it all—somewhat less than Phoenixlike but still alive. Little wonder that his prewar faith in utopian possibilities died somewhere in the Polish forests.

Mr. Sammler is weary of the over-many explanations, of the myriad theories purporting to account for the inexplicable.

> Intellectual man had become an explaining creature. Fathers to children, wives to husbands, lecturers to listeners, experts to laymen, colleagues to colleagues, doctors to patients, man to his own soul, explained. The roots of this, the causes of the other, the source of events, the history, the structure, the reasons why. For the most part, in one ear out the other. The soul wanted what it wanted. It had its own natural knowledge. (p. 3)

Now, at the opening of the novel, he has a new problem, a new phenomenon to explain. Coming home each afternoon from the New York Public Library, riding the bus through Columbus Circle, Mr. Sammler has noticed a handsome young Negro with smoked glasses and a camel's-hair coat, a methodical pickpocket. The police are not interested in his citizenly report, but he is perplexed. When the Negro realizes that Sammler has been observing him, he chases Mr. Sammler and ambushes him in the lobby of his apartment building. Then what? "The black man had opened his fly and taken out his penis. It was displayed to Sammler with great oval testicles, a large tan-and-purple uncircumcised thing—a tube, a snake. . . ." (p. 49) Not a word is spoken by the Negro. After this mysterious epiphany, Sammler finds *The Future of the Moon,* by V. Govinda Lal, stolen for him by his loving daughter.

The Negro pickpocket, the New York police, and the flight of manned spacecraft to the moon are enough to occupy a man's thoughts, but one of Sammler's former readers, now a professor at Columbia, invites the old man to lecture on the 1930s. The occasion is a disastrous drama of incomprehension and rudeness. The students are mostly bored by Sammler's increasingly excited memories of H. G. Wells and rationalism's dream of scientific progress. When he mentions George Orwell and Orwell's comments on the British navy which protected the British pacifists, he is interrupted:

> "That's a lot of shit."
> Sammler could not speak.
> "Orwell was a fink. He was a sick counterrevolutionary. It's good he died when he did. And what you are saying is shit." Turning to the audience, extending violent arms and raising his palms like a Greek dancer, he said, "Why do you listen to this effete old shit? What has he got to tell you? His balls are dry. He's dead. He can't come." (p. 42)

Although Sammler is tired of the old European "culture game," he is repelled by the New Left and the validation of ideas by phallic measurements. Before his lecture he had wondered at the popularization of the Enlightenment: "The dreams of nineteenth-century poets polluted the psychic atmosphere of the great boroughs and suburbs of New York." (p. 33) And fanatics roamed the streets. Mr. Sammler wonders if Western civilization can survive its own dissemination, can outlive the rage of millions morally repelled by the materialism that supports them.

Like Herzog, who wanted to be "marvelous," Mr. Sammler gives up Romantic dreams: "He was only an old Jew whom they had hacked at, shot at, but missed killing somehow, murdering everyone else with their blasts." (p. 197) When his nephew's son tells him he has booked a flight to the moon, Sammler answers, "I do not personally care for the illimitable. . . . I am content to sit here on the West Side, and watch, and admire these gorgeous Faustian departures for the other worlds." (p. 184) In his conversation with Dr. V. Govinda Lal, Sammler disdains the frantic effort to be original: "All mapmakers should place the Mississippi in the same location. . . ." (p. 228) In the country of those blinded by fanaticism, one-eyed Mr. Sammler is—or ought to be—the philosopher-king.

The many threads of the narrative are drawn together in the sixth chapter, wherein Dr. Lal recovers his manuscript, the pickpocket is struck down by Sammler's son-in-law (despite Sammler's attempt to stop the attack), and Elya Gruner dies. His uncle prays for him and calls him a good man because "he did meet the terms of his contract. The terms which, in his inmost heart, each man knows." (p. 313) Elya had carried out his "assignments," had performed surgical operations he disliked, had done his duty. In his raucous way, he had loved his family and had provided for them. These were the terms of the contract he had met.

To speak of human obligations with the metaphor of a legal document is to fly in stormy weather. For those presently alienated from middle-class America and attracted by the possibility of revolution for the hell of it, *Mr. Sammler's Planet,* with its references to Weimar and the Fabian Society and the plays of Racine, with its world-weary tone of resignation, is an affront. Intelligent critics have minimized the ironic distance between Bellow and his aged spokesman and have imagined a virtual identity between them, despite the fact that Sammler's experiences are quite unlike those of his creator.[41] John J. Clayton, author of an excellent study of Bellow's work through *Herzog,* has responded in anger to *Mr. Sammler's Planet*: "Saul Bellow, like Spiro Agnew and George Wallace, is disgusted with the lack of law and order in America. Like Agnew, he is revolted by young people in revolt and like Wallace, terrified of blacks." [42] This strikes me as a misinterpretation of the book. In the present climate of political opinion, Bellow's Mr. Sammler is no more likely to persuade the New Left than Thomas Mann's rationalist character, Settembrini, was able to convince Hans Castorp. Bellow has been condemned for his "bitterness" because his wisdom is unwelcome.[43] Nonetheless, mapmakers must put the Mississippi where it is and not where they wish it to be.

VI

The End of the Jewish People?

In 1965, the distinguished French publisher, Gallimard, issued a provocative book on Israel by a prominent sociologist who was also a Jew by ancestry and by the official classification of the Vichy government. The book was entitled *Fin du Peuple Juif?* The title was not simply a gimmick. It raised a fundamental question. How is the modern, secular culture of the State of Israel related to the ancient faith of Jewish people? It is, of course, common knowledge that Orthodox Judaism is the established religion of Israel and that Reform and secular Jews suffer under various legal disabilities (for example, both civil and mixed marriages are prohibited). It is not widely realized, argues Georges Friedmann, that the young Israelis have lost sympathy with Orthodox Judaism. "The young *sabras* [Israeli-born] refuse to be guided by the enthusiasms of a past in which, though it was certainly heroic, they did not share." [1] This comment strangely echoes Philip Roth's symposium response of 1961: "I cannot find a true and honest place in the history of believers that begins with Abraham, Isaac, and Jacob on the basis of the heroism of these believers or of their humiliations and anguish." [2] The *sabras* are rather *more* hostile to their past than Roth, who is—at least in the quoted statement—extremely respectful. They have no interest in the history and continuity of Jewish culture. The East European *shtetl*, which Americans view as the center

222

of *Yiddishkeit*, has no significance for them. Between the fall of Jerusalem in A.D. 70 and the establishment of the State of Israel in 1948, there is a long hiatus. Among the *sabras* of Israel there is even a sect, the Canaanites, who look back nostalgically upon a time *before* the advent of Judaism. On the basis of his comparative study of the problem of assimilation in Israel and in the United States, Friedmann concludes that there is no Jewish nation; there is only the State of Israel. Outside of Israel, Jewish culture is threatened by total extinction: "In the Diaspora the Jewishness of the assimilated Jew is to a large extent . . . ultimately maintained only by non-Jews who consider him a Jew." [3] Friedmann's own ambivalence about this prospect is demonstrated by the dialogue he carries on with himself in the last chapter of his book.

The ambivalence of many American Jews has, I hope, been indicated by this present study of Jewish literature within the context of Americanization. There are many other signs of anxiety. Greeting the beginning of a new decade in the spring of 1961, a spokesman writing in *Judaism* magazine asserted that American Jews share fully in the attributes of American national character; in the same article, he condemned assimilation as the goal of a heretical "minority of universalists, internationalists, and rabid anti-Zionists." [4] The shrillness and confusion of the article are by no means unusual. The same combination of satisfaction and fear is evidenced in the many conferences called to discuss the "crisis of freedom" faced by the Jewish community. In the fall of 1966, however, *Judaism* included an important article entitled "The Cost of Jewish Survival." The author urged Jewish education as the only means of survival within an ecumenical age. "Judging by the staggering rate of Jewish defections and the insufficient rate of Jewish reproduction," he wrote, "it is painfully evident that liberty is beginning to prove a greater national peril than persecution." [5] Liberty a greater peril than persecution? It all depends, of course, on which way you look at it. While Jewish organizations sponsor conferences and issue statements on the dangers of intermarriage (and of the lower fertility rate among Jewish women), young men and women, nominally Jews, consider themselves citizens of Woodstock Nation, a thoroughly nonsectarian social system. Who will explain to them that it is contrary to Mosaic law for men and women to wear each other's clothing? While distinguished scholars ask if Emancipation may not have been a mistake, from the point of view of communal survival,[6] their Jewish students use their freedom to marry whomever they please. Assimilation seems an irreversible process.[7] Of course, some unimaginable catastrophe may yet overcome American Jews and return them to the status of a bitterly persecuted scapegoat minority, but it seems much more likely that disaster, whatever its form, will not be correlated to the traditional religious categories. In 1971, anti-Semitism seems among the least of our worries.

The still unfinished Six-Day War of 1967 has complicated matters in at least two ways. In the first place, Israel's danger and her militarily triumphant response evoked enormous enthusiasm among American Jews, including many who thought they had no stake in Israel. Contributions of money rocketed upwards, numerous young Americans volunteered to serve or to settle in Israel, the anti-Zionist American Council for Judaism suffered a setback. But the mood of empathy has not meant any decrease in the rate of intermarriage. The confidence that Israel insures Jewish survival may even *lessen* the degree of observance of modern American Jews. With Golda Meir's picture on the wall, who needs a kosher kitchen? In the second place, some of the New Left, especially among the Black Panthers and their sympathizers, have sided with the Arabs in their war of "national liberation" against "Zionist imperialism." This sympathy for the Arab cause has led to the renewal of a certain amount of anti-Semitism in the United States. There is not, however, any indication that this phenomenon is very widespread. It may even be that hatred of Israel on the part of the militant Left will create "backlash" pro-Israeli sentiments elsewhere in society. All in all, the Six-Day War has probably slowed but by no means halted the trend toward assimilation.

There is no need to exaggerate. As I have attempted to point out in Chapter III and elsewhere, countertendencies exist. Nominal Jews rediscover their past. Suburban congregations decide to place greater emphasis on traditional rituals. The professor comes home with a menorah. Chassidic Jews of Williamsburg continue to forbid themselves radio, TV, film, and the perilous benefits of the public library.[8] But the rate of intermarriage continues to increase. It is very difficult

to believe that Henry Longfellow's observations on the Jewish cemetery at Newport were—in the very long run—all that wide of the
mark. The Jewish people has survived as a persecuted minority
through millennia, which does indeed seem a miracle, but hundreds
of thousands of Jews have, in the course of the last six thousand
years, disappeared into the people among whom they lived. Tradition has it that 80 per cent of the Jews remained in Egypt when
Moses led his people out of bondage. No one can say how many
Jews vanished into Hellenistic civilization. In Victor Perera's novel
The Conversion (1970), there is a sophisticated Spanish priest who
notices his mother's curious habit of lighting candles on Friday
evenings. From this he suspects the Jewish ancestors that countless
contemporary Spaniards, Italians, Germans—perhaps even Americans—have never dreamed of.[9]

Assimilation is, of course, a complicated process of give-and-take.
It has been the uncertain identity of this new man, this American,
which has made the assimilation of Jews and Catholics relatively
easy. The essence of our secular nationhood has yet to be established
and defined. The dominant Protestantism of the seventeenth and
eighteenth centuries was challenged in the nineteenth century. It is
common now for theologians to speak of the post-Christian United
States. Jews who once refused to adopt the religion of those who
called them "Christ-killers" feel thoroughly at home in the secular
city, which they too have helped to build. To argue in 1967—as
Milton Himmelfarb did—that the only choice for a Jew is whether
to be a Jew or a Christian is to falsify.[10] Assimilation has *not* erased
entirely the lineaments of the largely Protestant past, but the pot has
bubbled away and produced a new amalgam that the builders of Bay
Colony would be hard put to identify. The new amalgam, the new
man, has been shaped in some unquantifiable measure by Jewish
influences other than those felt by the Puritans in their search for
Old Testament models of political and religious life. The "entertainment industry" is very largely composed of secular Jews, many of
whom have changed their names, whose influence on Broadway,
Hollywood, and the television studios of metropolitan centers is extremely difficult if not impossible to assess. The political style of
urban and suburban America has unquestionably been influenced
by the Jewish minority. What will the future of American literature

be like after a period in which Saul Bellow, Norman Mailer, and Philip Roth are among the finest writers of fiction?

While most American Jews are gratefully committed to American institutions, many feel that this society is still too capitalistic, too imperialistic, and too racist to win their loyalty. The conversion to radicalism was the theme of Chapter IV, but I should like to suggest again that the radical movements of the 1960s and, presumably, the 1970s are even more nonsectarian than the society that gave them birth. The styles of William Sloane Coffin and Robert Lowell are different from the styles of Noam Chomsky and Norman Mailer; Father Daniel Berrigan has techniques unlike those of Jerry Rubin. Nonetheless, these outspoken men have more in common with each other than with coreligionists comprising the "silent majority." Among the younger radicals the terms "Protestant," "Catholic," "Jew" seem emptied of significance. The "flower children" are not greatly interested in the dogmatic differences for which men once fought and died.

If, however, the explanation for the phenomenal creativity of Jewish intellectuals is to be located in their peculiar marginality, in their double alienation from their own heritage and from the culture of the "host society," what happens to this creativity when the behavioral distinctions between Jews and Gentiles become insignificant? In other words, can marginality lead to creativity for Jews and not for Gentiles when both feel equally marginal (or equally at home)? It does not seem likely. Veblen's famous analysis no longer applies. Or, if it does, it applies to Gentiles as well as to Jews.

What are the *literary* consequences of the virtual conclusion of the process of Americanization? It is my personal conviction that the twenty-five years that followed World War II have been both "breakthrough" and climax. The assimilation of the Jewish writer has reached the point where Bellow, Mailer, and Roth can now find a national rather than the largely ethnic audience that Abraham Cahan, Ludwig Lewisohn, and Meyer Levin were forced to settle for (when they wrote of Jews rather than of Gentiles). In 1964, I rashly conjectured that the renaissance of Jewish writers had very nearly run its course. "If present tendencies continue," I remarked, "Negroes are more likely than Jews disproportionately to fill the ranks of dissent and to imagine in novel and in poem another country better than the one we live in now." [11] This does not yet strike me as a foolish remark. Paradoxically, the survival in America of a significant and identifiably Jewish literature depends upon the unlikely conversion to Judaism of a stiff-necked, intractable, irreverent, attractive generation that no longer chooses to be chosen.

.

Notes

I INTRODUCTION: *Emancipation, Assimilation, and the Crisis of Identity*

1 See Michael A. Meyer, *The Origins of the Modern Jew* (Detroit, 1967), p. 8.

2 A similar controversy arose when an Israeli Jew attempted to register his children as Jews although his wife was not a Jew; see the *New York Times,* January 24 and 29, 1970, March 11, 1970.

3 Abraham Joshua Heschel, *Between God and Man,* ed. Fritz A. Rothschild (New York, 1959), p. 81.

4 Mary Antin, *The Promised Land* (Boston, 1912), p. 129.

5 Cecil Roth, *A History of the Jews* (reprinted edition, New York, 1961), p. 132.

6 Howard M. Sachar writes that the Jewish Bolsheviks, "almost without exception," severed "their connections with the Jewish people, were fanatically Russian in their cultural orientation, and almost uncontrollably vindictive in their attitude toward Jewish nationalism" (*The Course of Modern Jewish History* (Cleveland, 1958), p. 301). See also Salo Wittmayer Baron, *The Russian Jew under Tsars and Soviets* (New York, 1964), pp. 202–05.

7 See Daniel Bell, "Reflections on Jewish Identity," *Commentary,* XXXI (June 1961), 471–78.

8 Milton M. Gordon, *Assimilation in American Life* (New York, 1964), p. 193; see also Gordon's "Marginality and the Jewish Intellectual," in Peter I. Rose, ed., *The Ghetto and Beyond* (New York, 1969), pp. 477–91, and Marshall Sklare, Marc Vosk, and Marc Zborowski, "Forms and Expressions of Jewish Identification," *Jewish Social Studies,* XVII (July 1955), 205–18.

9 Salo Wittmayer Baron, *A Social and Religious History of the Jews,* 14 vols. (New York, 1952—), I: 10, 12.

10 Herbert Gold, "Jewishness and the Younger Intellectuals," *Commentary,* XXXI (April 1961), 322–23.

11 Sidney Goldstein and Calvin Goldscheider, *Jewish Americans* (Englewood Cliffs, N.J., 1968), p. 240.

12 See especially Gordon, *Assimilation,* p. 190.

13 Karl Shapiro, *Poems of a Jew* (New York, 1958), p. ix.

14 Ernest Van den Haag, *The Jewish Mystique* (New York, 1969), p. 33.

15 For typical attempts to produce an acceptable definition, see Melville J. Herskovits, "Who Are the Jews?" in Louis Finkelstein, ed., *The Jews,* 2 vols. (New York, 1949), II: 1158; Jacob Agus, "Judaism vs. Jewishness," *Commentary,* IV (November 1947), 426–28; Salo Wittmayer Baron, "Who Is a Jew? Some Historical Reflections," *Midstream,* VI (Spring 1960), 5–16.

16 Sidney Hook, "Reflections on the Jewish Question," *Partisan Review,* XVI (May 1949), 482.

II   *The Promised Land*

1 Quoted in Roderick Nash, *Wilderness and the American Mind* (New Haven, 1967), p. 34.

2 The first American Jew was, however, Elias Legardo, who arrived in Virginia in 1621; see Anita Libman Lebeson, "The American Jewish Chronicle," in Louis Finkelstein, ed., *The Jews,* 2 vols. (New York, 1949), I: 317.

3 Of Spinoza, Julius Guttmann comments, "His philosophy stands in profound opposition to the Jewish religion, not only to its traditional dogmatic form, but also to its ultimate convictions" (*The Philosophies of Judaism* (New York, 1964), p. 265). See also Jacob Agus, *The Evolution of Jewish Thought* (New York, 1959), p. 299.

4 Printed in Joseph L. Blau and Salo Wittmayer Baron, eds., *The Jews of the United States, 1790–1840, A Documentary History,* 3 vols. (New York, 1963), I: 8.

5 Ibid., p. 9.

6 Quoted in Nathan Glazer, *American Judaism* (Chicago, 1957), p. 35.

7 Blau and Baron, *The Jews of the United States,* II: 658.

8 Quoted in Theodore Friedman and Robert Gordis, eds., *Jewish Life in America* (New York, 1955), p. 110.

9 *Poetical Works of Henry Wadsworth Longfellow,* 6 vols. (Boston, 1886), II: 33–36.

10 Digby Baltzell, *Philadelphia Gentlemen* (Glencoe, Ill., 1958), pp. 273–91.

11 The story of the assimilation of New York's German Jews is told in a popular and not entirely accurate fashion in Stephen Birmingham, *Our Crowd* (New York, 1967).

12 Glazer, *American Judaism*, p. 35.

13 Michael A. Meyer, *The Origins of the Modern Jew* (Detroit, 1967), p. 39.

14 Quoted in Glazer, *American Judaism*, pp. 151–52.

15 Ibid., p. 58.

16 Emma Lazarus, *Admetus and Other Poems* (New York, 1871).

17 On these and other writers, see Sol Liptzin, *The Jew in American Literature* (New York, 1966), Chapter 2.

18 Emma Lazarus, *Songs of a Semite* (New York, 1882).

19 Mary Antin, *The Promised Land* (Boston, 1912).

20 On life in the *shtetl*, see Mark Zborowski and Elizabeth Herzog, *Life Is With People* (New York, 1962).

21 The phrase is the title of Chapter 13.

22 Quoted in Glazer, *American Judaism*, p. 152.

23 Leslie A. Fiedler, "Genesis: The American-Jewish Novel through the Twenties," *Midstream*, IV (Summer 1958), 21.

24 Abraham Cahan, *Yekl: A Tale of the New York Ghetto* (New York, 1896).

25 See Sanford E. Marovitz, "*Yekl*: The Ghetto Realism of Abraham Cahan," *American Literary Realism*, II (1969), 271–73.

26 Nicholas Karl Gordon, "Jewish and American: A Critical Study of the Fiction of Abraham Cahan, Anzia Yezierska, Waldo Frank, and Ludwig Lewisohn" (Stanford University, Ph.D. dissertation, 1968), p. 55.

27 Abraham Cahan, *The Imported Bridegroom and Other Stories of the New York Ghetto* (reprinted edition, New York, 1968).

28 Abraham Cahan, *The Rise of David Levinsky* (New York, 1917).

29 For an excellent account of David's gradual apostasy, see David Singer, "David Levinsky's Fall: A Note on the Liebman Thesis," *American Quarterly*, XIX (Winter 1967), 696–706.

30 Quoted in Marshall Sklare and Joseph Greenbaum, *Jewish Identity on the Suburban Frontier* (New York, 1967), p. 3.

31 Quoted in Moses Rischin, *The Promised City* (Cambridge, Mass., 1962), p. 75.

32 The title of Chapter VI.

33 See also p. 380.

34 Melvin M. Tumin, "The Cult of Gratitude," in Peter I. Rose, ed., *The Ghetto and Beyond* (New York, 1969), pp. 69–82.

35 Isaac Rosenfeld, *An Age of Enormity* (Cleveland, 1962), p. 274; see also Jules Chametzky, "Boats against the Current," in David Mad-

den, ed., *American Dreams, American Nightmares* (Carbondale, Ill., 1970), pp. 87–93.

36 Beatrice Bisno, *Tomorrow's Bread* (Philadelphia, 1938), p. 305.

37 Anzia Yezierska, *Hungry Hearts* (Boston, 1920).

38 Quoted in Nicholas Gordon, "Jewish and American," p. 75.

39 Samuel Ornitz, *Haunch Paunch and Jowl* (New York, 1923).

40 Meyer Levin, *In Search* (New York, 1950), p. 515.

41 Ibid., p. 73.

42 Meyer Levin, *Reporter* (New York, 1929).

43 Meyer Levin, *Frankie and Johnnie* (New York, 1930).

44 Levin, *In Search,* pp. 75–76.

45 Louis Wirth, *The Ghetto* (reprinted edition, Chicago, 1956), p. 193.

46 Marcus Klein, "The Roots of Radicals," in David Madden, ed., *Proletarian Literature of the 1930s* (Carbondale, Ill., 1968), p. 155.

47 Meyer Levin, *The Old Bunch* (New York, 1937).

48 Irving Howe, "Daniel Fuchs' Williamsburg Trilogy: A Cigarette and a Window," in Madden, *Proletarian Literature,* p. 98.

49 Daniel Fuchs, *Homage to Blenholt* (New York, 1936), p. 144.

50 Ibid., p. 143.

51 Daniel Fuchs, *Summer in Williamsburg* (New York, 1934), p. 98.

52 Daniel Fuchs, *Low Company* (New York, 1937), pp. 313–14.

53 Fuchs, *Summer in Williamsburg,* pp. 50–51.

54 Irving Malin, *Jews and Americans* (Carbondale, Ill., 1965), p. 33.

55 Henry Roth, *Call It Sleep* (reprinted edition, New York, 1960).

56 Isaac Rosenfeld, *Passage from Home* (New York, 1946).

57 See C. Bezalel Sherman, *The Jew Within American Society* (reprinted edition, Detroit, 1965), p. 184; Erich Rosenthal, "Some Recent Studies about the Extent of Jewish Out-Marriage in the U.S.A.," in Werner J. Cahnman, ed., *Intermarriage and Jewish Life* (New York, 1963), p. 86.

58 Ruby Jo Reeves Kennedy, "Single or Triple Melting-Pot? Intermarriage in New Haven, 1870–1950," *American Journal of Sociology,* LVIII (July 1952), 56–59; Nathan Glazer, "What Sociology Knows About American Jews," *Commentary,* IX (March 1950), 284. Glazer relied on an earlier version of Mrs. Kennedy's study.

59 Rosenthal, "Extent of Jewish Out-Marriage," p. 89.

60 Ibid., p. 87.

61 Ibid., p. 88.

62 Albert I. Gordon, *Intermarriage* (Boston, 1964), p. 89.

63 Sherman, *The Jew Within American Society,* p. 188.

64 Judson T. Landis, "Marriages of Mixed and Non-mixed Religious Faith," *American Sociological Review,* XIV (1949), 401–7; Gordon, *Intermarriage,* pp. 195–96.

65 Sklare and Greenbaum, *Jewish Identity on the Suburban Frontier*, pp. 314–15.

66 Myron Kaufmann, *Remember Me to God* (Philadelphia, 1957), pp. 255–56.

67 Miriam Bruce, *Linden Road* (New York, 1951).

68 Barbara Probst Solomon, "Jewishness and the Younger Intellectuals," *Commentary*, XXXI (April 1961), 355.

69 Barbara Probst Solomon, *The Beat of Life* (Philadelphia, 1960).

70 Neal Oxenhandler, *A Change of Gods* (New York, 1962).

71 The exception among the *Partisan Review* critics is Jeremy Larner, who wrote that "Roth . . . seeks only to cheapen the people he writes about" ("The Conversion of the Jews," *Partisan Review*, XXVII [Fall 1960], 761).

72 Philip Roth, *Goodbye, Columbus* (Boston, 1959).

73 Joseph C. Landis, "The Sadness of Philip Roth: An Interim Report," *Massachusetts Review*, III (Winter 1962), 264.

74 Harvey Swados, *A Radical's America* (Boston, 1962), p. 174.

75 Leonard Baskin, "My Jewish Affirmation," *Judaism*, X (1961), 294.

76 Dan Isaac, "In Defense of Philip Roth," *Chicago Review*, XVII (1964), 92.

77 Theodore Solotaroff," Philip Roth and the Jewish Moralists," *Chicago Review*, XIII (Winter 1959), 92.

78 Isaac, "In Defense of Philip Roth," p. 94.

79 Irving and Harriet Deer, "Philip Roth and the Crisis in American Fiction," *Minnesota Review*, VI (1966), 359.

80 Philip Roth, "Jewishness and the Younger Intellectuals," *Commentary*, XXXI (April 1961), 351.

81 Philip Roth, *Letting Go* (New York, 1962).

82 Leslie A. Fiedler, "Genesis: The American-Jewish Novel through the Twenties," *Midstream*, IV (Summer 1958), 28.

83 Philip Roth, *Portnoy's Complaint* (New York, 1969).

84 Burt Blechman, *The War of Camp Omongo* (New York, 1963).

85 Bruce Jay Friedman, *A Mother's Kisses* (New York, 1964).

86 Stanley Elkin, *Boswell: A Modern Comedy* (New York, 1964), p. 364.

87 Henry David Thoreau, *Walden*, Chapter II.

88 Stanley Elkin, *Criers and Kibitzers, Kibitzers and Criers* (New York, 1966).

89 Ibid., p. 59.

90 Elkin, *Boswell*, p. 193.

91 Ibid., p. 259.

92 Ibid., p. 267.

93 Elkin, *Criers and Kibitzers*, p. 5.

94 Elkin, *Criers and Kibitzers*, p. 33.

95 Ibid., p. 11.

96 Ibid., p. 19.

97 Ibid., p. 36.

98 Stanley Elkin, *A Bad Man* (New York, 1967).

99 See Leslie A. Fiedler, "Saul Bellow," in Irving Malin, ed., *Saul Bellow and the Critics* (New York, 1967), pp. 2–4.

100 Howard W. Polsky, "A Study of Orthodoxy in Milwaukee," in Marshall Sklare, ed., *The Jews: Social Patterns of an American Group* (Glencoe, Ill., 1958), p. 332.

101 Sidney Goldstein and Calvin Goldscheider, *Jewish Americans* (Englewood Cliffs, N.J., 1968), p. 177.

102 Judith R. Kramer and Seymour Leventman, *Children of the Gilded Ghetto* (New Haven, 1961), p. 151.

103 Sklare and Greenbaum, *Jewish Identity on the Suburban Frontier*, pp. 63, 52.

104 Kramer and Leventman, *Children of the Gilded Ghetto*, p. 92.

105 *New York Times*, June 20, 1965.

106 Grace Paley, *The Little Disturbances of Man* (New York, 1959), pp. 62, 58, 63.

107 Sklare and Greenbaum, *Jewish Identity on the Suburban Frontier*, p. 6.

108 Ibid., p. 331.

109 Irving Greenberg, "Toward Jewish Religious Unity: A Symposium," in Peter I. Rose, ed., *The Ghetto and Beyond*, p. 158.

110 Vladimir Nahirny and Joshua A. Fishman, "American Immigrant Groups: Ethnic Identification and the Problem of Generations," *Sociological Review*, XIII (November 1965), 321.

111 Ibid., p. 322.

112 Werner J. Cahnman, "Suspended Alienation and Apathetic Identification," *Jewish Social Studies*, XVII (July 1955), 223–28.

113 Bernard Lazerwitz, "Contrasting the Effects of Generation, Class, Sex, and Age on Group Identification . . ." *Social Forces*, XLIX (September 1970), 50–59.

114 J. T. Borhek, "Ethnic-Group Cohesion," *American Journal of Sociology*, LXXVI (July 1970), 33–46.

115 See Lawrence H. Fuchs, *The Political Behavior of American Jews* (Glencoe, Ill., 1956); Nathan Glazer and Daniel Patrick Moynihan, *Beyond the Melting Pot* (Cambridge, Mass., 1963), pp. 166–71; Gerhard Lenski, *The Religious Factor* (Garden City, N.Y., 1961), p. 145; B. Z. and May L. Sobel, "Negroes and Jews: American Minority Groups in Conflict," in Peter I. Rose, ed., *The Ghetto and Beyond*, pp. 384–408. The last cited is especially important.

116 Oscar Handlin, *Adventure in Freedom* (New York, 1954), p. 255.

117 Alfred Kazin, *A Walker in the City* (New York, 1951).

118 Alfred Kazin, "Under Forty," *Contemporary Jewish Record,* VII (February 1944), 11.

119 Norman Podhoretz, *Making It* (New York, 1967).

III *One's Own People*

1 Horace Kallen, *Culture and Democracy in the United States* (New York, 1924), pp. 124–25.

2 Ibid., pp. 122–23.

3 Richard C. Hertz, *The American Jew in Search of Himself* (New York, 1962), p. 109.

4 Morris Raphael Cohen, *Reflections of a Wondering Jew* (Glencoe, Ill., 1950).

5 Mordecai Kaplan, *Judaism as a Civilization* (2nd ed., New York, 1957).

6 Mordecai Kaplan, *The Future of the American Jew* (New York, 1948).

7 Kaplan, *Judaism as a Civilization,* p. 47.

8 Meyer Levin, *In Search,* (New York, 1950), pp. 93–94.

9 See Sol Liptzin, *The Jew in American Literature* (New York, 1966), pp. 185, 190; *New York Times,* June 26, 1963; Ludwig Lewisohn, "To the Young Jewish Intellectuals," in Harold U. Ribalow, ed., *Mid-Century* (New York, 1955), pp. 168–75; Richard Rubenstein, *After Auschwitz* (Indianapolis, 1966), p. 174.

10 Norman Podhoretz, *Doings and Undoings* (New York, 1964), p. 119.

11 Maurice Edelman, "Seeking the Promised Land," *New York Times Book Review,* October 20, 1963.

12 Kurt Lewin, *Resolving Social Conflicts,* ed. Gertrude Weiss Lewin (New York, 1948), p. 193.

13 Ibid., pp. 195–96.

14 *New York Times,* September 4, 1967.

15 Ben Hecht, *A Jew in Love* (New York, 1931), p. 3.

16 James Yaffe, *The American Jews* (New York, 1968), p. 308.

17 Meyer Levin, "The East Side Gangsters of the Paper-Backs," *Commentary,* XVI (October 1953), 342.

18 Stuart E. Rosenberg, *America Is Different* (New York, 1964), p. 250.

19 Philip Roth, "Writing About Jews," *Commentary,* XXXVI (December 1963), 452; see also *New York Times,* June 19 and June 26, 1963.

20 "Taub East" appears in Ivan Gold's *Nickel Miseries* (New York, 1963).

21 Leslie A. Fiedler, *Waiting for the End* (New York, 1964), p. 70.

22 Cynthia Ozick, "America: Toward Yavneh," *Judaism,* XIX (Summer 1970), 273, 282.

23 Ludwig Lewisohn, *Up Stream* (New York, 1922).

24 Ludwig Lewisohn, *The Broken Snare* (New York, 1908).

25 Lewisohn, *Up Stream*, p. 219.

26 Ibid., p. 240.

27 Ludwig Lewisohn, *Roman Summer* (New York, 1927).

28 Ludwig Lewisohn, *The Island Within* (New York, 1928).

29 Ludwig Lewisohn, *Mid-Channel* (reprint edition, New York, n.d.), p. 99.

30 Ludwig Lewisohn, *Trumpet of Jubilee* (New York, 1937), p. 245.

31 Ludwig Lewisohn, *The Answer* (New York, 1939).

32 Ludwig Lewisohn, *The American Jew* (New York, 1950).

33 Salo Wittmayer Baron, *The Russian Jew under Tsars and Soviets* (New York, 1964), p. 172.

34 Meyer Levin, *Yehuda* (New York, 1931).

35 Michael Blankfort, *The Juggler* (Boston, 1952). On Blankfort's personal odyssey, see "The Education of a Jew" in Ribalow, *Mid-Century*, pp. 45–51.

36 See Harold U. Ribalow, "Zion in Contemporary Fiction," in Ribalow, *Mid-Century*, pp. 570–91.

37 Robert Alter, "Sentimentalizing the Jews," *Commentary*, XL (September 1965), 75.

38 Hugh Nissenson, *A Pile of Stones* (New York, 1965).

39 Hugh Nissenson, "Going Up," *Midstream*, XVI (November 1970), 49.

40 Oscar B. Goodman, "There Are Jews Everywhere," *Judaism*, XIX (Summer 1970), 283.

41 Tony Tanner, "Bernard Malamud and the New Life," *Critical Quarterly*, X (Summer 1968), 168. See also Samuel Bluefarb, "Bernard Malamud: The Scope of Caricature," *English Journal*, XXIII (July 1964), 319–26, 335, which compares Malamud to Sholom Aleichem.

42 See Frederick W. Turner III, "Myth Inside and Out: Malamud's *The Natural*," *Novel*, I (Winter 1968), 133–39; Earl R. Wasserman, "*The Natural:* Malamud's World Ceres," *Centennial Review*, IX (1965), 438–60.

43 Wasserman is especially good on Harriet Bird and Jung's "Mater Saeva."

44 Bernard Malamud, *The Natural* (New York, 1952).

45 Bernard Malamud, *The Magic Barrel* (New York, 1958).

46 Bernard Malamud, *Idiots First* (New York, 1963).

47 See James M. Mellard, "Malamud's Novels: Four Versions of Pastoral," *Critique*, IX, ii (1967), 5–19.

48 Benjamin Siegel, "Victims in Motion: Bernard Malamud's Sad and Bitter Clowns," *Northwest Review*, V (Spring 1962), 79.

49 Bernard Malamud, *The Assistant* (New York, 1957).

50 Alan W. Friedman, "Bernard Malamud: The Hero as Schnook," *Southern Review,* IV, iv (1968), 930.

51 Leslie A. Fiedler offers the "absurd" suggestion that Morris Bober might even be a *"lamedvavnik,* one of the hidden just for whose sake the world is preserved . . ."; see *No! In Thunder* (Boston, 1960), p. 110.

52 Sanford Pinsker, "The Achievement of Bernard Malamud," *Midwest Quarterly,* X (1969), 386.

53 See Samuel Irving Bellman, "Women, Children, and Idiots First: the Transformation Psychology of Bernard Malamud," *Critique,* VII, ii (Winter 1964–65), 123–38; Ruth B. Mandel, "Bernard Malamud's *The Assistant* and *A New Life:* Ironic Affirmation," *Critique,* VII, ii (Winter 1964–65), 110–22.

54 Robert Alter, "Malamud as Jewish Writer," *Commentary,* XLII (September 1966), 71.

55 Bernard Malamud, *The Fixer* (New York, 1966).

56 The contrary view is maintained in Gerald Hoag, "Malamud's Trial: *The Fixer* and the Critic," *Western Humanities Review,* XXIV (Winter 1970), 1–12.

57 Herman Wouk, *The Caine Mutiny* (New York, 1951).

58 Herman Wouk, *Marjorie Morningstar* (New York, 1955).

59 Herman Wouk, *Youngblood Hawke* (New York, 1962).

60 Arthur Cohen, *The Carpenter Years* (New York, 1967).

61 Chaim Potok, *The Chosen* (New York, 1967).

62 Chaim Potok, *The Promise* (New York, 1969).

63 Noah Gordon, *The Rabbi* (New York, 1965).

64 John Hollander, *Movie-Going and Other Poems* (New Haven, 1962), p. 6.

65 Karl Shapiro, "Christmas Eve: Australia," *Poems: 1940–1953* (New York, 1953), p. 26.

66 Karl Shapiro, *Poems of a Jew* (New York, 1958).

67 Irving Feldman, *Works and Days and Other Poems* (Boston, 1961).

68 Irving Feldman, *The Pripet Marshes and Other Poems* (New York, 1965).

69 Hollander, *Movie-Going,* p. 18.

70 John Hollander, *A Crackling of Thorns* (New Haven, 1958).

71 Lewisohn, *The Answer,* pp. 121–22.

IV *The Revolutionary Messiah*

1 Hugo Valentin, quoted by Louis Ruchames, "Jewish Radicalism in the United States," in Peter I. Rose, ed., *The Ghetto and Beyond* (New York, 1969), p. 229.

2 Ruchames, "Jewish Radicalism," p. 228. Similar arguments appear, for instance, in Robert St. John, *Jews, Justice, and Judaism* (Garden City, 1969).

3 Salo Wittmayer Baron, *A Social and Religious History of the Jews*, 14 vols., (New York, 1952—), IX: 192.

4 See Arthur Hertzberg, *The French Enlightenment and the Jews* (New York, 1968).

5 Ruchames, "Jewish Radicalism," p. 231; see also Anita Libman Lebeson, *Pilgrim People* (New York, 1950), p. 235: "The record will show that it was sectional, economic and personal interests that determined the reaction of Jews of America to the institution of slavery. . . . Conscience ran a poor second to the pocketbook."

6 Thorstein Veblen, "The Intellectual Pre-Eminence of Jews in Modern Europe," *Political Science Quarterly*, XXXIV (March 1919), 38, 41; see also Lewis Feuer's *The Scientific Intellectual* (New York, 1963), p. 315: "The revolt against the masochist asceticism of ghetto Judaism took many forms—psychoanalysis, Zionism, Socialism. All these modes of thought were linked, however, with the common denominator of the hedonist-libertarian ethic . . ." Feuer overstates his case.

7 Veblen, "Intellectual Pre-Eminence of Jews," p. 41.

8 Isaac Rosenfeld, *An Age of Enormity*, (Cleveland, 1962), p. 69; see also Irving Howe, "The Lost Young Intellectual: A Marginal Man, Twice Alienated," *Commentary*, II (October 1946), 361–67.

9 Robert E. Park, "Human Migration and the Marginal Man," *American Journal of Sociology*, XXXIII (May 1928), 891–92.

10 Emma Goldman, *Living My Life* (Garden City, N.Y., 1934).

11 Alexander Berkman, *Prison Memoirs of an Anarchist* (reprinted edition, London, 1926).

12 Quoted in Moses Rischin, *The Promised City* (Cambridge, Mass., 1962), p. 155.

13 Abraham Cahan, "The Apostate of Chego-Chegg," *Century*, LIX (November 1899), 96.

14 Joseph Freeman, *An American Testament* (London, 1936), p. 22.

15 See Nathan Glazer, *The Social Basis of American Communism* (New York, 1961), Chapter 4.

16 C. Bezalel Sherman, "Secularism and Religion in the Jewish Labor Movement," in Theodore Friedman and Robert Gordis, eds., *Jewish Life in America* (New York, 1955), p. 127.

17 Michael Gold, *Jews without Money* (New York, 1930).

18 Quoted in Daniel Aaron, *Writers on the Left* (New York, 1961), p. 88.

19 Albert Halper, *The Chute* (New York, 1937).

20 Isidor Schneider, *From the Kingdom of Necessity* (New York, 1935).

21 Isidor Schneider, *Comrade: Mister* (New York, 1934), unpaged.

22 Meyer Levin, *Citizens* (New York, 1940).

23 Daniel Aaron, "Some Reflections on Communism and the Jewish Writer," in Peter I. Rose, ed., *The Ghetto and Beyond* (New York, 1969), p. 266.

24 Paul Goodman, *People or Personnel* (New York, 1965), p. 44.

25 Paul Goodman, *The Facts of Life* (New York, 1945).

26 Paul Goodman, *Utopian Essays and Practical Proposals* (New York, 1962), p. 12.

27 Ibid., p. 226.

28 Paul Goodman, *Drawing the Line* (New York, 1962), p. 105.

29 Goodman, *People or Personnel*, p. 3.

30 Goodman, *Drawing the Line*, p. 61.

31 Paul Goodman, *Community of Scholars* (New York, 1962), pp. 159–60.

32 Paul Goodman, *Growing Up Absurd* (New York, 1960), p. 12.

33 Ibid., p. 39.

34 Paul Goodman, *Like a Conquered Province* (New York, 1967), p. 31.

35 Paul Goodman, *Parents Day* (Saugatuck, Conn., 1951).

36 Goodman, *Utopian Essays and Practical Proposals*, p. 234.

37 Joel Carmichael, "Unlust in Action," *Midstream*, V (Summer 1959), 103; the most helpful essay is by Sherman Paul, "Paul Goodman's Mourning Labor: *The Empire City*," *Southern Review*, IV, iv (1968), 894–926.

38 Paul Goodman, *Making Do* (New York, 1963).

39 Paul Goodman, "Lines," *Hawkweed: Poems* (New York, 1967), p. 88.

40 Norman Mailer, *Advertisements for Myself* (New York, 1959), p. 17.

41 Norman Mailer, *The Naked and the Dead* (New York, 1948).

42 Norman Mailer, *The Presidential Papers* (New York, 1963).

43 Norman Mailer, *Advertisements for Myself*, p. 94.

44 Norman Mailer, *Barbary Shore* (New York, 1951).

45 Edmond L. Volpe, "James Jones—Norman Mailer," in Harry T. Moore, ed., *Contemporary American Novelists* (Carbondale, Ill., 1964), p. 117.

46 Norman Mailer, *The Deer Park* (New York, 1955).

47 Mailer, *Advertisements for Myself*.

48 Leslie Fiedler, *Waiting for the End* (New York, 1964), p. 88.

49 Norman Mailer, *Cannibals and Christians* (New York, 1966), pp. 27–28.

50 Norman Mailer, *Armies of the Night* (New York, 1968), p. 23.

51 Christopher Lasch, *The New Radicalism in America* (New York, 1965), p. 347.

52 Norman Mailer, *An American Dream* (New York, 1965).

53 Tony Tanner, "On the Parapet: A Study of the Novels of Norman Mailer," *Critical Quarterly,* XII (Summer 1970), 165.

54 Elizabeth Hardwick, "Bad Boy," *Partisan Review,* XXXII (Summer 1965), 291.

55 Barry H. Leeds, *The Structured Vision of Norman Mailer* (New York, 1969), p. 126. Similar allegations have been made by Max F. Schulz in *Radical Sophistication* (Athens, Ohio, 1969) and by Helen Weinberg in *The New Novel in America* (Ithaca, N.Y., 1970): *"An American Dream* is an audacious romantic assertion that the embattled 'noble savage' in man, given the courage and strength and luck, can prevail against the establishment of the tyrannical snob" (Schulz, p. 91); "Through will and courage Rojack ultimately gains his freedom, a total freedom, although possibly not free of ghosts . . . The spiritual progress of the hero is toward this freedom: the self is reborn at the beginning of the novel through the murder of evil, in the middle of the novel through true orgasm, and at the end of the novel through the loss of love" (Weinberg, p. 139).

56 Leo Bersani, "The Interpretation of Dreams," *Partisan Review,* XXXII (Fall 1965), 604, 606.

57 William H. Pritchard, "Norman Mailer's Extravagances," *Massachusetts Review,* VIII (Summer 1967), 562–68.

58 Diana Trilling, "Norman Mailer," *Encounter,* XIX (November 1962), 55–56.

59 Quoted in Donald Kaufman, *Norman Mailer* (Carbondale, Ill., 1969), p. 88.

60 Benjamin DeMott, "Docket No. 15883," *American Scholar,* XXX (Spring 1961), 237.

61 Mailer, *Armies of the Night,* p. 48.

62 Norman Mailer, *Why Are We in Vietnam?* (New York, 1967).

63 Mailer, *Cannibals and Christians,* p. 71.

64 Norman Mailer, *Miami and the Siege of Chicago* (Cleveland and New York, 1968).

65 Clancy Sigal, *Going Away* (Boston, 1961).

66 Allen Ginsberg, *Howl and Other Poems* (San Francisco, 1956).

67 Allen Ginsberg, *Kaddish and Other Poems* (San Francisco, 1961).

68 *Howl,* pp. 9, 13

69 Ibid., p. 14.

70 Frederick Hoffman, *The Mortal No* (Princeton, 1964), p. 485.

71 Allen Ginsberg, *Reality Sandwiches* (San Francisco, 1963).

72 Ibid., p. 9.

73 Allen Ginsberg, *Planet News* (San Francisco, 1968), p. 90.

V   Mr. Bellow's America

1   Saul Bellow, "Two Morning Monologues," *Partisan Review*, VIII (May–June 1941), 234.

2   Saul Bellow, *Dangling Man* (New York, 1944).

3   Chester E. Eisinger, *Fiction of the Forties* (Chicago, 1963), p. 345.

4   Richard Lehan, "Existentialism in Recent American Fiction; The Demonic Quest," *Texas Studies in Literature and Language*, I (Spring 1959), 191.

5   Abraham Bezanker, "The Odyssey of Saul Bellow," *Yale Review*, LVIII (Spring 1969), 360.

6   Saul Bellow, *The Victim* (New York, 1949).

7   See also Leslie A. Fiedler's remarks in *Love and Death in the American Novel* (New York, 1960), pp. 360–61.

8   Jonathan Baumbach, *The Landscape of Nightmare* (New York, 1965), p. 45.

9   Keith Opdahl, *The Novels of Saul Bellow* (University Park, Penn., 1967), p. 59.

10   "Sermon by Doctor Pep," *Partisan Review*, XVI (May 1949), 455–62; "Address by Gooley MacDowell to the Hasbeens Club of Chicago," *Hudson Review*, IV (Summer 1951), 222–27.

11   Norman Podhoretz, *Making It* (New York, 1967), p. 165.

12   Saul Bellow, *The Adventures of Augie March* (New York, 1953).

13   On the links to Yiddish literature, see Gerald J. Goldberg, "Life's Customer, Augie March," *Critique*, III (Summer 1960), 15–27; Paul Levine, "Saul Bellow: The Affirmation of the Philosophical Fool," *Perspective*, X (1959), 163–76.

14   See W. M. Frohock, "Saul Bellow and His Penitent Picaro," *Southwest Review*, LIII (1968), 36–44.

15   Bernard Sherman, *The Invention of the Jew* (New York, 1969), p. 142.

16   Saul Bellow, *Seize the Day* (New York, 1956).

17   John J. Clayton, *Saul Bellow: In Defense of Man* (Bloomington, Ind., 1968), p. 128; see also William J. Handy, "Saul Bellow and the Naturalistic Hero," *Texas Studies in Literature and Language*, V (Winter 1964), 538–45.

18   Clayton, *Saul Bellow*, p. 129.

19   Opdahl, *The Novels of Saul Bellow*, pp. 116–17.

20   See J. C. Mathis, "Theme of 'Seize the Day,'" *Critique*, VII (Spring 1965), 43–45; Clinton W. Trowbridge, "Water Imagery in *Seize the Day*," *Critique*, IX, iii (1967), 62–73.

21   Richard Chase, "The Adventures of Saul Bellow," *Commentary*, XXVII (April 1959), 323, 330; see also Martin Price, "Intelligence and Fiction," *Yale Review*, XLVIII (March 1959), 451–64; Geoffrey Rans,

"The Novels of Saul Bellow," *Review of English Literature,* IV (1963), 18–30.

22 Charles Rolo, "Reader's Choice," *Atlantic Monthly,* CCIII (March 1959), 88; Donald Malcolm, "Rider Haggard Rides Again," *New Yorker,* XXXV (March 14, 1959), 171–73.

23 Ihab Hassan, *Radical Innocence* (Princeton, 1961), p. 321; see also Eisinger, *Fiction of the Forties,* p. 343; Abraham Bezanker, "The Odyssey of Saul Bellow," *Yale Review,* LVIII (Spring 1969), 371.

24 Michael Allen, "Idiomatic Language in Two Novels by Saul Bellow," *Journal of American Studies,* I, ii (1967), 275–80.

25 Robert G. Davis, "The American Individualist Tradition," in Nona Balakian and Charles Simmons, eds., *The Creative Present* (Garden City, N.Y., 1963), 111–41.

26 Daniel J. Hughes, "Reality and Hero," *Modern Fiction Studies,* VI (1960), 345–64; for an essay that sees greater contrast between the American and the African scenes than I do, see Ralph Freedman, "Saul Bellow: The Illusion of Environment," *Wisconsin Studies in Contemporary Literature,* I (Winter 1960), 50–65.

27 Saul Bellow, *Henderson the Rain King* (New York, 1959).

28 See also Michael A. Goldfinch, "A Journey to the Interior," *English Studies,* XLIII (October 1962), 439–43.

29 See Robert Detweiler, "Patterns of Rebirth in *Henderson the Rain King,*" *Modern Fiction Studies,* XII (1966), 405–14.

30 Elizabeth Hardwick, "A Fantastic Voyage," *Partisan Review,* XXVI (1959), 299–303.

31 J. C. Levenson, "Bellow's Dangling Men," *Critique,* III (Summer 1960), 13.

32 Marcus Klein, "A Discipline of Nobility," *Kenyon Review,* XXIV (Spring 1962), 203–26.

33 Saul Bellow, *Herzog* (New York, 1964).

34 David D. Galloway, "Moses-Bloom-Herzog: Bellow's Everyman," *Southern Review,* II (Winter 1966), 73.

35 See Franklin R. Baruch, "Bellow and Milton: Professor Herzog in His Garden," *Critique,* IX, iii (1967), 74–83.

36 John W. Aldridge, "The Complacency of Herzog," in Irving Malin, ed., *Saul Bellow and the Critics* (New York, 1967), p. 210.

37 Stanley Trachtenberg, "Saul Bellow's *Luftmenschen:* The Compromise with Reality," *Critique,* IX, iii (1967), 58.

38 Irving Malin, *Saul Bellow's Fiction* (Carbondale, Ill., 1969), p. 148; see also Earl Rovit, *Saul Bellow* (Minneapolis, 1967), p. 9.

39 Saul Bellow, *Mosby's Memoirs and Other Stories* (New York, 1968).

40 Saul Bellow, *Mr. Sammler's Planet* (New York, 1970).

41 See John J. Clayton, "Bellow and the Planet of Our Discontent," *The Valley Review,* I (December 1970), 14–15; Alfred Kazin, "Though

He Slay Me," *New York Review of Books,* XV (December 3, 1970), 3-4.

42 Clayton, "Bellow and the Planet of Our Discontent," p. 14.

43 Edward Grossman, "The Bitterness of Saul Bellow," *Midstream,* XVI (August–September 1970), 3–15.

VI The End of the Jewish People?

1 Georges Friedmann, *The End of the Jewish People?* (Garden City, N.Y., 1967), p. 126.

2 Philip Roth, "Jewishness and the Younger Intellectuals," *Commentary,* XXXI (April 1961), 351.

3 Friedman, *The End of the Jewish People?* p. 240.

4 Lothar Kahn, "Another Decade: The American Jew in the Sixties," *Judaism,* X (Spring 1961), 110.

5 Immanuel Jakobovits, "The Cost of Jewish Survival," *Judaism,* XV (Fall 1966), 426. A similar view is expressed in Robert Gordis, *Judaism in a Christian World* (New York, 1966), pp.vii–xxxiv.

6 Joseph L. Blau, *Modern Varieties of Judaism* (New York, 1966), Chapter 6.

7 See Herbert J. Gans, "American Jewry: Present and Future" and "The Future of American Jewry," *Commentary,* XXI (May, June 1956), 422–30, 555–63.

8 On the Chassidic Jews of Williamsburg, see Solomon Poll, *The Hassidic Community of Williamsburg* (New York, 1969).

9 See especially J. O. Hertzler, "The Sociology of Anti-Semitism through History," in Isacque Graeber and Steuart Henderson Britt, eds., *Jews in a Gentile World* (New York, 1942), p. 84n.

10 See Milton Himmelfarb, "Secular Society? A Jewish Perspective," *Daedalus* XCVI (Winter 1967), 220–36.

11 Allen Guttmann, "The Conversions of the Jews," *Wisconsin Studies in Contemporary Literature,* VI (Summer 1965), 175–76.

Supplementary Bibliography

This bibliography is a highly selective list of fiction, poetry, drama, and autobiography not mentioned in the text. It is, therefore, meant to supplement and not include textual references.

Adler, Edward. *Notes from a Dark Street.* New York, 1962.
Angoff, Charles. *Journey to the Dawn.* New York, 1951.
———. *To the Morning Light.* New York, 1952.
———. *The Sun at Noon.* New York, 1955.
———. *Between Day and Dark.* New York, 1959.
———. *The Bitter Spring.* New York, 1961.
———. *Summer Storm.* New York, 1963.
Astrachan, Sam. *An End to Dying.* New York, 1956.
———. *The Game of Dostoevsky.* New York, 1965.
Bisno, Beatrice. *Tomorrow's Bread.* Philadelphia, 1938.
Bogner, Norman. *Seventh Avenue.* New York, 1967.
Bruce, Miriam. *Linden Road.* New York, 1951.
Charyn, Jerome. *Once Upon a Droshky.* New York, 1964.
———. *On the Darkening Green.* New York, 1965.
———. *The Man Who Grew Younger.* New York, 1967.
———. *Going to Jerusalem.* New York, 1967.
———. *American Scrapbook.* New York, 1969.
Dahlberg, Edward. *Bottom Dogs.* New York, 1930.
———. *Because I Was Flesh.* Norfolk, Conn., 1964.
———. *The Leafless American.* New York, 1967.
Davidman, Joy. *Letter to a Comrade.* New Haven, 1938.
Faust, Irvin. *Roar Lion, Roar.* New York, 1964.
———. *The Steagle.* New York, 1966.
Fiedler, Leslie Aaron. *Pull Down Vanity.* Philadelphia, 1962.

———. *The Second Stone*. New York, 1963.
———. *Back to China*. New York, 1965.
———. *The Last Jew in America*. New York, 1966.
———. *Being Busted*. New York, 1969.
Fruchter, Norman. *Coat upon a Stick*. New York, 1963.
———. *Single File*. New York, 1971.
Funaroff, Sol. *The Spider and the Clock*. New York, 1938.
Glass, Montagu. *Potash and Perlmutter*. New York, 1909.
Gold, Herbert. *Birth of a Hero*. New York, 1951.
———. *The Prospect Before Us*. Cleveland, 1954.
———. *The Man Who Was Not with It*. Boston, 1956.
———. *The Optimist*. Boston, 1959.
———. *And Therefore Be Bold*. New York, 1960.
———. *Love and Like*. New York, 1960.
———. *Salt*. New York, 1963.
———. *Fathers*. New York, 1966.
———. *Great American Jackpot*. New York, 1969.
Gold, Ivan. *Nickel Miseries*. New York, 1963.
———. *Sick Friends*. New York, 1969.
Goldberg, Gerald Jay. *The National Standard*. New York, 1968.
Goldman, William. *The Thing of It Is*. New York, 1967.
Gordon, Noah. *The Rabbi*. New York, 1965.
Granit, Arthur. *The Time of the Peaches*. New York, 1959.
Hecht, Ben. *Erik Dorn*. New York, 1921.
———. *A Jew in Love*. New York, 1931.
———. *A Child of the Century*. New York, 1954.
Horowitz, Eugene. *Home Is Where You Start From*. New York, 1966.
Ignatov, David. *Poems: 1934–1969*. Middletown, Conn., 1970.
Israel, Peter. *The Hen's House*. New York, 1967.
Jacobs, Paul. *Is Curly Jewish?* New York, 1965.
Katkov, Norman. *Eagle at My Eyes*. Garden City, N.Y., 1948.
Kaufman, Bel. *Up the Down Staircase*. Englewood Cliffs, N.J., 1964.
Lebowitz, Albert. *Laban's Will*. New York, 1966.
Liben, Meyer. *Justice Hunger*. New York, 1967.
Lieber, Joel. *Move!* New York, 1968.
Longstreet, Stephen. *The Pedlocks*. New York, 1951.
———. *Pedlock and Sons*. New York, 1966.
Markfield, Wallace. *To an Early Grave*. New York, 1964.
Mirsky, Mark. *Thou Worm Jacob*. New York, 1967.
Nemerov, Howard. *Federigo, or, The Power of Love*. Boston, 1954.
———. *The Salt Garden*. Boston, 1955.
———. *Mirrors and Windows*. Chicago, 1958.
———. *New and Selected Poems*. Chicago, 1960.
———. *The New Room of the Dream*. Chicago, 1963.
———. *The Blue Swallows*. Chicago, 1967.

Neugeboren, Jay. *Corky's Brother*. New York, 1969.

Odets, Clifford. *Awake and Sing*. New York, 1935.

Paley, Grace. *The Little Disturbances of Man*. Garden City, N.Y., 1959.

Papier, Judith B. *The Past and Present of Solomon Sorge*. Boston, 1967.

Plutznik, Hyam. *Apples from Shinar*. Middletown, Conn., 1959.

Popkin, Zelda. *Herman Had Two Daughters*. Philadelphia, 1968.

Reznikoff, Charles. *By the Waters of Manhattan*. New York, 1930.

Renek, Morris. *Siam Miami*. New York, 1969.

Rosen, Norma. *Joy to Levine!* New York, 1962.

———. *Green*. New York, 1967.

———. *Touching Evil*. New York, 1969.

Rosenthal, Irving. *Sheeper*. New York, 1967.

Roskolenko, Harry. *When I Was Last on Cherry Street*. New York, 1968.

Rothberg, Abraham. *The Song of David Freed*. New York, 1968.

Rothchild, Sylvia. *Sunshine and Salt*. New York, 1964.

Rukeyser, Muriel. *Theory of Flight*. New Haven, 1935.

———. *A Turning Wind*. New York, 1938.

———. *U.S. 1*. New York, 1938.

———. *Waterlily Fire: Poems, 1935–1962*. New York, 1963.

Schwartz, Delmore. *The World Is a Wedding*. Norfolk, Conn., 1948.

———. *Summer Knowledge*. New York, 1959.

Simckes, L. S. *Seven Days of Mourning*. New York, 1963.

Sontag, Susan. *The Benefactor*. New York, 1963.

Speicher, John. *Looking for Baby Paradise*. New York, 1967.

Stern, Richard G. *Golk*. New York, 1961.

———. *Europe*. London, 1962.

———. *Stitch*. New York, 1965.

Stolzfus, Ben. *The Eye of the Needle*. New York, 1967.

Swados, Harvey. *Out Went the Candle*. New York, 1955.

———. *On the Line*. Boston, 1957.

———. *False Coin*. Boston, 1959.

———. *Nights in the Garden of Brooklyn*. Boston, 1961.

———. *The Will*. Cleveland, 1963.

Wallant, Edward Lewis. *The Human Season*. New York, 1960.

———. *The Pawnbroker*. New York, 1961.

———. *The Tenants of Moonbloom*. New York, 1963.

———. *The Children at the Gate*. New York, 1964.

Wilner, Herbert. *Dovish in the Wilderness*. Indianapolis, 1968.

Yaffe, James. *The Good-for-Nothing*. Boston, 1953.

Yellen, Samuel. *The Passionate Shepherd*. New York, 1957.

———. *The Wedding Band*. New York, 1961.

Index